Qualitative Research Ethics

RESEARCH METHODS

Qualitative Research Ethics

ROSE WILES AND RICHARD CHENHALL

BLOOMSBURY ACADEMIC
LONDON · NEW YORK · OXFORD · NEW DELHI · SYDNEY

BLOOMSBURY ACADEMIC
Bloomsbury Publishing Plc, 50 Bedford Square, London, WC1B 3DP, UK
Bloomsbury Publishing Inc, 1359 Broadway, New York, NY 10018, USA
Bloomsbury Publishing Ireland, 29 Earlsfort Terrace, Dublin 2, D02 AY28, Ireland

BLOOMSBURY, BLOOMSBURY ACADEMIC and the Diana logo are
trademarks of Bloomsbury Publishing Plc

First published in Great Britain 2012

This edition published 2026

Cover design: Charlotte James
Cover image © shuoshu / iStock

A catalogue record for this book is available from the British Library.

A catalog record for this book is available from the Library of Congress.

ISBN: HB: 978-1-3504-2503-3
PB: 978-1-3504-2502-6
ePDF: 978-1-3504-2504-0
eBook: 978-1-3504-2505-7

Series: Bloomsbury Research Methods

Typeset by Deanta Global Publishing Services, Chennai, India
Printed and bound in Great Britain

For product safety related questions contact productsafety@bloomsbury.com.

To find out more about our authors and books visit www.bloomsbury.com and
sign up for our newsletters.

CONTENTS

About the Authors viii
Series Foreword ix

1 Introduction 1

Key Terms 4
  Moral Judgements 4
  Ethics 4
  Ethical Frameworks 5
  Consequentialist Approaches 5
  Non-consequentialist Approaches 5
  Principlist Approaches 5
  Ethics of Care 6
  Virtue Ethics 6
  Ethical Regulation 6
  Ethical Guidelines 7
  Informed Consent 7
  Capacity 7
  Duty of Confidentiality 8
  De-identification 8
  Risk 8

2 Thinking Ethically: Approaches to Research Ethics 11

Introduction 11
The Development of Contemporary Research Ethics 12
Ethical Frameworks 18
Legal, Regulatory and Professional Frameworks Professional Ethical Guidelines 23

Ethical Regulation 24
Legal Regulation 25
   Making Ethical Decisions 33
Research Ethics, Integrity and Governance 35
Summary 36

3   Informed Consent 37

Introduction 37
Providing Information 40
   Encouraging Participation: Incentives, Encouragement and
      Acknowledgement 52
   Recording Consent 53
   Consent in Online Research 55
Summary 63

4   Anonymity and Confidentiality 65

Introduction 65
Confidentiality 66
Breaking Confidentiality 67
Accidental Disclosures 72
'Off the Record' Comments 76
Anonymization and Pseudonymization 77
Identification 78
Visual Data and De-identification 80
Summary 82

5   Risk and Safety 83

Introduction 83
Risks for Research Participants 83
Assessing Risk of Harm 84
Types of Risk 87
The Risk of Exploitation and Harm 90
Minimizing Risks of Harm 92
   Risks to Researchers 93
Physical Risks 94

Emotional Risks 97
Professional Risks 100
Summary 102

6   Ethical Dilemmas 103

Introduction 103
Ethical Dilemmas 103
Making Ethical Decisions 119
Summary 120

7   Where Next for Research Ethics? 121

Introduction 121
Developments in Research Methods 121
Decolonizing Methods: Yarning 122
Visual and Creative Methods 124
Participatory Methods 126
Digital and E-research 128
Data Sharing and Big Data 131
Data Sovereignty 136
Artificial Intelligence 137
Where Next for Research Ethics? 139
Summary 144

Further Reading and Resources 145
General Guidance on Research Ethics 145
Risks and Safety 147
Consent 147
Ethical Issues in Relation to Specific Methods 148
Professional Guidelines and Codes 150
Latin America and the Caribbean 152
Pacific Countries 152
Asia and SE Asia 153
References 158
Index 192

ABOUT THE AUTHORS

Rose Wiles retired from academia in 2016 after a research career in qualitative research methods and the sociology of health at the University of Southampton, UK. She was a member of both institutional and National Health Service research ethics committees during her career. She continues to take an interest in issues relating to research ethics.

Richard Chenhall is a medical anthropologist at the Melbourne School of Population and Global Health at the University of Melbourne, Australia. Richard has spent his academic career working with Indigenous communities to build research capacity in areas related to the social determinants of health. He has Chaired Human Research Ethics Committees at the University of Melbourne for over ten years.

SERIES FOREWORD

The idea behind this book series is a simple one: to provide concise and accessible introductions to frequently used research methodologies and methods, as well as to current issues in research methodology. Books in the series have been written by experts in their fields with a request to write about their subject for a broad audience.

The series has been developed through a partnership between Bloomsbury and the UK's National Centre for Research Methods (NCRM). The original 'What is' series emerged from the eponymous strand at NCRM's popular Research Methods Festivals, which began in 2004 and moved online in 2021 for its ninth run.

This relaunched series reflects changes in the research landscape, embracing research methods innovation and interdisciplinarity. Methodological innovation is the order of the day, and the books provide updates to the latest developments while still maintaining an emphasis on accessibility to a wide audience. The format allows researchers who are new to a field to gain an insight into its key features while also providing a useful update on recent developments for people who have had some prior acquaintance with it. All readers should find it helpful to be taken through the discussion of key terms, the history of how the method or methodological issue has developed, and the assessment of the strengths and possible weaknesses of the approach through analysis of illustrative examples.

In *Qualitative Research Ethics*, Rose Wiles and Richard Chenhall have provided an updated edition of their critical book on research ethics in qualitative research within the social sciences. Within it, they introduce longstanding ethical considerations as well as emerging concerns. They introduce three central premises. First, they contend that researchers need to attend to ethical concerns throughout the research process. Second, they introduce ethical frameworks and perspectives, arguing that being familiar with various philosophical approaches will support researchers as they grapple with ethical dilemmas. Third, they suggest that the majority of ethical concerns will be 'relatively mundane and everyday, but no less important for that'. Significantly, Wiles and Chenhall conclude the book by providing a broader sense of the guidelines, regulations and legislation that are shaping ethics in qualitative research.

Across the book's seven chapters, Wiles and Chenhall introduce opportunities for readers to engage with core concepts and considerations related to research ethics. Ultimately, this affords an opportunity for readers to develop what they call 'ethical literacy' – which they conceptualize as involving more than knowing how to acquire ethical approval. Rather, it 'means encouraging researchers to understand and engage with ethical issues as they emerge . . .' and evolve. Usefully, their book provides a much-needed balance by introducing researchers to the core concepts of research ethics and the pragmatic implications of enacting ethical practice. Importantly, Wiles and Chenhall's updated edition provides readers with clear understandings of new developments in research methods that are impacting ethics. This includes attention to decolonising methods, emergent technologies, and visual and creative methods, among other areas.

While the books within this series do not provide information about their subject matter down to a fine level of detail, they are designed to equip readers with an understanding of the basis for why particular methodological concepts and practices, such as research ethics, are worth careful study. This book is no exception. Here, the authors have once again provided an accessible and incisive overview for readers to engage deeply with qualitative research ethics.

Jessica Nina Lester and Mark Elliot

CHAPTER 1

Introduction

This book provides an introduction to research ethics relevant to qualitative research across the social sciences. It outlines approaches for thinking about ethical issues in qualitative social research and the key ethical issues that need consideration. It is intended to have relevance for researchers and students working across a range of social science disciplines and it explores ethical issues relating to 'traditional' research approaches, such as ethnography, interviews and focus groups, as well as those relating to new and emerging methods and approaches, particularly visual, online and Indigenous methods and the use of Artificial Intelligence (AI) and data sharing.

There has been an increasing interest in research ethics in the twenty-first century in the light of the increasing ethical regulation of social research. Various authors working in qualitative social science, particularly ethnographers, have contested the appropriateness of ethical regulation in social research. These academics have argued that qualitative research poses minimal risks to participants and that ethical review of research by research ethics committees is both unnecessary and detrimental to social science research (Atkinson, 2009; Dingwall, 2008; Hammersley, 2009). An alternative view is that social science research is never risk free and that systems of ethical review encourage researchers to think through ethical issues and to develop their ethical thinking (Boulton et al., 2004; Traianou, 2020). Despite considerable critiques of regulation, systems of ethical review have become embedded in most research institutions. This has heightened researchers' awareness of ethical issues and highlighted the need for training and resources to enhance researchers' 'ethical literacy' (Kara and Pickering, 2017).

Much of the drive for researchers in this area has been to enable them to manage the institutional ethical review process and a number of excellent resources have been developed with this aim in mind (e.g. the NESH Research Ethics Library at https://www .forskningsetikk.no/en/resources/the-research-ethics-library/; the CO:RE Knowledge Base at https://core-evidence.eu/).)

However, enhancing 'ethical literacy' means more than learning how to achieve ethics approval. 'Ethical literacy' means encouraging researchers to understand and engage with ethical issues as they emerge throughout the process of research and not merely to view research ethics as something that is completed once a favourable opinion on a proposed research project has been granted by a research ethics committee. While it may be the case that some ethical issues can be anticipated prior to a study commencing, often ethical issues emerge as research proceeds, sometimes in unexpected and surprising ways.

An argument frequently put forward by social researchers is that ethical decision-making is inevitably situational and contextual and cannot be determined by appeal to predetermined codes and principles. It is argued that decisions about ethical issues that emerge in the process of research need to be decided on 'in the field' in the light of the specific issue, the people involved and the likely consequences. This is sometimes used as an argument against ethical regulation in general which is viewed as limiting researchers' ability to act on the situation that arises. It is also used as an argument against the use of ethical frameworks (particularly principlism) in ethical decision-making. It is argued that a 'one size fits all' approach such as principlism, in which issues such as informed consent and anonymity are viewed as essential principles to be upheld in all social research, is limiting and prevents researchers making ethical decisions in the context of their research in the ways that meet the needs of their research participants.

It is a central theme of this book that consideration of ethical frameworks is important in helping to guide researchers in thinking through the ethical challenges with which they are confronted. This is not to argue that ethical dilemmas are anything other than situational and contextual; consideration of ethical frameworks does not preclude individual deliberation on the part of researchers. The ethical dilemmas that researchers encounter in research are essentially moral dilemmas. Researchers may have a 'gut feeling' about the morally 'right' course of action in a situation that they encounter. However, ethical frameworks can help them to think about, evaluate and justify these 'gut feelings'. Ethical frameworks do not provide clear answers to such dilemmas, simply a means of thinking about them and assessing what an appropriate and defensible course of action might be. Such actions might differ according to the ethical framework used and an individual researcher's moral views. The important issue is that researchers use a framework that fits with their moral views and which enables them to explore and justify the decisions they make.

The focus of this book is based on three premises: first, that researchers need to consider ethical issues throughout the entirety of their research; second, that gaining an understanding of the different philosophical approaches to research ethics and identifying an approach that fits with their moral and intellectual framework will help them to engage with issues that emerge as their research unfolds; and third, that, despite the well-known horror stories of unethical conduct, most ethical issues with which researchers grapple are relatively mundane and everyday, but no less important for that. The book focuses primarily on ethical issues that emerge for researchers and research participants in the conduct of research. Researchers also have ethical responsibilities to the research team with whom they may be working, to their discipline, to the wider research community and to the public. It is incumbent on researchers to consider ethical issues within this broader context.

The book commences with an exploration of ethical frameworks as well as various forms of guidelines and regulation that guide or inform ethical decision-making. This chapter also outlines relevant legislation with which researchers are obliged to comply.

The following three chapters explore three of the core issues in research ethics and the ways that researchers have engaged with them: informed consent; anonymity and confidentiality; and risk. In each of these chapters, the meaning of these concepts is explored and their application, and in some cases their relevance, in different types of research approaches is outlined. In each of these three chapters, examples are provided from the literature of the ways in which researchers have managed these ethical issues in their research. Examples are also drawn on from a research project on informed consent conducted with Rose Wiles's colleagues Sue Heath, Graham Crow and Vikki Charles as part of the Economic and Social Research Council (ESRC) Research Methods Programme as well as a project on ethical issues in visual methods conducted with Rose Wiles' colleagues Jon Prosser, Amanda Coffey, Sue Heath and Judy Robison. Each of these projects involved interviews or focus groups with researchers exploring their views about ethical issues in qualitative research and how these issues were managed in the context of their research.

Chapter 6 discusses common ethical dilemmas that researchers experience and through detailed case studies, discusses the deliberation and management of such dilemmas. Finally, Chapter 7 explores developments in research methods over the last decade and the ethical challenges that these raise. Developments in Indigenous methodologies, participatory, visual, digital and e-research methods, data sharing and big data and Artificial Intelligence are discussed and the extent to which these demand new approaches to research ethics or the reworking of familiar issues in new contexts. A list of resources where further information on the various issues discussed in this book is provided.

There are a number of key terms used in the literature on ethics. These are explained throughout this book. A brief definition of the key terms is given here; further information on them can be found in the relevant chapters.

Key Terms

Moral Judgements

Moral judgements are concerned with intentions and actions which are good (or the 'right' thing to do) contrasted with those that are bad or wrong. A moral judgement is made when a person decides what the right course of action is in a specific situation. Ethical dilemmas in research involve people making moral judgements.

Ethics

Ethics is the branch of philosophy which considers moral issues. The terms ethics and morals are often used interchangeably. Research ethics is concerned with moral behaviour in research contexts.

Ethical Frameworks

Ethical frameworks provide a means of thinking about ethical dilemmas (or moral behaviour). They provide some criteria against which researchers can consider what is right or wrong to do when presented with an ethical dilemma. Common ethical frameworks are consequentialist, principlist, non-consequentialist, ethics of care and virtue ethics.

Consequentialist Approaches

Consequentialist approaches argue that ethical decisions should be based on the consequences of specific actions so that an action is morally right if it will produce a good outcome for an individual and wider society.

Non-consequentialist Approaches

Non-consequentialism is a normative ethical theory which suggests that the right or wrong of an action is not determined by its consequences. No matter what good comes of a certain action, a non-consequentialist might argue that the action is morally wrong based on some other feature or rule inherent to the action itself, such as a sense of duty, a law or a specific right. For a non-consequentialist, telling the truth is the right thing to do irrespective of the fact that it may bring either good or bad results. There are many different types of non-consequentialist approaches. Deontologists argue that there are certain rules or principles that must be followed. Kantian non-consequentialism suggests that it is our duty to follow rules and that we have an ethical obligation to act according to principles that are universalizable (i.e. to have good intentions, to treat people with dignity and respect). Other examples of non-consequentialism are those that view the construction of rules and/or principles through a process of consensus building through social contracts.

Principlist Approaches

Principlist approaches draw on the principles of respect for people's autonomy, beneficence, non-maleficence and justice in making and guiding ethical decisions in research. Respect for *autonomy* relates to issues of voluntariness, informed consent, confidentiality and anonymity. *Beneficence* concerns the responsibility to do good, *non-maleficence* concerns the responsibility to avoid harm and *justice* concerns the importance of the benefits and burdens of research being distributed equally. People using principlist approaches make ethical decisions on the basis of these specific principles. Principlist approaches hold that consent to participate in research should be freely given and that potential participants should not experience any form of coercion to encourage them to take part in research.

Ethics of Care

An ethics of care approach means that ethical decisions are made on the basis of care, compassion and a desire to act in ways that benefit the individual or group who are the focus of research. An ethics of care approach means that researchers make decisions about ethical issues in relation to a particular case and by drawing on the notion of 'care' in relation to research participants, rather than applying universal rules.

Virtue Ethics

Virtue ethics focus on the virtue or moral character of the researcher rather than principles, rules or consequences of an act or decision. Virtue ethics draw on the notion of researcher integrity and seek to identify the characteristics or virtues that a researcher needs in order to behave in morally (or ethically) 'good' ways.

Ethical Regulation

Most research conducted by researchers in the UK and North America, and much research conducted in other European countries and indeed in the Western world, is subject to ethical regulation. The form this takes is review by a recognized ethics committee.

Ethical Guidelines

Professional ethical guidelines and codes provide frameworks to enable researchers to think through the ethical dilemmas and challenges that they encounter in their research. In most cases, these guidelines are very general and with the exception of some specific issues, such as confidentiality or matters that might result in accusations of research misconduct, they do not provide answers to how researchers should manage the specific situations that they might encounter in their research. Social researchers in many (but not all) disciplines can, and do, conduct research without being members of a professional organization. It is also the case that guidelines are not legally enforceable. Nevertheless, a researcher may be excluded from membership of a professional organization, damage their reputation and have difficulty getting their work published or gaining grants if they disregard these guidelines in ways that challenge disciplinary norms of ethical behaviour.

Informed Consent

Informed consent involves providing participants with clear information about what participating in a research project will involve and giving them the opportunity to decide whether or not they want to participate.

Capacity

The term 'capacity' or 'competence' is used to refer to people's ability to give consent to participate in research. There are some groups for whom questions of capacity or 'competence' to provide consent are raised. These groups include children and young people, people with intellectual disability and people with some physical and/or mental illness and disability. People are assumed to lack capacity to consent if they are not able to understand what participating in research will involve, to weigh up the risks and benefits to them of participating or to reach their own decision about this and/or other matters that affect their life. Assessing capacity to consent is, in many cases, a judgement made by researchers but there are some legal issues that need consideration and specific issues are relevant for research with children and young people.

Duty of Confidentiality

In the research context, the duty of confidentiality is taken to mean that identifiable information about individuals collected during the process of research will not be disclosed. Additionally, the duty of confidentiality may mean that specific information provided in the process of research will not be used at all if the participant requests this. Confidentiality is closely connected with anonymity. However, de-identification of data either through anonymization or pseudonymization does not cover all the issues raised by concerns about confidentiality.

De-identification

The primary way that researchers seek to protect research participants from the accidental breaking of confidentiality is through the process of anonymization or pseudonymization. Applying a pseudonym to replace a participant's real name, organization or place offers a certain degree of confidentiality. However, there might be other identifiers that could be used to identify a participant. Anonymization is where data is rendered in such a way that it is it no longer possible to be associated with an identifiable person. This would include removing direct identifiers, such as names, addresses or an ID number and consideration of indirect identifiers such as age, gender, ethnicity, disability or details about a specific public event or occurrence that could lead to identification.

Risk

Supporting the safety and well-being of research participants is an important element of ethical research practice. While much qualitative research may pose only minimal risks to participants, it is important not to disregard the risks that can occur, particularly in research on topics which are in some way 'sensitive' because they focus on personal issues, taboo issues or issues which pose a threat for those participating in the research. Assessments of risk should also focus on risks for researchers which may arise from lone working or from the nature of the research.

CHAPTER 2

Thinking Ethically

Approaches to Research Ethics

Introduction

Researchers inevitably experience ethical issues in the process of conducting research. Sometimes these issues are anticipated and planned for and may form part of decision-making about a project before it commences. However, often ethical challenges and dilemmas are unexpected and emerge as research unfolds. Guillemin and Gillam (2004) have distinguished between procedural ethics and 'ethics in practice' as a framework to think about the relationship between planning for and undertaking ethical research. While there are a number of 'common' ethical issues, and the following three chapters in this book explore these, research is always situated and contextual and the specific issues that arise are often unique to the context in which each individual research project is conducted. However, while ethical issues are often unique to a specific context, the management of such issues nevertheless needs to be informed by a range of ethical frameworks, approaches, regulation and guidelines. In this chapter the various guidelines, approaches and frameworks that inform, guide and in some cases constrain, ethical decision-making are outlined. An understanding of these provides an important basis from which researchers can think through, and argue their ethical decisions.

The Development of Contemporary Research Ethics

Contemporary understanding of research ethics in social research has its roots in the history of medical research. The Nuremberg Code (1947) was developed as a result of the Nuremberg trials after the Second World War at which abuses to research subjects arising from experimentation by Nazi doctors were identified. The code set out ten key principles to underpin medical and experimental research, central to which were issues of consent and avoidance of risk to research participants. The World Health Organisation's Declaration of Helsinki (1964) developed this code and has been identified as central in subsequent legislation and ethical codes of conduct (Israel & Hay, 2006). However, despite the existence of these codes, further cases of abuse arising from medical and scientific research conducted during the 1960s and 1970s occurred. The most well-known of these cases is the Tuskegee syphilis study which took place between 1932 and 1972, in which the effects of syphilis in 400 poor African American men were studied over a prolonged period even though treatment for the disease had become available. This was not an isolated case and a number of other ethical scandals relating to biomedical studies were identified in which people were experimented on to examine disease progression and/or to develop medical treatments (see Israel & Hay, 2006). It was the Tuskegee study in particular that has been identified as being instrumental in establishing the United States' National Commission for the Protection of Human Subjects in Biomedical and Behavioural Research in 1979 and the subsequent Belmont Report and the formation of Institutional Review Boards (IRBs) for reviewing research in the United States. The Belmont Report (1979) has been highly influential and provides the underlying principles by which research ethics committees across the Western world evaluate research proposals (see Whitney, 2023). It identified three key principles, respect for persons, beneficence and justice, to which Beauchamp and Childress (1979), in a widely used book in the field of bioethics, added a fourth, that of non-maleficence (Macfarlane, 2009). These principles are discussed further here.

The ethical frameworks used in social research have emerged from the frameworks developed in relation to medical research. This is an issue that is a concern for many social scientists who view the risks of social research to be far less significant than for medical research. Nevertheless, it is important to recognize that the social sciences have not been immune from accusations of unethical behaviour. Stanley Milgram's (1963) obedience to authority experiment, Phillip Zimbardo's (see Haney, Banks and Zimbardo, 1973) Stanford Prison experiment and Laud Humphreys' (1975) study on sexual encounters between men are commonly cited, yet debated, ethical 'horror stories' in the social sciences (Tolich, 2014). While these now infamous studies have been cited frequently (Tolich, 2014), there are more recent examples of ethical dilemmas in the social sciences (see for example Taquette & Souza, 2022). A key concern, is the risk that poorly designed qualitative studies may contribute to discrimination and stigma against communities or groups who are economically disadvantaged; belong to racial, ethnic, gender or sexual orientation minorities; are living with a stigmatized illness or disability; have limited access to health services; or for whom health care issues intersect with social, political, or economic factors (Gabbidon & Chenneville, 2021). Gabbidon and Chenneville (2021) emphasize that qualitative researchers have a duty to safeguard their participants and uphold the integrity of the research process. This involves practicing reflexivity, fostering opportunities for community involvement at every stage of the research and recognizing the community as the expert when it comes to assessing risks and addressing needs. In discussing projects related to children in care, Boddy et al. (2023) argue that researchers carry an increased responsibility to carefully manage the risk of reinforcing or perpetuating 'othering'. This involves being reflexively aware of how research knowledge is produced within political and economic systems. Rather than contributing to discourses of vulnerability, research should be transformative – constructing counter-narratives that are grounded within these broader systems (Thomson et al., 2024: 30; see also Fine, 2016). Focusing on the ethical implications of conducting qualitative research within a framework of 'epistemic' justice is a fundamental orientation of this book (see Chapter 3 for further discussion of epistemic justice).

The regulation of social research has increased significantly over the last decade, particularly in Europe and North America (see Whitney, 2023). In the United States, Institutional Review Boards (IRBs) have, since the 1970s, screened research on and with 'human subjects'. Their powers have been identified as considerable and wide-ranging and their scope increasing (Haggerty, 2004). The US Department of Health and Human Services has codified its regulations in law for the protection of human subjects in research. The 'common rule' regulations found at 45CFR 46 were largely drawn from the Belmont Report and include components outlining the protections for human research subjects additional protections for certain populations and registration requirements for Institutional Review Boards (IRBs). In Canada, the Tri-Council Policy Statement on the Ethical Conduct for Research Involving Humans (TCPS2, 2022) provides standards for researchers and human research ethics committees. In the UK, funding bodies, such as the Economic and Social Research Council (ESRC), have established ethical frameworks (ESRC, 2025) resulting in the widespread formation of research ethics committees in universities and other research organizations (Tinker & Coomber, 2004; Guillemin et al., 2012; Kohn & Shore, 2017). Research ethics committees had already been operating for some time for researchers conducting research in UK health care settings and, more recently, for research in social care. Similar developments have occurred in the European context, for example for research funded by the European Commission (Wiles et al., 2011). In Australia, the National Health and Medical Research Council (NHMRC, 2018;2025) and in New Zealand the National Ethics Advisory Committee (NEAC, 2021) provide standards, values and principles to guide researchers and human research ethics committees.

Despite guiding principles provided in countries such as the UK, Canada, Australia and New Zealand, there is evidence to suggest that different research ethics committees use a range of different application systems and governance requirements that impact ethical review (Karram Stephenson et al., 2020; Dudi-Venkata et al., 2021). Furthermore, while there are similarities in the identification of key ethical principles across countries, there are significant variabilities in how they are applied as Goodyear-Smith et al. (2002) have demonstrated in a study examining international variations in ethics committee requirements across five Westernized nations.

Virtually all research conducted by researchers in the UK, North America, Australia and New Zealand and much research conducted in European countries and indeed in the Western world, is subject to some form of ethical regulation by a recognized ethics committee. In addition, there has also been significant growth of ethics committees in the Global South, including both low- and middle-income countries (see Hummel et al., 2021a). This growth of institutional ethical review processes is viewed as moving social research in the direction of the highly regulated system of review by IRBs in the United States and is a development that has been widely criticized by social scientists in the UK (Haggerty, 2004; Dingwall, 2008; Hammersley, 2009) as well as social scientists in other countries (Haggerty, 2004; Israel & Hay, 2006; Gorman, 2011; Kohn & Shore, 2017). Concerns have been raised by researchers that increasing levels of review will encourage uniform approaches to 'ethical' issues such as anonymity and consent that avoid any level of risk; this has been identified as threatening the future of good quality social research and posing particular difficulties for researchers using ethnographic approaches (Murphy & Dingwall, 2007; Bell & Wynn, 2023), online (Orton-Johnson, 2010), visual and creative methods (Prosser & Loxley, 2008) and approaches that involve the use of covert methods (Spicker, 2011; Calvey, 2018).

Various other concerns have been raised about the ethical review of qualitative research. Researchers have commented on the increasing bureaucratization of ethical review, the lack of transparency and consistency of institutional ethical review committees and the promotion of biomedical conceptions of risk and harm that do not align with qualitative epistemologies and approaches (see Guta et al., 2013; Burr & Reynolds, 2010). Haggerty (2016), in his dual role as academic and research ethics board member, described the ever-expanding reach and power of the ethics bureaucracy over research practice as 'ethics creep' (see also Iphofen and Tolich, 2018). Guta and colleagues (2013) have documented how various researchers have since used 'ethics creep' to describe various issues they have had with formal ethics review and its threat to academic freedom.

Guta et al. (2013) and others, such as Kohn and Shore (2017), have sought to contextualize the growth of ethical regulations within the rise of the 'audit culture' and managerialism in universities and their concerns about legal liability and reputation. Such shifts are also concerned with the increasing regulation around research governance than ethics per se (Gorman, 2011).

Alongside critics of the system, various other authors have identified the importance of researchers engaging with systems of review, so that committees are informed methodologically and ethically (Iphofen, 2009; Israel & Hay, 2006: 141; Pauwels, 2008; Wiles et al., 2011). This is a position with which this book aligns itself. Iphofen (2009), among others, has noted that while there is limited empirical evidence, ethical review can have an important educative function and one which does not of itself limit social research. Guta et al. (2013: 308) argue that concerns over ethical freedom point to somewhat ethnocentric and biased perspectives of 'academic benevolence' in a contemporary context where privatization, globalization and issues related to the production of knowledge, decolonization of research, data governance and sovereignty require both general and local ethical standards and review. More recently, researchers such as King (2021) have contributed to considerations for the development of ethics procedures built on a 'culture of care', that emphasize principles of support, openness, collaboration and relationships.

Other researchers have argued that human research ethics committees should recognize the situated nature of qualitative research and the challenges of applying generalized guidelines uniformly across all types of research. In an online ethnographic study of Spanish bloggers, Estalella and Ardèvol (2011) explain that many existing guidelines for online research have been shaped by fixed assumptions about research design (such as chats, mailing lists and blogs), as well as the nature and classification of online interactions (public or private). Advocating for a more dialogical and situated ethical practice, the researchers suggest that ethics committees need to be receptive to the specific contexts in which research takes place. Iphofen and Tolich (2018) has suggested a complete turnaround for human research ethics committees (accounting for qualitative epistemologies), whereby the researcher takes a more active role in providing information to the committee and the ethics committee members more passive in learning and listening to researchers. Questions framing this approach would include:

1 What is the research project about?

2 What ethical issues does the researcher believe are raised by this project?

3 How does the research plan to address these ethical problems?

4 What contingencies are in place if the research project changes its focus after the research has been approved and has begun? (Iphofen & Tolich, 2018: 4)

Consideration of the links, overlaps and differences between morals, ethics, ethical approaches, ethical frameworks, ethical regulation and legal regulation are an important starting point for thinking about ethics.

The decisions that researchers make about the ethical issues that they anticipate encountering in the research planning stage and those that emerge as research unfolds are influenced by several issues: professional guidelines; disciplinary norms; ethical and legal regulation and an individual's ethical and moral outlook. Figure 2.1 illustrates this diagrammatically. Each of these issues is explored in this chapter.

All individuals have a moral outlook about what is right and wrong that guides their behaviour. This moral outlook is shaped by individuals' experiences and interactions and the specific moral beliefs held are inevitably individual (see Gregory, 2003). Nevertheless, society has a large amount of agreement on specific

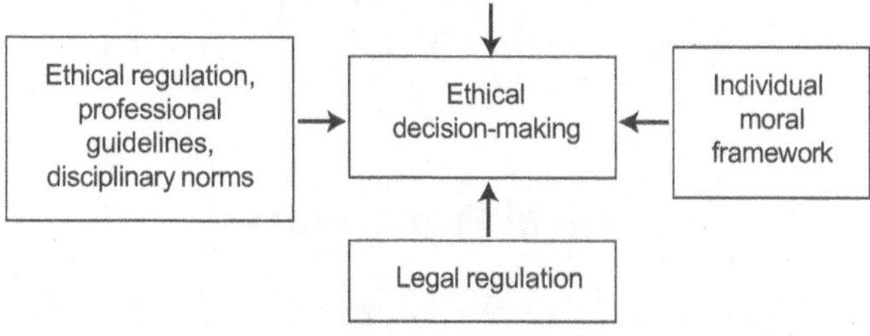

FIGURE 2.1 *Factors shaping ethical decision-making in research.*

moral *principles* about right and wrong (such as justice and fairness), even though there is considerable disagreement about the application of these principles to particular circumstances and contexts. Ethical approaches are the application of key moral norms (or principles). Ethical behaviour in research demands that researchers engage with moral issues of right and wrong. To do this, they draw on ethical principles identified by the research community to which they belong. The specific ethical issues that researchers identify in their research are informed by their own moral outlook and their understanding of ethics in research. The frameworks for thinking about and managing them are informed largely by the ethical principles derived from the various approaches to ethics which are set out in professional ethical guidelines as well as various textbooks on the topic. Some of these ethical issues can be considered prior to the research commencing but many are emergent and become apparent only as the research proceeds. Researchers can draw on a range of resources from the literature and the research community to assist their thinking in how to manage such issues. It is crucial that they resolve the issues in ways that accord with their moral beliefs but also in ways that do not contravene the established ethical standards of their profession. Researchers' ethical decision-making is also strongly influenced by ethical and legal regulation. Researchers are legally obliged to conform with legal regulation relating to their research. Ethical regulation does not carry such weight but nevertheless researchers are generally obliged to comply with ethical regulation by their institution or by the organizations they are conducting research with or for. It should be noted that conforming with ethical or legal regulation does not necessarily equate with ethical (or moral) behaviour; compliance with regulation in many contexts is often the minimum requirement and ethical behaviour demands more careful consideration of the issues involved. These frameworks, guidelines and regulation that impact on ethical decision-making are explored here.

Ethical Frameworks

A range of approaches to research ethics can be identified (see Israel & Hay, 2006; Macfarlane, 2009; Mertens & Ginsberg, 2009;

Iphofen & Tolich, 2018; Iphofen, 2020). These approaches or frameworks provide a means of thinking about moral behaviour. They provide some criteria against which researchers can consider what is right or wrong to do when presented with an ethical dilemma. These frameworks do not provide clear answers to such dilemmas but rather a means of thinking about them and assessing what an appropriate and defensible course of action might be. Consideration of these frameworks is therefore important in helping to guide researchers in thinking through the ethical challenges with which they are confronted. One of the challenges of engaging with these frameworks is that the criteria that each uses to inform moral decisions vary and thus the decisions that researchers may make will differ according to which framework is used. It is also the case that some of the criteria (or principles) *within* certain frameworks may lead people to reach different decisions about the ethical challenges they encounter according to which principle within a framework they give primacy to. The most common approaches are consequentialist, principlist, non-consequentialist, ethics of care and virtue ethics.

Consequentialist approaches argue that ethical decisions should be based on the consequences of specific actions so that an action is morally right if it will produce a good outcome for an individual or for wider society. What is good for a particular individual may not, however, be good for society and vice versa. In consequentialism, the more 'good' consequences that result from an act, the better or more right is the act; no act is seen as inherently *wrong* as judgements are based on the outcome of the act. Using a consequentialist approach, a researcher would assess what the outcome of a specific decision might be and decide on an action that they believe would result in the most beneficial outcome. For example, a researcher might argue that it would be acceptable to undertake covert visual research, for example on youth crime, if the findings of the research could be seen as benefiting society as a whole. Similarly, a researcher might argue that it is morally right to disclose confidential data from one participant if that might lead to a better outcome for a larger group of people. An example of consequentialist arguments is provided by Laud Humphreys' (1975) study of homosexual behaviour. This research has been widely criticized for being unethical but was defended by Humphreys on consequentialist grounds (Warwick, 1982). Humphreys argued that increasing knowledge about sexual encounters between men was essential to bringing about a change in repressive laws and attitudes (Lenza, 2004). Further detail about Laud Humphreys' study is provided in Chapter 6 (see also Perlstadt, 2024b). Common critiques of consequentialist approaches highlight the difficulty of accurately determining whether the benefits truly outweigh the risks, the tendency to overemphasize potential benefits while minimizing possible harms, the prioritization of the researcher's perspective over that of participants, and the treatment of individuals as means to research ends rather than as ends in themselves (Kau et al., 2023: 356).

People using non-consequentialist approaches argue that consideration of matters other than the ends produced by actions needs to be considered and that ethical decisions should be based on specific rules or principles (based on legal, moral or justice frameworks) regardless of the consequences. A researcher adopting a non-consequentialist approach might, for example, argue that it is morally right to maintain a confidence even if the consequences of that might not be beneficial or in the interests of the wider society.

Principlist approaches draws on the principles of respect for people's autonomy, beneficence, non-maleficence and justice in making and guiding ethical decisions in research (see Beauchamp & Childress, 2001). Respect for autonomy relates to issues of voluntariness, informed consent, confidentiality and anonymity. Beneficence concerns the responsibility to do good, non-maleficence concerns the responsibility to avoid harm and justice concerns the importance of the benefits and burdens of research being distributed equally. People using principlist approaches make ethical decisions on the basis of these specific principles. Central to a principlist approach is that consent must be freely given and that potential participants should not be subject to any encouragement (or coercion) to take part, such as that arising from payment for participation or power relations between the researcher and participant. Each of the principles is viewed as important, but it is recognized that they may conflict with each other, and in such cases, it is necessary to make a case for why one might need to be chosen over another. Principlist approaches are widely used and commonly form the basis of the evaluation of applications for ethical approval by research ethics committees (Israel & Hay, 2006: 37). Some authors, such as John Traphagan (2013) have been critical of principlist approaches, explaining that they are inadequate as a universal moral category because culture influences how people think about autonomy. Drawing from perspectives from medical anthropology, Traphagan shows that, in contrast to the United States, where autonomy is largely constructed as an ideology that emphasizes the rights of individuals, in Japan, autonomy is seen as embedded in social relationships. Ethical decisions are not based on a universalized principle but rather decisions are made in response to specific contexts, situations and in relations to the interests and needs of others.

Another approach much more in line with this thinking is an ethics of care approach. An ethics of care approach was originally identified by Carol Gilligan (1982) and has been developed by other feminist theorists (Mauthner et al., 2002; Held, 2006; Larrabee, 2016). In this approach, ethical decisions are made on the basis of care, compassion and a desire to act in ways that benefit the individual or group who are the focus of research, recognizing the relationality and interdependency of researchers and research participants. This contrasts with the approaches outlined above which involve using rules or principles to address ethical dilemmas. An ethics of care approach means that researchers make decisions about ethical issues in relation to a particular case and by drawing on the notion of 'care' in relation to research participants, rather than applying universal rules. Held (2006) has identified some key features of the approach and argues that it involves: meeting the needs of others; recognizing emotions; recognizing people's relationality and interdependence; and respecting and seeking the views of others and their moral claims. This is an approach used in much feminist and participatory research where researchers develop close relationships with their participants (see Edwards & Mauthner, 2012). It has been viewed by some as a form of virtue ethics (see below) in that researchers need to develop particular characteristics or virtues in relation to the research they conduct. Miller et al. (2012) have developed some guidelines for a feminist ethics of care which draws on the key features identified above. These comprise questions for researchers to consider in deliberating on ethical dilemmas (Miller et al., 2012: 11).

Virtue ethics is person-based; it focuses on the virtue or moral character of the researcher rather than principles, rules or consequences of an act or decision. Virtue ethics draws on the notion of researcher integrity and seeks to identify the characteristics or virtues that a researcher needs in order to behave in morally (or ethically) 'good' ways. There is also the expectation that it is the researcher's responsibility to carry out the research in a way that is most likely to produce valid conclusions. Macfarlane (2009: 42) has identified the demands that different phases of the research process place on researchers and the moral virtues that researchers need to manage these challenges at each stage. He also identifies the corresponding 'vices' that characterize a deficit or excess of each virtue that researchers may exhibit when they fall short of a desired virtue. The virtues identified are courage, respectfulness, resoluteness, sincerity, humility and reflexivity. It is recognized that these virtues are ideals which researchers strive for and that the vices are what can occur when these ideals cannot be met. As Macfarlane notes (2009: 42), 'This set of virtues and vices represent the ideal character of the researcher and the temptations they face during what is a demanding social and intellectual process'. In relation to ethical dilemmas, a virtue ethics approach would expect a researcher to ask what a virtuous researcher would do in the given situation.

An ethical dilemma, based on one from Chenhall's own experience, may help to clarify the actions that might be taken on the basis of these different frameworks. An ethical dilemma commonly experienced by researchers relates to the issue of confidentiality. For example, a study involving an Indigenous Australian alcohol and drug (AOD) rehabilitation centre involved ethnographic research with all staff and residents to find out their views and experiences of culturally specific AOD treatment (Chenhall, 2007). During the course of Chenhall's ethnographic research, he became aware of a participant resident using drugs on the property (Chenhall et al., 2011). Should staff be informed of the resident breaking the rules of the Centre so that this could be addressed or should Chenhall not intervene, given that to do so would involve breaches of confidentiality? A consequentialist would look to the possible outcomes of acting and perhaps would argue that the greatest good would come from disclosing this information in order to protect the safety of all residents at the centre. A principlist would be likely to argue that upholding the principle of confidentiality should be paramount and that information should not be disclosed. An ethics of care approach would look to the impact of disclosing information on the participants and would explore what the most beneficial outcome would be for them. A virtue ethics approach would explore what a 'virtuous' researcher would do in this context, which would ensure *all* participants were treated with respect. In this case, this would be likely to mean maintaining confidentiality or following Traphagan above to act in a way that respects the cultural protocols embeddedness in the network of social relationships and processes. The different ethical frameworks described above provide researchers with the tools to guide decision-making in research. However, there are a range of other factors which shape, influence or constrain ethical decision-making. These are discussed here.

Legal, Regulatory and Professional Frameworks Professional Ethical Guidelines

There are many professional guidelines and codes aimed at providing frameworks to enable researchers to think through the ethical challenges that they encounter in their research (see e.g. American Sociological Association, 2018; Association of Social Anthropologists, 2021; British Psychological Society, 2021; British Sociological Association, 2017; European Science Foundation, 2023; RESPECT guidelines, 2004; Social Research Association, 2021 and Komić et al., 2015 for a survey of research ethics terminology used by different professional codes). There are also specific guidelines and codes on particular methods or approaches which raise ethical challenges, such as online research (Ess & the AOIR Ethics Working Committee, 2002; British Psychological Society, 2007; Franzke et al., 2020; Kristiansen, 2022) and visual methods (British Sociological Association Visual Sociology Group's statement of ethical practice, 2009; Papademas and International Visual Sociology Association, 2009). These guidelines inform the decisions that researchers make about procedural and emergent ethical issues. They are drawn, to varying degrees, from the ethical approaches outlined above, particularly principlist approaches. Such guidelines are necessarily very general. Except in relation to some very specific issues, such as confidentiality or matters that might result in accusations of research misconduct, they do not provide answers to how researchers should manage the specific situations that they might encounter in their research. Rather, they outline principles to enable researchers to think through the specific situations that occur (Wiles et al., 2006). These guidelines recognize the situated and contextual nature of the ethical challenges that arise when conducting research. The principles addressed in these codes generally relate to issues of the well-being and rights of research participants, informed consent, privacy, confidentiality and anonymity. Social researchers in many disciplines can, and do, conduct research without being members of a professional organization; as such not all researchers are subject to the guidelines and even if they are, these are not legally enforceable. Nevertheless, a researcher may be excluded from membership of a professional organization, damage their reputation and have difficulty getting their work published or gaining grants if they disregard these guidelines in ways that challenge disciplinary norms of ethical behaviour. They might also be subject to disciplinary sanctions if they do not comply with institutional requirements of ethical research behaviour.

Ethical Regulation

Most researchers are subject to ethical review procedures through a research ethics committee (REC). Committees vary widely in the ways in which they assess applications for review and the conclusions they come to, even in highly regulated and established systems such as that for the review of research in the UK National Research Ethics Service, the Australian Human Research Ethics operating under the National Statement on ethical conduct in Human Research and the Office for Human Research Protections in the United States (Edwards et al., 2004; Israel, 2004; Office for Human Research Protections, 2021). The US Department of Health and Human Services has collated over 1,000 laws, regulations and guidelines that govern human subject protections in 131 countries, organized into region-specific compilations (https://www.hhs.gov/ohrp/international/compilation-human-research-standards/index.html). Generally, the various principles in these regulations and guidelines are fairly uniform and are likely to comprise voluntary informed consent, the confidentiality of information provided by participants, the anonymity of study participants, the avoidance of harm and researcher integrity. These are issues that researchers are advised to consider carefully in preparing applications to RECs.

RECs have the power to determine the way that various ethical issues will be managed within a research project. RECs generally focus on procedural or anticipated ethical issues; it appears that social researchers tend not to seek advice from RECs on ethical issues that emerge once research has commenced unless they are obliged to do so (Wiles et al., 2012). As noted above, some concerns have been raised that ethical regulation places limitations on research, particularly certain types of research such as ethnography, online research and visual methods. Prosser has argued that visual research methods sit uneasily within conventional ethical practice and regulation in social research and that this poses problems in relation to the review of visual research by research ethics committees or boards (Prosser, 2000; Wiles et al., 2011). Proponents of visual research have noted the importance of visual researchers developing ethical practice and becoming members of the committees or boards which conduct ethical review to improve the ethical review and decision-making processes in relation to visual research (Pauwels, 2008).

Many resources exist to assist researchers through the ethical review process (see e.g. Oliver,2010 or Smyth et al., 2016). As well as the importance of preparing a good application that addresses the central ethical issues, researchers can adopt other strategies to maximize their chances of gaining approval. These include finding out how a local REC operates, opting for a committee that might be sympathetic, identifying a committee member to champion the application and being prepared to discuss the application with committee members (Wiles et al., 2012; Israel & Hay, 2006). While RECs have considerable power in determining how ethical issues will be managed in research, there is some evidence that researchers have developed ways to work with ethics committees to modify their impact (Wiles et al., 2012). Increasingly, research has investigated what makes a good research ethics review and how this can be improved (Sidaway et al., 2023; Handal et al., 2021).

Legal Regulation

Research is subject to a number of legal considerations with which researchers are obliged to comply. When considering legal issues it is important to bear in mind that these provide a framework of the minimum standards that need to be adhered to but that these, by themselves, do not necessarily equate with ethical or moral practice. Masson (2004: 43) notes:

> There is a close relationship between law and ethics but not everything that is legal is ethical. Frequently law . . . attempts only to set the minimum acceptable standard. The aspirations of ethical practice are higher . . . It can never be appropriate to defend proposed practice solely on the basis that it is legal.

Specific laws vary across countries, but similar laws exist in most Western countries. There are a number of laws that have a bearing on research; these relate to consent, confidentiality, privacy, data protection and copyright. The information given here does not constitute legal advice and researchers with specific concerns should seek legal advice from their institution. In the UK, more detailed information on the legal issues identified here can be found at the UK Research and Innovation for the Economics and Social Research Council (UKRI, 2022). In other countries, frameworks include, for example, Australia's National Health and Medical Research Council's (NHRMC) National Statement on Ethical Conduct in Human Research (2025) and Canada's Tri-council policy statement on Ethical Conduct for Research Involving Humans (Canadian Institutes of Health Research, 2022). Institutions receiving funding through these government bodies are required to comply with the regulations and gain ethics approval from a registered human research ethics committee. In the United States, institutions that receive federal funding are governed by the Code of Federal Regulations, Title 45, Part 46 (45 CFR 46), referred to as the Common Rule. A second set of regulations has jurisdiction over privately funded research administered by the US Food and Drug Administration (see Babb, 2021 for a discussion of the increasing privatization of governance of human research ethics in the United States). In Europe, legislative frameworks have been discussed by Steinkamp et al. (2007) and Orzechowski et al. (2021). Other countries are in various stages of developing legislative frameworks as documented by Aguilera et al. (2022) for Latin America and the Caribbean. India has developed legislative frameworks for biomedical and health research through the Indian Council of Medical Research (see Behera et al., 2019).

In the UK, adults who lack the capacity to make the decision whether or not to participate in research are covered by the Mental Capacity Act or the Adults with Incapacity (Scotland) Act. The Act applies to all people who lack the capacity to make a decision at the time it is sought, whether or not the lack of capacity is permanent or temporary. Researchers undertaking research with adults who lack the capacity to consent must have their ethics application approved by a medical or social care research ethics committee who will assess the validity of the project and the necessity of people with limited capacity being involved in it. In Australia, adults who lack the capacity to consent to research can have a substitute decision-maker provide consent on their behalf, or in certain circumstances, research may be conducted without consent in emergencies. The Medical Treatment Planning and Decisions Act 2016 and the Guardianship and Administration Act 2000 outline the legal framework for these situations (see Holmes et al., 2022).

The law around the process of consent for children under the age of sixteen to participate in research is complex (see Alderson & Morrow, 2020; Spencer, 2021). Generally, children who are able to understand the implications of participation in a research study are viewed as having the 'capacity' to make a decision about whether or not to take part in research. Parental consent is needed if a child is not viewed as having the capacity to consent. However, in practice, researchers often seek parental consent (in addition to children's consent) regardless of a child's capacity to consent in order to safeguard them from any problems that might arise. However, this should not adversely impact a child's safety, emotional and psychological security and well-being. These issues are explored in more detail in Chapter 3. In line with legislation in England and Wales, Disclosure and Barring Service (DBS) checks are also necessary for researchers working with children and with other groups deemed 'vulnerable'. In Australia, individual States and Territories are responsible for the implementation of National Standards for Working with Children Checks following a Royal Commission into Institutional Responses to Child Sexual Abuse in 2017. Readers are encouraged to make sure you check what police/criminal record checks are required for work with children or vulnerable adults in your country. See the Ethical Research Involving Children (ERIC) website for useful information and resources (https://childethics.com/).

Legislation related to confidentiality varies across countries. In Australia, the Privacy Act (1988) establishes fundamental rules for how organizations manage personal data and includes provisions that allow the use of personal information without consent under certain circumstances (Blank, 2025). There is no specific legislation relating to confidentiality in the UK but there is a common law duty of confidentiality such that there is an expectation that information given in confidence to a researcher will not be disclosed without prior consent. The UK GDPR and Data Protection Act requires protection of personal information, with some exceptions for consent, overriding public interest or legal obligations. There are other situations in which commitments to confidentiality may be overridden. Failure of a researcher to take appropriate action in cases where a child discloses that they are being seriously harmed or mistreated could result in legal liability. In the UK, people who suspect a child is being mistreated are not legally obliged to report this. However, a range of professionals (such as teachers and social workers) are obliged to do so under Local Authority child protection procedures. This is the case for other countries; however, in Australia, for example the legislation differs across the States and Territories according to who is required to report, what types of abuse and neglect have to be reported, the 'state of mind' that activates the reporting duty, and who to report to (AIFS, 2024). If a qualitative researcher does not fall under a prescribed profession that is mandated to report (and this may not always be clear if the researcher is also a registered psychologist or social worker), their institution may have specific policies or an individual may have the right to voluntarily report and be protected by legislation with regard to confidentiality and immunity from legal liability. In the UK, there is no law regarding actions in the case of data relating to less serious crime and researchers are left to make their own decisions on appropriate actions, if any. In the case of adults, there is no law that obliges researchers to pass data on adults engaged in criminal activity to the legal authorities. However, researchers should be aware that research data given in confidence do not enjoy legal privilege and they may be liable to subpoena by a court (Crow & Wiles, 2008). There are no cases of this occurring in the UK but cases have been reported in other countries. These issues are discussed further in Chapter 4.

In Australia, the Privacy Act (1988) regulates how organizations collect and handle personal information, with the Privacy Commissioner providing two sets of legal guidelines that researchers must follow when handling personal information without individuals' consent and that provide guidance to Human Research Ethics Committees in deciding whether to approve research applications (Australian Government, 2024). In the UK, research privacy is primarily governed by the UK General Data Protection Regulation (UK GDPR) and the Data Protection Act 2018 (DPA, 2018). These laws ensure personal data is processed lawfully, fairly and transparently, with specific provisions for research, archiving and statistical purposes. Article 8 of the European Convention on Human Rights, incorporated into UK law through the Human Rights Act 1998, guarantees the right to respect for private and family life, home and correspondence. Observing, photographing or filming someone in a place where they might have a reasonable expectation of privacy, or indeed using personal data, might be considered an invasion of privacy. Additionally, researchers are also subject to the UK Data Protection Act which demands that data are kept securely and do not lead to any breach of agreed confidentiality and anonymity.

Copyright law is of relevance to researchers using still or moving images. Copyright rests with the person taking the image, or their employing institution. A research participant who agrees to have their photograph taken or be subject to video recording has no legal rights over the subsequent use of their image. This also applies to the archiving and reuse of visual data. In the case of respondent-generated visual data (e.g. photos a study participant has taken), copyright rests with the respondent and it is necessary for them to assign copyright to the researcher for their subsequent use in a research project (Wiles, Prosser et al., 2008). Issues of copyright are also relevant in relation to online research where clear citation of internet sources must be provided and permission given for the use of images.

The European Union's General Data Protection Regulation (GDPR) is probably one of the largest regulatory changes that sought to harmonize data protection laws across the EU. It took effect on 25 May 2018 and was originally intended to protect online consumers from having their personal data misused for marketing process, but also applies to universities and research institutions (Lynskey, 2015). The GDPR establishes a set of formal requirements around the collection, treatment and dissemination of data on research participants with new requirements around such areas as accountability, data security and informed consent. The GDPR has had a global impact with different countries introducing their own versions, such as China's Personal Information Protection Law, the State of California and Colorado passing similar privacy acts as well as Switzerland and the UK introducing their own GDPR. The EU GDPR impacts any organization or company that processes the personal data of EU-based data subjects, regardless of where that processing occurs. Data processing is defined as any operation that is performed on personal data from collection and recording to dissemination or destruction. Personal data is information related to a person which can be used to identify them directly or indirectly. Indirectly refers to a situation where someone else can identify an individual through a researcher's data set by having access to other data, even when the researcher cannot make the data identifiable. If personal data has undergone 'pseudonymisaton', the GDPR applies, as this data could be attributed to a person by combining different data or other information. 'Anonymisation' is where the data is rendered in such a way that is it no longer possible to be associated with an identifiable person and thus the GDPR does not apply (however the GPPR does apply when data is first handled to anonymize it).

A number of issues concerning the protection of personal data are relevant to qualitative researchers, although various challenges have been identified in applying GDPR regulations to the social sciences (see Raposo et al., 2022). In qualitative research, verbal or written consent is informed by national regulations and guidelines and usually focuses on protecting participants' voluntary and informed participation and preventing coercion. Under Article 4(11), the GDPR defines consent as: 'any freely given, specific, informed and unambiguous indication of the data subject's wishes by which he or she, by a statement or by a clear affirmative action, signifies agreement to the processing of personal data relating to him or her' (European Union Agency for Fundamental Rights, 2019). In this context, researchers must gain consent about how they intend to process their data including what personal data will be collected, why this will be collected, the legal ground for processing a participant's personal data, who has access to their personal data, information about the reuse of data and what rights a participant has with regard to processing their data. While researchers may not know the specific purpose of data processing at the time of data collection, GDPR does allow for research to gain consent for broader research areas. This is relevant for open ended qualitative research, such as ethnographic, narrative or community-based participatory research, where the specific purpose of the research may be unclear at the beginning of a project.

Also, of relevance for qualitative researchers is around the identifiability either directly or indirectly of participants. Under Article 9, the GDPR defines sensitive data as

> personal data revealing racial or ethnic origin, political opinions, religious or philosophical beliefs, or trade union membership, and the processing of genetic data, biometric data for the purpose of uniquely identifying a natural person, data concerning health or data concerning a natural person's sex life or sexual orientation shall. (Article 9. GDPR)

While researchers who are working with larger data sets that in themselves are not sensitive, when these are combined with other data enabling inferences, this data can become sensitive in nature (see Quinn, 2021; Quinn & Malgieri, 2021). It is very difficult to completely anonymize qualitative data. Specific information about a community context, a person's background, their age, even community events can become possible identifiers. While some efforts can be made to pseudonymize data, it can be difficult to remove all identifiers that may link to specific individuals. Various research has demonstrated the ease with which individual participants in research can be identified through data such as gender, postcode and date of birth (see El Emam, 2011). As required by the GDPR, research involving sensitive data requires that researchers follow a set of principles in processing personal data (data minimization, purpose limitation), researchers must facilitate data subject rights (rights of erasure, to object to processing and to data portability), meet certain administrative requirements (including having an appointed Data Protection Officer and Data Protection Impact

Assessment) and provide a legal base for processing data around, for example, informed consent.

The impacts of the GDPR have been variously discussed by social science disciplines, most notably in anthropology (Sleebom-Faulner & Mcmurray, 2018). These discussions underscore more extensive explorations of the tensions in ethnographic forms of inquiry that emphasize 'thick description' alongside protecting the identity of participants through anonymization (e.g. see Rhoads', 2020 discussion of anonymization issues related to her own work on fraternity life and the work of Alice Goffman in her book on fugitive life in an American city (2009). Reporting on a workshop of anthropologists in London, Yuill (2018) lays out a number of problematic areas for conducting ethnographic research within the GDPR requirements. The need for specificity around communicating with participants' consent for research activities does not account for the more fluid nature of participant observation where consent is negotiated over time and the scope of fieldwork can change depending on events, participant/research preference and other factors. The need for all aspects of data, including field notes, to be open access or shared stimulated debates on the nature of field notes that are often written as memory aids to be written up as fuller ethnographic descriptions at a later point (pseudonymization often occurs at this point). Field notes are often not shared because they can be highly identifiable and personal in nature and complete anonymization can be very difficult. Workshop participants, Yuill (2018) tells us, expressed that anonymization (involving the removal of both direct and indirect personal identifiers) strips away the very strengths of ethnographic approaches that strive to write about people, their lives and their practices in specific contexts. Reflecting on the controversy around Nancy Scheper-Hughes (2000) research on mental illness in a rural Irish village, where the 'pseudonymised' village was later identified and written up in a series of articles for the *Irish Times*, de-identification can cause research participants distress where they are excluded or do not agree with the way they have been portrayed in qualitative research.

> 'Naming', then, creates the possibility for more robust fieldwork and reporting of findings, and it enhances the ethical conduct of researchers who, without the protection of anonymity, can no longer conceal poor evidence. (Yuill, 2018)

This is particularly pertinent for participatory research approaches where the GDPR would have issues with research participants being named as co-authors or choosing to be identified in the co-production of knowledge. One response to these issues has been the issuance of statements from various anthropological and sociological associations, who have appealed to Article 85(2) of the GDPR that allows for a number of provisions to prevent undue restrictions for the humanities and social sciences around 'academic expression' (see e.g. https://www.theasa.org/downloads/Joint%20ASA%20BSA%20ESA%20RGS%20statement%200418.pdf and https://easaonline.org/wp-content/uploads/2025/06/EASA-statement-on-data-governance.pdf).

Making Ethical Decisions

How can these ethical frameworks, guidance and regulation be used in practice in making decisions about ethical issues that are anticipated prior to a study commencing or that emerge throughout the process of research? There are various resources which provide researchers with advice about managing the 'standard' ethical issues that need to be addressed in the process of obtaining approval from a research ethics committee (see, e.g. Iphofen, 2009 and Iphofen & Tolich, 2018). These guidelines and resources do differ by country. In European and Scandinavian countries, research ethics guidelines have a deontological focus where the aim is to protect the rights of individuals as autonomous citizens, whereas in the UK, United States, Canada, Australia and New Zealand guidelines are more utilitarian in focus asking researchers to consider whether the potential harms are outweighed by potential benefits of research (Franzke et al., 2020). Other ethical perspectives include Indigenous emphases on relationality and social justice (Kara, 2018)

In preparing applications for committees, researchers obviously have to draw on the various frameworks, guidance and regulation outlined above. Committees also play a role in monitoring and advising on the management of ethical issues at the anticipatory stage of research. More challenging are the ethical issues that emerge during the process of conducting research (see Guillemin & Gillam, 2004). Such challenges are often unique to the context of a research project, are unexpected and unplanned for; researchers are often presented with an ethical issue for which they feel ill-prepared and unsure about how best to resolve.

Various strategies exist that researchers use to manage such ethical challenges. The strategies that researchers use to make decisions draw on various elements of the frameworks outlined above, although researchers' deliberations may not always involve a conscious engagement with these frameworks. Often researchers may resolve their ethical dilemmas by drawing on their moral judgement about the appropriate course of action, but this is invariably one that is informed by ethical frameworks. While researchers may argue that research is situated and contextual and that ethical dilemmas cannot be resolved by appeal to higher principles and codes, the argument presented in this book is that an understanding of moral codes and principles does not force researchers into specific predetermined decisions but rather assists them in making sound, justifiable ethical decisions.

Various models to guide decision-making in the face of ethical challenges have been identified. Israel and Hay (2006: 132), for example, outline a seven-step process involving: (i) identifying the nature of the problem and the stakeholders involved; (ii) identifying various options for resolving the dilemmas; (iii) identifying the range of consequences of each option for different stakeholders; (iv) considering the short and long-term implications of decisions; (v) considering the options by reference to moral principles such as honesty, trust, autonomy, fairness and equality; (vi) integrating consequences and principles to reach an independent and justifiable decision; (vii) reflecting on the decision. Israel and Hay (2006: 135) provide a number of questions that researchers can ask themselves as part of the process of reflecting on the morality of the proposed action to be taken to resolve the ethical dilemma:

> Several prompts can be used to reflect on the action that is about to be adopted. MacDonald (2002) urges us to consider the following: will I feel comfortable telling a close family member such as my mother or father what I have done; how would I feel if my actions were to attract media attention; how would I feel if my children followed my example; and is mine the behaviour of a wise and virtuous person?

A similar model is proposed by Kitchener and Kitchener (2009: 9) who identify the different levels of reasoning that underpin ethical decision-making. They note that researchers can move up through the levels according to the complexity of the decision. At level 1 is a researcher's moral sense which is informed by their beliefs and values. At level 2 are the various ethical codes and disciplinary frameworks which guide moral decision-making and which form the 'accumulated wisdom' of a profession or discipline. If ethical dilemmas cannot be resolved at these levels, they need to be critically evaluated in relation to ethical principles such as beneficence, non-maleficence, honesty and fairness to reach a sound and justifiable ethical decision.

Research Ethics, Integrity and Governance

Research ethics, integrity and governance are often used interchangeably, causing confusion for research and institutional administrators (Kolstoe & Pugh, 2023; see also Pretova & Barclay, 2019 and Kolstoe & Carpenter, 2023). Research integrity has been described as a form of social virtue whereby a researcher adheres to a set of moral principles in conducting research, such as honesty, transparency, rigour, collaboration and so on (Kolstoe & Pugh, 2023; see also Joynson & Leyse, 2015). Characteristics of research integrity are often disciplinary specific and framed by institutional culture and education. However, researchers generally share a common understanding of research integrity as a combination of honesty, transparency and objectivity (Shaw & Satalkar, 2018). The moral principles upon which a researcher plans to organize and conduct their study are assessed by a research ethics committee. Human research ethics relates to the moral principles supporting the design and execution of research projects that involve other people's lives. A research ethics committee makes a judgement as to whether a particular piece of research should be conducted as proposed. Human research ethics committees are guided in their judgements by different ethical frameworks, such as principlism, but they must also be sensitive to the practical realities of conducting research (see *Introduction*). Finally, research governance is related to the research duties required by researchers and institutions as laid out in laws and policies that are assessed by research officers. Governance is related to how institutions manage, oversee and regulate research on the basis of specific laws, insurance requirements, indemnity obligations, employment contracts and other local regulations. In England and Wales, the Health Research Authority (HRA)/ Health and Care Research Wales under the National Health Service provides various guidance on legal and compliance issues, including special consideration of qualitative research and protocols (www .hra.nhs.uk). Where the NHS has duty of care, researchers can submit one application that will receive an assessment of governance and legal compliance in addition to an independent ethical opinion by a research ethics committee. Other countries also have national organizations that provide guidance to the internal activities of institutions conducting human research (see e.g. the Australian National Health and Medical Research handbook on Research Governance 2011). Kolstoe and Pugh (2023) describe that ethical opinion provided by research ethics committees should be kept separate from research governance, because they relate to fundamentally different considerations. Ethics consider societal norms and principles; governance, legal/policy compliance. However, good governance should be contingent on being viewed favourably by a research ethics committee. While research integrity, ethics and governance are linked, it is important that they are clearly identified in promoting and conducting good research.

Summary

This chapter has outlined the various guidelines, approaches and frameworks that inform, and in some cases constrain, ethical decision-making. These include ethical frameworks, professional guidelines and ethical and legal regulation. An understanding of these provides an important basis from which researchers can think through, and argue the case for, their ethical decisions.

CHAPTER 3

Informed Consent

Introduction

Informed consent is a central concept in ethical research practice and is one of the key principles underpinning professional guidelines for social scientists (in the UK see e.g., British Psychological Society, 2021; British Sociological Association, 2017; Social Research Association, 2021; in Australia, see for example, The Australian Sociological Association, 2025, the Australian Anthropological Association, 2012, Australian Psychological Society, 2007, in the United States see American Psychological Association, 2016, American Anthropological Society, 2025, American Sociological Association, 2018). It involves providing participants with clear information about what participating in a research project will involve and giving them the opportunity to decide whether or not they want to participate (Wiles et al., 2008). Specifically, research participants need to be made aware of: what the research is about; why it is being conducted; who is funding it; what will happen to the results and how they will be disseminated; what their participation in the project will involve; what the potential risks and benefits of their involvement might be; and how issues of anonymity and confidentiality will be managed. Potential research participants should also be made aware that they are not obliged to take part and that they can withdraw from the study if they later change their mind about participating.

While at first glance informed consent may appear a relatively straightforward issue, a closer examination of the issues involved reveals that the process is far from straightforward. Social researchers have to balance a number of factors in managing issues of informed consent. Obviously, they have to comply with any legal frameworks and regulations as discussed in Chapter 2, but additionally they have to balance a range of sometimes competing interests, such as the aims of the research, what they consider to be the best interests of research participants as well as the interests of formal or informal gatekeepers. They also have to operationalize and be reflexive about issues of 'information', 'consent' and 'competence'. This chapter explores general issues of informed consent as they apply to qualitative research across methodological approaches.

Notions of informed consent imply that participants will always be fully informed about what participating in research will involve. While recognizing that intentions to 'fully inform' participants may be problematic, which is discussed below, it is also important to note that there are some research projects in which participants cannot be fully informed about the research before it takes place; to do so would render the research impossible to undertake. Various research projects in psychology, for example, explore behaviour in specific contexts that would change if study participants were made aware of the aims of the study. In research projects such as these, participants are consented to the research on the basis of limited or false information about the study aims but they should always be fully debriefed after the data have been collected and at this point be given full information about the study and have the opportunity to give full consent for their data to be used; they would be expected to have the right to withdraw themselves, and their data, from the study if they wished to do so. In the light of concerns raised about unethical experiments conducted by social psychologists in the 1960s and 1970s, such as the well-known Milgram experiment on obedience to authority and the Stanford Prison experiment (see http://www.experiment-resources.com /milgram-experiment-ethics.html), there are very strict ethical controls on how informed consent is managed in studies when some level of limited disclosure is necessary for the research to be conducted (see British Psychological Society, 2021).

Covert research is another type of research in which informed consent prior to the research commencing is not possible (see Marzano, 2021). There have been some important studies which have conducted research covertly, particularly in the area of criminology. Typical examples are studies of football hooligans, of neo-Nazi groups and of corporate activities (see Scratton, 2004). Some proponents of covert research have argued that it is in the interests of the general public to expose how some organizations or institutions operate and, in some cases, the only way this can occur is through covert means. However, various criticisms of covert research have been raised, including that it violates the principle of informed consent, invades privacy, betrays trust and 'spoils the field' for other researchers (for a discussion of these issues see Herrera, 1999; Homan & Bulmer, 1982; Homan, 1991; Punch, 1986; Spicker, 2011). In the face of increasing ethical regulation of research, research conducted completely covertly has become relatively rare. Nevertheless, it is still the case that much research, while not expressly covert, may take place without participants being fully aware of to what they are consenting (see Chapter 7 for a discussion of informed consent in Web 2.0 and Web 3.0 research contexts). A good example of this is the use of various social media as research data and the challenges that researchers face in protecting confidentiality and seeking informed consent for the use of publicly available information in, for example, YouTube videos, Instagram posts or Twitter/X tweets (see Chojnicka, 2024, for a discussion of ethical issues related to studying gender transition narratives in Polish social media).

In research that involves visual methods, there are additional challenges around consent. Consent should be obtained for taking and using images generated in a research project, especially when such images identify individuals. However, this in itself is not always straightforward in that it may not be possible to obtain consent for all people in images and, even if consent is obtained, respondents may not be able to fully appreciate what the implications of being identified may be. The fact that it is increasingly the preference of both researchers and respondents that study participants are *not* anonymized in visual research findings raises a further set of ethical considerations, not least that this presents a challenge to established ethical practice.

In conducting research in other countries and cultural contexts, the notion of informed consent and personal autonomy may be differently interpreted. For example, Akpa-Inyang and Cham (2021) have argued that western European concepts of a libertarian rights-based autonomy do not always align with African values and norms.

Values such as communalism, traditional customs, spirituality and relational autonomy play a central role in many African societies. These are reflected in African moral philosophies, which prioritize the collective good over individual rights. Their study also revealed that factors such as language, education levels, poverty, and cultural beliefs create obstacles to obtaining informed consent in African communities and that an approach which emphasizes a more relational approach to informed consent is more appropriate.

Providing Information

The provision of information about a project is an important part of ensuring that potential participants understand what participating in a research project might entail. However, many issues need to be taken into consideration in making decisions about this; these include how much information to provide, when to provide it and how often to repeat it. In terms of the *amount* of information to provide, it is clearly important to provide comprehensive information about the project so that participants can understand what being a participant will involve for them. However, giving very comprehensive information that runs to several pages is likely to be very off-putting; not only are people unlikely to read it or take it in, it also risks putting them off participating. Various researchers have also pointed out the specific challenges in providing understandable information when working in cross-language qualitative research studies (Mohamad-Nasri et al., 2021). Ethical regulation, particularly for research conducted in health care settings and subject to review by national bodies such as the National Research Ethics Service (NRES) in the UK, may pose severe restrictions on researchers' ability to provide information in a non-standard way. In the United States, informed consent in medical research is governed by federal regulations outlined in the Common Rule (45 CFR 46) under 46.116 General Requirements (https://www.ecfr.gov/current/title-45/subtitle-A/subchapter-A/part -46#p-46.111(a)(8)).

Consideration of *how* information is provided is also important. It is obviously crucial that information is presented in a user-friendly way. This involves giving consideration to the layout, colour, size of text, type of language and the inclusion of graphics in the provision of information. For researchers working with children, young people or groups with limited comprehension, innovative ways often need to be identified to engage with participants to enable them to understand what participating in a study might involve. This is likely to involve keeping written information to a minimum and incorporating pictures and other graphics into the information provided. Researchers have experimented with a range of ways of providing information to meet these needs including the use of photos, comic strips and video (Clarke et al., 2011). Beck et al. (2025) have produced guidelines for the creation of accessible consent materials and procedures when conducting research with people living with autism and intellectual disabilities. They suggest the following

1   Involve people with lived experience on the research team.
2   Seek out collaborators with expertise in human research participant protections.
3   Start with checklists instead of templates.
4   Improve written language and formatting.
5   Use participant-centred language.
6   Use precise phrasing.
7   Structure information in a logical order.
8   Integrate visuals.
9   Simplify and integrate authorization language, as applicable (Beck et al., 2025: 5).

A further practical issue involves consideration of *when* to provide information. In some research contexts, particularly if the research is complex, it may be appropriate to provide some introductory information to potential participants about the research and to provide full information only if they express an interest in participating. This is one way of dealing with potential information overload for participants. In longitudinal studies or research with repeated stages of data collection, it may be appropriate to provide information, and gain consent, for each stage of data collection to ensure that participants give their continuing consent to participate in the study. This approach highlights the importance of viewing consent as a process that is ongoing throughout a project rather than as a one-off event that occurs when recruiting people to a study. Some researchers, regardless of the type of study or its methodology, view adopting a model of 'process consent' as appropriate, in which consent is discussed and negotiated throughout the whole period of a study because it ensures that participants have the opportunity to review their participation and the use of their information (Goodenough et al., 2004; Cameron et al., 2004; Cutliffe & Ramcharan, 2002). This is an approach adopted particularly by researchers working in participatory research and ethnographic paradigms (Klykken, 2022). Renold et al. (2008) provide a good example of this approach in their study of the everyday lives and identities of children in care, in which consent was negotiated at all stages of the project:

> Children's 'consent' forms (requested by the university ethics committee) were purposively constructed as open-ended, partial and provisional, ensuring that children and young people could choose how to engage in a research project. Our overall aim was to use a language that framed their participation as always negotiable. For example, they could choose whether or not they wished to sign the consent form and a designated part of the leaflet was formed in which they could outline their own expectations or desires about the project and our own role as researchers . . . our approach [was] to engage in an ongoing dialogue from the outset, which involved developing personalized ethical protocols 'in the moment' with children and young people. (Renold et al., 2008: 443)

Underlying these practical issues of how much information to give, how to present it and when and how often to give it, are a number of challenges inherent in the research process which give rise to ethical dilemmas that impact on the decisions that researchers make about these issues. The first is the difficulty in providing comprehensive information to research participants about a study. In qualitative research, the specific focus and outcomes of a research study, and perhaps even the phases of data collection, are often not known at the start of a study as study design is generally emergent. So, for example, at the outset of a study, a general research focus or set of questions may have been designed but the number of study participants, the number of interviews to be carried out with each individual and the specific direction of the research is often dependent on the data collected and the emerging analysis. This is particularly the case for ethnographic research. The use of digital media, in addition to other creative approaches, to establish a range of communication needs and preferences, has been identified as a good way to support continued engagement with some population groups, such as children and young people (see Sherwood & Parsons, 2021).

A related issue concerns the ways in which the data collected will be written up and disseminated in public arenas which are unlikely to be known at the start of a research project; indeed, the dissemination of research findings may continue for many years after the completion of a project. While researchers have varying views about whether or not consent should refer only to participation in a study rather than the way data are used in publications, it is, nevertheless, an important issue for consideration in relation to consent and one which links closely to issues of anonymity and confidentiality and ownership of data. Clearly, if data are in any sense 'owned' by participants (such as photographs they have taken) or if participants are potentially identifiable, then consent needs to be extended to the ways in which data are used. The point here is that the ability to give comprehensive information at the beginning of a study about what participating will involve for an individual and what will happen to the data produced is often impossible. It is also the case, of course, that it is impossible to know what participating in a research project will be like for specific individuals. Researchers cannot know what particular issues an individual might feel sensitive about or find distressing or what the experience of participating will be like for them. Various authors have noted that it is unlikely that participants can ever fully understand to what they are consenting and what researchers' intentions are (Miller & Bell, 2002; Prosser, 2000; Wiles et al., 2007). The best a researcher can do is to aim to give optimal information, to anticipate what risks could arise from the project and to inform participants of them, to consider the stages at which consent is necessary and to make plans for achieving such consent. More recently, in the era of open access and 'big data', there are new complexities for researchers for gaining informed consent (see Mills, 2017 and Chapter 7). The Qualitative Data Repository (2017–2023) housed at the University of Syracuse is a dedicated archive for storing and sharing data generated by qualitative researchers (https://qdr.syr.edu/). QDR provides advice and templates as to how to manage informed consent for long-term storage and data sharing encouraging researchers to communicate to participants who will be able to access the data, what the data will be used for and details about confidentiality protections, in addition to specifying options around data availability, such as redactions/omissions of certain portions of information (https://qdr .syr.edu/guidance/human-participants/informed-consent).

A second challenge inherent in the research process is that it is often difficult to provide information (and gain consent) from everyone involved in a research project. This is particularly the case when conducting research in public settings, such as at public events, in shopping malls, libraries, art galleries, schools or hospital waiting rooms. In such cases it might be possible to inform key individuals, but providing detailed information to everyone who might be observed or in some way 'participate' in a study in a public setting is likely to be impractical if not impossible. It is generally the case that researchers attempt to inform people in public arenas that research is being undertaken by, for example, putting up posters informing people about a project and when data collection is taking place. This provides the possibility for individuals to remove themselves if they do not wish to 'participate', or, if practical, request that they are excluded from data collection. Even in research in less public settings, such as in people's homes, it can be the case that others contribute, such as in cases when a spouse or friends of a research participant are present during an interview and contribute to it. It is a moot point whether or not people who have contributed in a minor, and unexpected, way to a research project should be considered as participants for whom consent is needed. In general, this is likely to depend on the level of their involvement.

A third challenge involves the role of gatekeepers to research participants (Singh & Wassenaar, 2016). Some research projects necessitate researchers gaining consent from various gatekeepers, such as managers, headteachers or hospital consultants, before it is possible to approach the individuals who are to be invited to be research participants. There is a growing body of research around informed consent and gatekeepers with various population groups, such as children and young people (Sherwood & Parsons, 2021), staff from institutions and governments (Christian et al., 2022; Komil-

Burley, 2021; Kars et al., 2016), people with disabilities (Williams, 2020), people who have experienced gender-based violence (Miller et al., 2022) and 'vulnerable' and minority populations more generally (Kay, 2019; McAreavey & Das, 2013; Walker & Read, 2011). While gatekeepers may need to give permission for individuals in their employ or care to be approached, this does not negate the need to seek consent from the specific individuals being invited to participate in a study. It may be that gatekeepers view themselves as able to consent for others they are responsible for, but researchers should ensure that in addition to gatekeeper approval, approval from individual participants is also sought. This can be difficult to do in some institutions where gatekeepers view themselves as in a position to give consent on behalf of those for whom they are responsible or who are in their care as may be the case in prisons or schools. Even if approached to give consent, the extent to which consent is freely and voluntarily given in contexts in which power dynamics form part of the relationship with the gatekeeper can be difficult; schools, prisons and residential institutions are clear examples where gaining consent from participants may be difficult because of a culture of compliance. In cases where someone in a powerful position in an organization who has sanctioned a research project will know that an individual has refused to participate, it may feel that, in effect, an individual's choice whether or not to consent is limited. The onus is on researchers to identify ways in which research participants are enabled to make decisions whether or not to participate in research, free from any influence from gatekeepers.

This will involve researchers spending time with participants to explore their wishes. It may also involve identifying ways to keep their decisions confidential from gatekeepers. Heath et al. (2009: 33) identify a range of strategies that researchers working in educational contexts have used to enable children and young people to decline to participate in research without their teacher's knowledge. These include providing alternative activities for participants to do when ostensibly participating in research. Research with children and other (so-called) 'vulnerable groups' who are viewed as lacking the 'capacity' (or 'competence') to give consent raises related but specific issues, and these will be explored in a separate section in this chapter.

Another key related set of issues is the critiques around informed consent from Indigenous commentators, who have explained that research ethics committees often marginalize Indigenous approaches to knowledge construction and dissemination (Tauri, 2018; West-McGruer, 2020). For many Indigenous communities, Tauri (2018) explains, the notion of informed consent is based on the liberal democratic tradition of the autonomous individual. However, in many Indigenous communities, individual rights are defined by the collective, as Butz notes in Canada:

> Conventional informed consent guidelines as exemplified by the [Canadian] Tri-Council Policy Statement presuppose an individuated liberal humanist research subject that is incommensurate with the subjectivities of our actual research participants as they experience them, and as the theoretical perspectives upon which much qualitative research is based conceptualise them. (2008: 241)

Indigenous writers have repeatedly emphasized that informed consent is an ongoing two-way process that is based on notions of cultural systems of authority and collectivity. As Pique notes for Canadian First Nation peoples

> When investigating knowledge that the community considers sacred, researchers must get consent from the keeper of this knowledge before seeking consent from various individuals who are willing to become research participants. The idea of sacred knowledge as a group's intellectual property highlights the distinction that needs to be made between individual knowledge and collective knowledge. (2001: 76)

Tauri (2018) notes that institutionalized ethics procedures can be viewed as a politics of containment that disempowers Indigenous voice and perspectives. Thus, decolonizing the structures of power and perspectives that support ethics committees is important. Countries such as Australia, New Zealand and Canada, among others, have developed Indigenous ethics guidelines and resources, alongside a growing literature in this area.

Similarly, in migrant health research, the eurocentrism informing principles of informed consent and its problematic interpretation in refugee and migrant contexts has been criticized (Ijsselmuiden

& Faden, 1992). Various researchers have discussed the cultural differences in understanding and interpreting informed consent, in addition to power differentials and living conditions of migrants that may make autonomy difficult in the consent process (see Zapata-Barrero & Yalaz, 2020 for a roadmap for migration scholars around qualitative migration research ethics). Hugman and colleagues (2011), in an article exploring the ethics of research involving refugees and other vulnerable groups, argue that while the principle of 'informed consent' is ethically sound, evidence from studies with refugee populations suggests that it falls short, as it misrepresents the extent to which research participants are able to exercise moral autonomy. It is not that participants do not understand consent, rather Hugman and colleagues (2011: 2078–9) explain that

> it reflects the quite tangible and stark power differentials between them and those who want to involve them in the research process and also the implications of the context in which consent is being sought. This makes asking for permission to interview people in such vulnerable situations or take photographs highly problematic, to say the least. Indeed, as one researcher asked, 'what does "informed consent" mean in an isolated . . . camp with security problems and no proper interpreters?' (Pittaway and Bartolomei, 2003: 37), to which the answer has to be that it may mean very little, unless researchers attend to their considerable responsibilities to respect the humanity of participants, to pursue beneficence and non-maleficence and to seek justice.

Citing power imbalances between researchers and refugee research participants, Hugman and colleagues (2011) advocate embedding informed consent within participatory, relational models to ensure that research relationships are empowering, reciprocal and reflexive (see also McCracken 2020 for a discussion of the ethical challenges when research participants encounter the positivistic frameworks of human research ethics committees in community based participatory research).

These discussions align with recent conversations about what has been termed 'epistemic injustice' (Kau et al., 2023; Hopman et al., 2023). Epistemic injustice involves denying individuals from marginalized groups the opportunity to produce knowledge or to be recognized as legitimate sources of their own understanding (see also discussion of data sovereignty in Chapter 7). Epistemic injustice can arise from academic research processes that uphold hegemonic power structures, determining who has the legitimate authority to create and disseminate knowledge about others. This includes

> exclusion and silencing; invisibility and inaudibility (or distorted presence or representation); having one's meanings or contributions systematically distorted, misheard, or misrepresented; having diminished status or standing in communicative practices; unfair differentials in authority and/or epistemic agency; being unfairly distrusted; receiving no or minimal uptake; being co-opted or instrumentalized; being marginalized as a result of dysfunctional dynamics. (Kidd et al., 2017: 1)

Epistemic injustice supports neo-colonialism by manifesting power inequalities in various relationships, both geopolitical (Global North/Global South) and local (universities and academics/ populations, such as migrants, Indigenous people and those living with disabilities). Pratt and De Vries (2023) highlight the urgent need to address the epistemic injustice caused by the exclusion of Global South perspectives in bioethics and propose a tripartite framework—focused on knowledge production, application and inclusion—as a foundation for reorienting global health ethics through understanding, dialogue and structural change. This aligns with other calls for epistemic justice, such as Guishard et al'.s (2018) appeal to reimagine the APA Ethics Code to better support social justice-oriented qualitative research by addressing epistemological gaps, emphasizing reflexivity, intersubjectivity and power dynamics and challenging conventional norms of knowledge production.

Informed consent has been an important consideration in ethical debates around epistemic injustice. In a study of the development rights of children in Moroccan controlled Western Sahara, Hopman argues that covert research without informed consent can be carried out in contexts of authoritarian regimes. Hopman (2021: 562) suggests that covert research is ethically permissible when:

1   the research aims to contribute to the protection of human rights,

2   the research participants remain anonymous, and

3   there is no other, overt way to obtain the necessary data.

In an article critiquing Hopman's use of a consequentialist paradigm, Kau and colleagues (2023) argue that Hopman's arguments are problematic in that they support various forms of epistemic injustice. Kau and colleagues (2023) challenge extractive research practices that employ international human rights frameworks that deny situated frameworks and concepts used by participants themselves. They argue that Hopman's conceptualization of informed consent omits the principles of autonomy and agency, instead limiting it to a right to information related to data privacy. Kau and colleagues seek to reframe research participants as active, legitimate bearers of knowledge. Kau and colleagues (2023), argue that when conducting research, researchers should follow a decolonial approach that emphasizes epistemic justice, which includes processes to support cross-cultural dialogue, reflexivity and reciprocity. Such approaches seek to support participants role in the active participation in knowledge production and avoid extractive data process that dismisses the credibility of participants. Hopman (2023) wrote a reply to the critique, acknowledging some of the points raised, while also justifying and clarifying her original argument in addition to providing a testimonial from a participant who was involved in the research study. Hopman contends that when informed consent is impossible due to the potential for human rights violations, covert research at specific phases of the study is ethically justifiable, provided the aim is to protect the human rights of participants. Hopman also provides important comments about the personal impact of rebuttals and academic exchange (Hopman 2023: 392–393).

Alongside these discussions, there has been a growing critique of the static, hierarchical researcher-participant relationships that the informed consent process can often represent. Following new materialist ontologies (Fox & Alldred, 2015), qualitative researchers, such as Klykken (2022), have called for a decentring of the researcher's authority and argued for perspectives that privilege the 'assemblematic' nature of the research processes that are relational, continuous and do not constantly assume participant vulnerability. Drawing on an ethnographic inquiry in an educational setting, Klykken (2022) emphasizes the concepts of 'response-ability' and 'thinking with care', framing informed consent as a reflexive and ethical tool applied throughout all phases of the research—pre-fieldwork, fieldwork and post-fieldwork. Guishard and colleagues (2018) likewise challenge the notion of knowledge production in research as neutral and objective, advocating for a deeper engagement with social justice. Current ethical codes are grounded in individualistic assumptions about rights, benefits and harms, which, as Guishard et al. (2018) explain, reduce 'complex cultural, structural, and systemic issues to individual behaviors, attributions, and responsibilities'. They call for new codes of ethics that emphasize collective, holistic and relational forms of knowledge production, that are reflexive and work towards social justice. Drawing on a range of research collaborations by the Public Science Project (PSP) at the Graduate Centre of CUNY, Fine (2016) also describes a critical participatory approach that seeks to reshape how knowledge is produced. This approach enables the rich documentation of counter-narratives and challenges dominant hegemonic discourses in collaboration with research participants who have historically been misrepresented as 'Others' (Fine, 2016: 47).

A fourth challenge around negotiating research participants consent and participation in research concerns operationalizing their right to withdraw from research. Part of informed consent concerns giving people the right to withdraw from their participation in a study at any point. This implies the need for researchers to ensure that they have people's ongoing consent to participate in a study (as discussed above) and that they are sensitive to recognizing participants' expressions of desire to opt out of a study. It is generally expected that information sheets and consent forms would state that participants have the right to withdraw from a study at any stage. However, researchers have noted that it is common, particularly for some groups, to be reluctant to state they do not want to continue being involved with a project (Alderson, 2004). So, for example, children might find it difficult to tell an adult that they no longer want to participate in a study or that they do not want to answer a particular question. The same issue can apply to people in a range of contexts because of the power relations that can exist between the researcher and the researched or simply a lack of awareness that they can say no to something to which they have previously agreed. Researchers need to be vigilant to participants' unspoken expressions of reluctance to continue to participate during data collection, such as an apparent lack of interest or irritation with the data collection (see Langston, Abbott, Lewis & Kellet, 2004;

Rodgers, 1999). In research with children and people with limited communication, some researchers have used 'stop' cards that participants can hold up if they do not want to answer a particular question or no longer want to participate (Wiles, Heath, Crow & Charles, 2005). If this type of method is to be used, it is important that participants practice using it before the data collection proper commences.

In reality, wholesale promises that participants can withdraw from a study at any time may be difficult to uphold and researchers need to think through the process whereby they can manage individual requests to withdraw from a study. It may be that enabling participants to withdraw is actually time-limited. While it may be straightforward for individuals to decline to participate in a specific phase of data collection, the withdrawal of data from an individual once analysis has taken place can be difficult, if not impossible. The limits to withdrawal from a study need to be made clear to research participants.

A final challenge is that, in some areas of research, people are often keen to take part because of an interest in the topic, because they do not want to appear uncooperative by saying 'no', because they are unaware of any risks that participation might involve or because they trust the researcher. In these cases, study participants often disregard researchers' explanations of what the research will involve or are reluctant to take the time needed to read information sheets properly. It can be very difficult to be sure that participants understand what they are consenting to in such contexts. One interviewee in a study on informed consent, for example, noted (Wiles et al., 2007: 6):

> We do what we can just to hold back young people's enthusiasm for taking part because on the whole most young people are very keen to take part and to be listened to . . . we as researchers can be sort of overwhelmed by young people's enthusiasm and just think 'yeah they understand, fine let's get on' . . . 'that's informed consent' and I, you know, I don't think it is . . . they just think 'oh great, this sounds fun'.

This can be particularly challenging in projects involving inter-national collaborations involving multiple countries, researchers and universities and where there can be variations not only in local ethical guidelines but approaches and traditions around informed consent (see Glasdam, Cathaoir & Stjernswärd, 2024).

Encouraging Participation: Incentives, Encouragement and Acknowledgement

The issue of whether or not some form of recompense, either financial or material, should be given to research participants as part of the process of consent is a subject of some debate (Largent & Fernandez Lynch, 2017; Różyńska, 2022). Recompense can be viewed as an incentive or inducement that may offer considerable encouragement for some groups to participate in research, who might without the 'reward' offered decline to participate. On the other hand, some researchers view such 'rewards' to be a just recompense for the time and effort of being involved in a research study. Nevertheless, the issue of payments raises questions about the role of 'rewards' when these are offered as part of the information given to participants about a study and whether this impacts negatively on the extent to which informed consent can be freely given. Various guidelines have been developed for researchers by funding bodies with regards to payment to participants (NHS, 2024; NHRMC, 2019).

It is clearly important that study participants are not out of pocket as a result of participating in research; travel expenses and any expenses relating to loss of income as a result of participating in research cannot be seen as an undue inducement. Payments, or other rewards such as gift vouchers, might arguably be viewed in a different light. Decisions about offering 'rewards' of some type are hampered by the fact that some groups, particularly various professional groups, are unlikely to agree to participate in research unless they are paid for their time. This has led some researchers to the view that, in the interests of fairness, all research participants should be paid a fee, not just those who demand it. In relation to 'hard to reach' groups, who have been traditionally excluded from research, ways need to be identified to encourage participation and these might include some form of 'appropriate reward'. Whether or not the importance of gaining insight into these previously excluded groups should override concerns about incentives would need consideration and justification. There is also the issue that some researchers, particularly those working in areas of deprivation and need, may view it as important to be able to 'give something back' to participants by way of acknowledging them for their time and effort. Such 'rewards' might be personal to an individual participant or to an organization or community. In Smyth's (2004: 53) study on segregation in South Africa, for example, food was given to interview participants and a donation made to a local organization that worked in the community. The challenges that 'rewards' for participation pose for informed consent can be offset by not informing participants that they will be paid until after they have agreed to participate. In this way, any payment or benefit becomes a 'thank you' for participating rather than an incentive. The difficulty with this is that it is not always possible to keep this a surprise when research takes place among a bounded group of participants, as word of mouth is likely to circulate quickly so a 'thank you' can soon become an incentive.

Recording Consent

The process of gaining consent involves researchers obtaining evidence that participants have consented to take part in a research project and have an understanding of the key issues involved. Consent should cover a general agreement to participate as well as confirmation that participants understand how data will be recorded, how anonymity and confidentiality will be managed and how the study will be disseminated. If specific consent is needed for the use of material owned by participants and/or it is intended that data will be archived for secondary analysis, there should be a space for participants to indicate whether or not they consent to this. Where the research design is complex or where consent is sought for a range of different activities, a consent form should include options so that participants can give or withhold their consent for each of them.

Iphofen (2009: 74) notes that consent 'should be gained in the most convenient, least disturbing manner for both researcher and researched'. In practice, it is common that researchers use signed consent forms; indeed, with the rise of ethical regulation, signed consent forms have become the norm in social research. The perceived advantages of using signed consent forms are that they increase the likelihood that participants understand what participation involves and that they protect the researcher from any subsequent complaints from study participants (Coomber, 2002). However, asking an individual for a signature can be problematic in some research contexts, particularly in research that relates to socially unacceptable behaviour or in particular cultural contexts (see Wynn & Israel, 2018). Researchers such as Coomber (2002) and the Domestic Violence Research Group (2004) have noted that the use of signed consent forms may compromise issues of confidentiality and anonymity which are important issues where participants are in need of protection. Participants may fear that signed consent forms may make the information they provide traceable to them, which may put them at risk of physical harm (in the context of research topics such as domestic violence) or vulnerable to potential investigation and prosecution by the criminal justice system (in the case of illegal activities). Coomber (2002) has noted that individuals may want to protect their identities from the researcher and expecting them to divulge it runs counter to other ethical principles. He notes that individuals involved in illegal activities who are asked to sign consent forms are unlikely to want to participate in research and, if they do so, they are likely to give a false name, thereby making the process meaningless. Furthermore, Coomber notes that signed consent forms are not in the interests of researchers as they may force them to be complicit in the prosecution of research participants which would contravene researchers' responsibilities to participants. In an even more critical analysis, ethnographers have critiqued the written consent form as a 'fetished' object that is representative of Western traditions of cultural bureaucracy, removing local meanings and constructions of the consent process (Wynn & Israel, 2018).

Additionally, signed consent is problematic when working with people who are illiterate or have language or communication problems or indeed when working with people who do not have a good command of the language in which the research is taking place. It is also the case that the need to obtain a signature in other contexts might be problematic in that it makes the process a formal one, and this might be seen as off-putting for some people. Researchers have developed a range of ways of obtaining consent without the use of signatures which may be appropriate in some circumstances, such as the use of tape-recorded consent, providing marks on a consent form, or, in the case of people with limited verbal communication skills, holding up red or green cards to indicate yes or no. While the opportunities to use alternatives to signed consent forms may be limited by ethical regulation, nevertheless a case can be made, in certain circumstances, for different approaches to recording consent. The challenge for researchers is to find a way to record that study participants give their informed consent to participate in a project. Signed consent does not necessarily achieve this any better than other methods.

Consent in Online Research

Online research raises particular challenges for consent which differ according to the specific online research method being used. More detailed information on these issues can be found in Hooley et al. (2012), Ess (2002), Zimmer and Kinder-Kurlanda (2017), Woodfield (2017) and on the Exploring Online Research Methods website, http:// www.restore.ac.uk/orm/ethics/ethcontents.htm

In relation to online interviews with people identified through personal contacts, online forums or discussion groups, consent can be gained through the use of a consent form, either in hard copy or electronic. One difficulty raised is that in the virtual world it is impossible to know if a study participant is who they say they are. Assessing their capacity to give informed consent may be difficult and it may not be possible to ascertain their age, status or vulnerability. Researchers have recently drawn attention to increasing issues related to 'imposter participants' in online interview studies both at the recruitment and interview stages (Giles et al., 2025). Imposter participants may be internet 'bots' or humans that complete multiple surveys seeking payments and monetary rewards. Giles et al. (2025) provide valuable case studies of online surveys that experienced fraudulent responses related to individual participants answering surveys multiple times on a very large scale. They suggest researchers need to plan their recruitment process carefully and to use careful prescreening processes to filter out non-genuine participants, including the use of strict verification checks, screening software and targeted recruitment methodologies.

Data collected needs to go through manual validation assessments to check for consistency and plausibility (Giles et al., 2025; see also Hokke et al., 2019). A key risk of these extra security measures is that participants can be deterred from being involved and can have concerns about confidentiality.

More significant challenges in relation to informed consent are raised by online ethnography. There are often difficulties in identifying and providing information about research, and gaining consent, from all members of an online community who may be observed. As Hooley et al. (2012) note, in online communities there are a small number of participants who are very active and a larger group who may interact with the community only sporadically but who remain part of the community. Maintaining ongoing consent with what may be a changing group of participants is also problematic. Some researchers may view it as appropriate to observe behaviour in an online group without the consent of the participants. This might sometimes be done in the early stages of a research project when a researcher is seeking to understand how a community operates and how they might best introduce their research project to the group. This 'lurking' in online communities has been identified as unethical and potentially damaging to the group observed. While it may not be necessary to gain consent from all participants prior to observing an online group, it is nevertheless essential that participants are aware of a researcher's identity and their interest in the group. Kozinets (2010: 148) has identified the central tenets of ethical research practice in online ethnography which include the need for researchers to openly identify themselves as researchers, to describe their research focus and how they will conduct their research with the group.

There are some types of information provided in online environments which are viewed as 'public' and for which consent for their use is perceived as unnecessary. This refers largely to postings for mass and public communications. There has been much debate about what is public and what is private on the internet and it is recognized that users may have varying views about the public or private nature of their contributions. It has been suggested that informed consent should always be sought for research focusing on communications which people view as private and which take place in private or semi-private forums but that this may not be essential in open access forums which are acknowledged and understood as public. The Association of Internet Researchers (Ess & the AOIR Ethics Working Committee, 2002: 5) notes 'the greater the acknowledged publicity of the venue, the less obligation there may be to protect individual privacy, confidentiality and the right to informed consent'. See also Chapter 7 for a discussion of these issues in relation to digital and e-research.

The growth of Web 2.0 (user-generated content and social interaction) and Web 3.0 (decentralized, semantic and AI-driven experience with increased user control and privacy) and the proliferation of paid platforms, such as Prolific and M-Turk that recruit and manage participants for researchers, pose specific challenges. As noted earlier, distinguishing between what is public and private on the web is problematic. Snee (2008) notes that the Web 2.0 environment complicates this in that social networking sites encourage the sharing of personal and even intimate information. The extent to which such information is viewed by the author as being in the public domain is not necessarily easy to gauge. There are also issues relating to anonymity because, even if people or institutions are de-identified in research reports, information collected from the internet is often easily traceable via a search engine. Identifying when some form of de-identification should be used and when it is appropriate to cite an internet user as an author by name is again not straightforward. It is certainly the case that not all internet users want to remain anonymous. This may apply particularly to authors of blogs. To de-identify people in such circumstances could be seen as infringing copyright and raise issues of intellectual property. All these issues are complicated by the fact that in online research geographical boundaries do not exist and thus different legal and ethical regulation applies to the data collected.

Organizations such as M-Turk, Prolific and Cloudsearch are now commonplace crowdsourcing sites that provide recruitment services for researchers and opportunities for the general public to participate in research (Hauser et al., 2019). Like other platforms, Prolific provides advice to researchers about their responsibilities in ensuring they have fulfilled their obligations with respect to human research ethics approvals, in addition to how consent should be managed on their platform. Prolific provides a further layer of data protection and privacy to participants and researchers and is registered as a data controller with the UK

Information Commissioner's Office. Of relevance to privacy and consent is that crowdsourcing sites are also storing participant data (and sometimes third parties are involved in handling data). This data, including participant names, email addresses, home address and correspondence with the researcher, may be processed for a variety of reasons. There are no explicit consent processes associated with this although users are referred to the General Data Protection Regulation law in the UK if they wish to contact Prolific in relation to their personal data. Qualitative researchers have been increasingly turning to crowdsourcing sites, especially when trying to reach traditionally hard-to-reach populations. For example, Strickland and Victor (2020), discuss the confidentiality provided by crowdsourcing platforms for their study of people who use drugs, allowing for increased trust when participants choose to share sensitive information.

There has been increasing critique of Web 2.0 given the centralization and control of major social media (and crowdsourcing) platforms by a few corporations and authorities. Concerns over data leaks and hacks in addition to the ways in which personal information has been used for targeted advertising and interlinked identification mechanisms that construct and utilize user profiles have also been raised (see Singh, 2019). Web 3.0 technologies promise a more democratic, decentralized user-controlled experience, enabling users to monetize their data directly. Platforms such as *Lens Protocol* (a modularized user-owned social media platform that allows people to build their own 'social graph' and decide how they want their data to be monetized if at all) and *Mirror* (a decentralized publishing platform utilizing crypto-native business models around tokens) are examples of Web 3.0 initiatives. In terms of informed consent, researchers need to engage more directly with users as owners of the platform in negotiating their research. This has the potential to improve the validity and engagement of participants in research, but also to sidestep important protocols or ethical requirements, a critique that has been directed towards different crowdsourcing platforms (see Peer et al., 2022).

In common with the concerns raised by researchers using visual methods, it has been noted that ethical review committees lack knowledge about Web 2.0/3.0 and that researchers may need to educate committee members as well as the wider research community. Eynon et al. (2009: 26) note that despite concerns that online research raises specific ethical challenges, there has more recently been a convergence in the view that research ethics for online research can be drawn from existing frameworks for offline settings. Similarly, Snee (2008: 20) found that most internet researchers did not feel that a specific 'Web 2.0' ethics is needed. Nevertheless, it is recognized that some special considerations are necessary when researching online and that issues of confidentiality, anonymity, disclosure, informed consent and privacy are cast in a different light in online research (see e.g. Morey et al., 2012).

There are some groups for whom questions of capacity or 'competence' to provide consent are raised. These groups include children and young people, people with intellectual disability and people with some physical and/or mental illness and disability. These groups of people are sometimes referred to as 'vulnerable' in relation to research. However, this term has been criticized as giving rise to negative stereotypes, 'fetishing' vulnerability and supporting assumptions of research participants who are viewed as lacking agency, are helpless and powerless (van den Hoonaard, 2020). These biased perspectives are repeated in ethics guidelines and codes and operationalized in various ways, such as around assumptions of freedom and capacity to consent (van den Hoonaard, 2020). In unpacking what vulnerability means for research ethics, different issues are raised in relation to consent according to the specific capacity issue that is raised. If people are not able to understand what participating in research will involve, to weigh up the risks and benefits to them of participating or to reach their own decision about this and/or other matters that affect their lives, then they would be assumed to lack capacity.

If research is being conducted in England and Wales with adults who lack the capacity to consent, then the 2005 Mental Capacity Act applies. In accordance with the Act, researchers must consult with someone close to the individual (proxy or surrogate) to advise whether s/he would want to be involved with the study. In all cases, proposals for the research need to be assessed by an approved NHS or social care research ethics committee (see Parker et al., 2010 for a discussion of the impact of the act on qualitative research). Recent work has pointed out the lack of information available to proxies on the legal and ethical basis of their decision-making (Shepherd et al., 2019). In other countries, such as Australia, there is no Commonwealth legislation that deals with the legal requirements for an adult who lacks capacity to provide consent to participate in research, with each State and Territory having its own legislative regime (see Rallis Legal, 2016). In the State of Victoria, the Guardianship and Administration Act (1986) applies, which outlines a four-step procedure for authorizing research where an adult person lacks the capacity to consent, including: approval by a human research ethics committee; an assessment of whether the person is likely to recover capacity to consent within a reasonable period of time; the giving of consent by a responsible person; and the performance of the research on the basis of procedural authorization (https://www.legislation.vic.gov.au/repealed-revoked/acts/guardianship-and-administration-act-1986/089).

Assessing capacity to consent is, in many cases, a judgement made by researchers. Many researchers believe it is possible to explain research in ways that the great majority of participants, even young children and people with disabilities, can understand. This involves being sensitive to the needs of particular individuals, providing appropriate materials to help to explain the research and engaging with them in ways that suit their styles of communicating. Rodgers (1999: 428), for example, notes in her research with people with learning difficulties that 'given careful explanations, many people with learning disability can understand and make decisions'. Identifying ways in which individuals can indicate their wish to discontinue participating has also been identified as important and part of the issue of ongoing consent. This is likely to involve becoming familiar with the ways in which individuals convey assent and dissent. In relation to both of these points, the ways in which this can be achieved is likely to be different for different groups and individuals. Kelly et al. (2025) have provided in-depth guidelines for people experiencing autism and intellectual disabilities and suggest the following for the consent process:

1 Minimize environmental and executive functioning barriers.
2 Provide options for a range of communication needs.
3 Offer decision-making support.
4 Consider whether a competence assessment is necessary.
5 Consider people with decisional impairment.

Proxy consent, that is consent given by someone, usually a relative or carer, on behalf of someone else, is rarely used in social research. While a proxy may be approached to assist in understanding whether an individual would be willing to participate in research, it is generally viewed as important that the assent of the individual concerned is also attained, and that this is monitored over the timeframe of the research. Certainly, ethical review committees would want a strong justification for the use of proxy consent. As noted above, many researchers hold the view that it is generally possible to explain a study in ways that someone can understand whatever (within reason) their level of 'competence'. If this is not possible, including an individual in a study raises significant ethical concerns and needs a strong justification in accordance with the relevant local legislation.

Research with children and young people raises a different set of issues and there is considerable debate, and some uncertainty among researchers, about researchers' legal obligations (Alderson & Morrow, 2020). In practice, unless there is clear guidance, interpretations of the age of competence to consent are varied. In law, children are generally seen as not competent to make decisions (in various areas of life) until the age of sixteen, although this has been challenged through the legal distinction around mature minors (see Griffith, 2016).

One example of a medical law related to the consent of mature minors is the Gillick competency developed in England and Wales and adopted by Australia and New Zealand. Scotland's Children Act was amended in 2020, and the mature minor doctrine was adopted in some states in the United States and Canada. In the United Kingdom, Gillick competency is based on the assumption that a young person under sixteen years of age with 'sufficient understanding' can provide consent in their own right and that their parent has no right to override their wishes. The Fraser Guidelines set out by Lord Fraser in his judgement of the Gillick case in the House of Lords relate specifically to contraceptive advice but are regarded as applicable to social research. They imply that children under the age of sixteen, providing they can demonstrate an understanding of research, are able to participate in a project without their parents' permission. Masson (2004) notes that if a researcher has not sought parental permission (or consent), they are not at risk of legal proceedings brought by parents unless a claim of harm is made by the child. It is important to note that only the prospective research participant can consent to take part in research. Parental 'consent' relates only to consent to approach the child. Obtaining parental permission for the child to be approached is therefore distinct from the ethical principle of consent. Nevertheless, it may be good practice to seek permission from parents if not to do so might lead to upset on the part of parents, given researchers' responsibility not to cause distress in the process of conducting research (particularly from an ethics of care or virtue ethics perspective). There is certainly a tension here as the implication of this decision can potentially deny a child's autonomy.

There are some areas of research in which researchers might view it as problematic for parental permission to be sought. Examples are sexual behaviour, personal relationships and drug use where young people might not want their parents to know about their involvement in specific behaviours or they might be concerned about the interest from their parents that involvement in the research might generate. Heath et al. (2009: 27–28) provide some examples, both positive and negative, of the ways that research ethics committees have responded to researchers' proposals not to obtain permission from parents in research with young people on sensitive topics (see also Spriggs, 2010, 2023).

However, despite the Gillick ruling, many researchers do seek parental permission, as well as consent from children, for participation in research. Partly, this is because establishing whether a young person has 'sufficient understanding' to give informed consent is problematic. Although there have been some attempts at developing tools to assist researchers in assessing competence to consent (see Boceta et al., 2021). An additional factor driving this is that institutional gatekeepers to children and young people tend to request parental permission (or consent) for children or young people to participate in research as a condition of gaining access. The advice from various guidelines in relation to research with children is that parental permission should generally be sought in order to protect children as well as researchers. However, this should always be in conjunction with consent from the children and young people themselves and parental wishes should not override those of the child; that is, if the parent gives permission but the child does not want to participate, then they should be excluded from the research. A more problematic situation occurs if the parent refuses permission but the child wishes to participate. In such cases, a researcher might use one of the ethical frameworks described above to help make a decision about an appropriate way forward.

Summary

Informed consent is not a straightforward concept. Obviously, researchers must comply with any legal frameworks and regulation but additionally they have to balance a range of sometimes competing interests, such as the aims of the research, what they consider to be the best interests of research participants as well as the interests of formal or informal gatekeepers. They also have to operationalize and be reflexive about issues of 'information', 'consent' and 'competence'.

CHAPTER 4

Anonymity and Confidentiality

Introduction

Issues of anonymity and confidentiality are key considerations in ethical research practice and, in common with informed consent, are concepts that underpin professional research guidelines for social scientists. The management of confidentiality and anonymity is closely linked with the management of consent in that participants need to be informed about how confidentiality and anonymity will be managed and what the implications of taking part will be in relation to these issues before consenting to participate. In other words, they need to be made aware of what will happen to the data, how they will be reported, whether it will be possible for them to be identified from these data and what the implications of that might be for them. Consideration of the implications of participating in relation to confidentiality and anonymity is something that the individual participant needs to assess in the light of their views about what is public and what is private and the risks involved. However, they need to be guided in this by the researcher who will know how the research will be disseminated and who the likely audiences will be.

The terms confidentiality and anonymity tend to be conflated in research but are in fact distinct but related concepts. Iphofen (2009: 91) usefully notes that confidentiality is a continuous variable in that some information is 'mundane' and does not need to be kept private while other information may be viewed as highly confidential by research participants and not for sharing with others. Anonymity, on the other hand, is a dichotomous variable – a person's identity is either known or is anonymous and there are no identifying data that can link the information to a participant. Nevertheless, in most qualitative research, confidentiality (through the process of anonymity or pseudonymity) cannot be assured; researchers can tell participants that they will endeavour to ensure that they are not able to be identified but they cannot guarantee this will be the case. While de-identification either through anonymization or pseudonymization of research participants has traditionally been the norm in social research, there is an increasing awareness that research participants may want to be identified in research outputs. Indeed, in some types of research identification of research participants is accepted practice.

This chapter will discuss the concept of confidentiality in relation to social research and the situations in which deliberate and accidental breaches of confidentiality can occur. It will also explore processes of de-identification through anonymization and pseudonymization and debates around the identification of research participants.

Confidentiality

Confidentiality is commonly understood as akin to the principles of privacy and respect for autonomy (Oliver, 2010; Gregory, 2003) and is taken to mean that information given to another person will not be repeated without their permission. In the research context, confidentiality is taken to mean that identifiable information about individuals collected during the process of research will not be disclosed and that the identity of research participants will be protected through various processes designed to de-identify them, unless they specifically choose to be identified. Additionally, confidentiality may mean that specific information provided in the process of research will not be used at all if the participant requests this (sometimes referred to as 'off the record' comments). The concept of confidentiality is closely connected with de-identification; in social research, de-identification (either through anonymization or pseudonymization) is the vehicle by which confidentiality is operationalized. However, de-identification of data does not cover all the issues raised by concerns about confidentiality. Confidentiality of data also includes not deliberately or accidentally disclosing what has been said in the process of data collection with others in ways that might identify an individual. A deliberate breach of confidentiality would involve, for example, telling a parent what a child had said in an interview or telling a health professional what a patient participant had said without the study participant's consent. An accidental breach of confidentiality would involve, for example, someone being identified through information that a researcher provided about an individual even though they had not named them.

Breaking Confidentiality

The intentional breaking of confidentiality by researchers is an action which is frowned upon by the research community. However, it is recognized that there may be occasions when researchers might be obliged, or feel they need, to break confidentiality (see e.g. Gibson et al., 2012; Surmiak, 2020). Legal and regulatory frameworks influence how these issues are dealt with (Yip et al., 2016; Masson, 2004; Montgomery, 2002; Blank, 2025). This is particularly the case in some areas of research, such as in research with children and in health contexts. Regulatory frameworks, such as research governance procedures or ethical guidelines, may also influence the freedom researchers have to make decisions on these issues. Legal frameworks in the United Kingdom include Article 8 of the Human Rights Act 1998, the Children's Act 1989, 2004 and the Data Protection Act 1998, 2018 which have relevance to confidentiality in relation to research (Montgomery, 2002). In the United States, protecting confidentiality in research relies on a combination of federal laws, institutional review board (IRB) regulations, and ethical guidelines. Key legal frameworks include the HIPAA Privacy Rule for health data (Health Insurance Portability and Accountability Act of 1996), the Certificate of Confidentiality issued by the Health and Human Services, and various state laws (see Palys & Lowman, 2000). For a comparison of data protection and privacy frameworks between India, China and Australia see Singh (2018).

In general, researchers have a common law duty of confidentiality to research participants but there are certain circumstances which may override this duty, for example, if there is an overriding duty to the public, such as might occur in relation to a serious criminal offence or in life-threatening circumstances. In addition, researchers may feel a moral duty (although there is no legal *obligation*) to disclose information if a study participant reports being a victim of crime or if a researcher feels a study participant is at risk of harm. This issue is particularly pertinent, and has been widely debated, in relation to child abuse (Bostock, 2002); where researchers view a child or young person at risk of physical or psychological harm, it would be expected that they would take some action to report it (Allen, 2009). Practitioner researchers, such as social workers and teachers, have a professional responsibility (a 'duty of care') to report situations or individuals they have concerns about to their managers or other professionals. They are at risk of disciplinary action if they do not do so (Masson, 2004; Allmark, 2002). There is, in addition, specific regulation in relation to the work of particular professionals and some groups (e.g. specific local authority child protection procedures in the UK as set out in the Children's Act 1989, 2004; see Mathews and Bross, 2015 for an international perspective). Health professionals may also feel a 'duty of care' as part of their professional registration to inform others if they have concerns about individuals that are uncovered during research, for example, those perceived to be at risk of serious ill health by not complying with a medical regimen. There are additionally some diseases that must, by law, be notified to public health authorities. Surmiak (2020) discusses researcher perspectives in Poland, where they explained that they were only willing to break confidentiality if they learnt about sexual or physical harms, especially when it related to children. While Poland has fairly limited institutional ethical controls, data privacy does fall under specific legal, constitutional and European frameworks and laws. Surmiak (2020) found that there were three reasons for researchers to maintain confidentiality in situations where they received knowledge of illegal activity, crimes and harm including: where researchers constructed their projects as neutral and that their aim was to collect data and not intervene; where researchers predicted the consequences of breaking confidentiality on research participants and where researchers held specific personal values about reporting such events.

Situations in which promises of confidentiality might need to be breached should be minimized by researchers thinking through the circumstances in which they might feel they need to break confidentiality prior to approaching research participants (Surmiak, 2020). Study participants should be alerted to these as part of the consent process (Ritchie & Lewis, 2003; Wright et al., 2004; DVRG, 2004). This means that participants are made aware of the circumstances in which confidentiality cannot be maintained and leaves the decision with the participant whether or not they identify them. In identifying the issues that warrant breaking confidentiality, researchers need to consider participants' safety and well-being and also various legal, regulatory and professional frameworks to which they are subject. This involves giving careful consideration to the types of issues that might emerge in the context of a specific research project that a researcher might feel it is in the best interests of research participants to report to others and setting these out when they consent people to a study. This might involve, for example, saying to research participants 'everything you tell me will be kept confidential unless you tell me something about you or someone else being harmed or being at risk of harm. If this happens, I will need to talk to you about what we should do about it'. Research ethics committees are likely to expect to see evidence that researchers have given careful consideration to these issues. However, a difficulty arises if issues emerge that researchers had not expected and had not alerted participants to as part of the consent process. The expectation is that, should unanticipated issues emerge during a study, the researcher should always discuss the need to disclose this and get participants' permission before doing so (Ritchie & Lewis, 2003; Wright et al., 2004; Othman & Hamid, 2018).

A problem arises for the researcher if the participant does not agree to the issue being disclosed and there is little discussion in the literature on how this should be managed. Most researchers appear to feel that unless a research participant gives permission for information about them to be disclosed, then researchers should not do so (Wiles, Crow et al., 2008). The exception to this would be cases of people (especially minors) at risk of serious harm, although, of course, what constitutes 'serious harm' in different research contexts will be subject to varying interpretations. In such cases, discussion of the issue with supervisors, peers or a research ethics committee prior to taking action is appropriate. If the decision to disclose information without the permission of the participant is made, it would be expected that participants are informed of this decision. It is clearly important that researchers are aware of what their legal responsibilities are and that they think through and can justify, their moral duty to participants in such cases. One researcher participant taking part in a research study on informed consent noted:

> Well I think it's a bit of a grey area because the teachers have a duty to report [but] do researchers? I think we may not be covered by the letter of the law but I think in the spirit of the law we have to report. I think I would have to say to the child, the promise of confidentiality would have to be framed in terms of the fact that if I find they're in danger, then I would have to speak to somebody but I'd try and do it with them. (Wiles, Crow et al., 2008: 420)

Criminological research raises some specific issues in relation to confidentiality in that information about illegal or criminal activity might be identified in the process of the research. The identification of illegal activity, or activities on the boundaries of legality, such as drug taking, falsely claiming benefits, underage drinking or sexual activity might of course arise in any research project. The decision about whether or not illegal or immoral activity should be kept confidential may be a difficult one (see Surmiak, 2020). Reporting of criminal activity identified through a research project inevitably risks alienating research participants and perhaps preventing subsequent research from being conducted. In Wiles et al.'s (2008) research project on informed consent, they found that researchers did not feel obliged to report criminal or immoral activity, providing no one was at risk of physical harm. Indeed, in some research contexts concerning illegal activity, the fieldwork is conducted on the understanding that the information provided will be kept confidential. Other researchers have discussed ethical dilemmas related to responding to disclosures of harm or illegal activities during research with people with disabilities, calling for more nuanced responses that avoid erroneous assumptions about the vulnerability of certain groups of people (Ribenfors & Blood, 2023). Disclosure and responsibilities of reporting violence, including family and domestic violence, have also been discussed, with recent researchers urging for trauma-informed approaches that support survivors' choice, control, and empowerment to (Campbell et al., 2019; see also Ellsberg & Heise, 2002; Peterman et al., 2023). Researchers need to be aware that they may be forced to breach confidentiality and provide information should the authorities become aware that they have it. The research literature indicates there have been very few legal cases where social researchers have been forced to reveal information collected for research purposes in the UK, Australia and New Zealand (see Lowman & Palys, 2014 for three notable examples), although such cases have been reported in the United States and Canada (Lee, 1993: 164; Leo, 1995; van den Hoonard, 2002: 8; Khan, 2019). This appears to be an area of great uncertainty for researchers, which involves them having to balance issues of legality and morality in how they manage their research. Iphofen (2009: 101) sums this up in this way:

> The prime dilemma is to balance the moral stance of confidentiality, with the legal position, while also judging the 'seriousness' of any reported offence and balancing that against the potential danger to 'as yet unknown' others who could be harmed by non-reporting.

Most researchers in the UK, Australia and New Zealand working in these areas appear to work in ways that enable them to avoid any legal pressure to divulge information. However, increasing levels of ethical regulation and concerns with risks to institutional reputation may present a challenge to these ways of working (see Adler & Adler, 2002). Researchers working in such areas should seek advice from their organization's legal representative or research support office prior to conducting research. However, as Ulatowski and Walker (2021) have demonstrated through discussion of key cases in Canada and the United States with regards to subpoenaed records, universities often fail to protect both their employers and research participants around court-ordered disclosure of confidential information (see also Palys and Lowman (2000) for discussion of legal and ethical issues and case studies related to confidentiality in Canada and United States)

Accidental Disclosures

Accidental breaches of confidentiality can occur in a range of ways. Accidental disclosures can occur when researchers discuss their research with peers (or others), in the process of presenting research at conferences or other forums and in publications. It needs to be remembered that the anonymization of individuals does not mean that they cannot be identified by others. Clark (see Wiles, Prosser et al., 2008: 30), for example, found that despite his best efforts at anonymization, someone attending a presentation he gave was able to accurately identify the specific individual presented in a quote. In this specific case, the presence of visual clues about an anonymized place provided enough information to enable the participant to be identified:

> Despite our best efforts, we did not entirely resolve the challenges of anonymising place. In some instances a failure to anonymise place can also unwittingly reveal the identities of individual participants as well. For example, the use of a quotation positioned alongside a particular photograph (in this case, of a patch of waste-ground in my research site) during a seminar paper I gave was sufficient to enable one member of the audience who was familiar with the research site to identify the participant who gave the quotation, even though I believed I had anonymised both participant and name of the fieldsite and ensured there was, seemingly, no identifying feature in the photograph.

Particular difficulties with disclosure of confidentiality occur in research projects involving high-profile and distinctive individuals, such as government ministers or a CEO of a company. It may be impossible to anonymize such individuals, and not necessarily desirable to do so. Indeed it may be that individuals such as these choose to be identified and to speak 'on the record'. These individuals are likely to be clear about what they are willing and not willing to discuss in a research interview and the implications of doing so. For these individuals, concerns about confidentiality may be minimal.

Research involving individuals who have distinct roles and who choose to be anonymous, such as a head teacher of a school or hospital manager, may pose greater difficulties in relation to confidentiality, particularly when a study involves one or a small number of organizations or groups. In part, the risks to confidentiality arise because, even though a research site and an individual may be anonymized, views expressed often need to be identified by a particular position (e.g., head teacher) in various dissemination fora for the research to make sense. Confidentiality of individuals can often be easily breached by the inclusion of contextual information, such as a general location (e.g. a city on the 'South Coast of England' or on the 'west coast of Australia' can be only a few places), a description of an organization, or some factual information about it. It is often easy to take an educated guess on the basis of descriptive information or to conduct a Google search that will identify, for example, the identity of a school on the basis of a national reporting scheme (Ofsted Report in the UK or ACECQA in Australia) or the identity of a hospital on the basis of waiting times for specific surgical procedures. Once an organization is identified, readers may feel they are able to guess at the identity of an individual's views set out in a report of the research. Although, of course, this may be only a guess on their part, this will not necessarily prevent consequences flowing from it. Research with people who have distinct experiences which might enable them to be easily identified is another group for whom confidentiality issues are raised.

As well as considerations of confidentiality to the external world, there are considerations of internal confidentiality to consider; that is, confidentiality of participants to other participants in the same organization or group. Study participants within an organization taking part in research are likely to know who else is taking part and may ask a researcher what their colleagues have said, or indeed a manager may ask what their employees have said about it. While it may be clear that such requests for information should not be met, a researcher may nevertheless inadvertently recount a seemingly innocuous event or comment to a participant that has arisen through the research that has unanticipated consequences for another participant. Additionally, participants within a specific organization or group that are the subject of research are likely to be able to take an educated guess at people's identities within a research report, and this can have unintended consequences. These issues of internal confidentiality are not necessarily confined to research taking place in organizations and may equally apply to research focusing on families or friendship networks (see Tolich, 2004). In research taking place in organizations or with networks of individuals, great care needs to be taken to ensure that confidentiality is maintained and that sensitive material is managed in ways that do not jeopardize individuals' well-being and their relationships with others. It has been noted that a number of harms might arise from confidentiality breaches which, depending on the context, may range from embarrassment to violence (Lee, 1993: 191). A researcher interviewed in a study on informed consent (Wiles, Crow et al., 2008: 424) noted in the context of research within families that a number of difficult issues arise in relation to this:

> There are really difficult issues when you are interviewing members of a family or couples, or people who are in a relationship and you are putting their accounts side by side. There are some very difficult issues there and we often try to side-step them by changing enough so that we're hoping that the person they're talking about won't be able to recognise themselves if they read it. It's very common for people to tell you things that you think would be hugely problematic if their relatives knew they'd said that . . . I think it's important to exercise judgement about the impact that that could have in the network that the person comes from.

In situations where accidental disclosures of confidentiality might occur, various steps can be taken to limit disclosure (see Lee, 1993). In some cases, it may be possible to write about particular findings in general ways, and to avoid the use of direct quotations to limit the risk of identification. However, in other cases, it may be necessary to omit some data, especially when data are particularly sensitive or when its inclusion could have negative consequences if the individual were identified. Sometimes it may be necessary to exclude individual cases altogether in order to protect people's identities, especially in cases where dramatic situations are described which are likely to make individuals identifiable. Another strategy is to change some aspect of the identity of an organization or an individual in the description of a case or in the attribution given to various individuals when quotes are used. So, for example, an individual might be ascribed a different gender, job or medical condition in order to reduce the likelihood of their being identified. However, if such an approach is used, great care needs to be taken to ensure this doesn't affect the integrity of the data. Some researchers are very much against the idea of 'tampering' with data in this way and methods textbooks and research guidelines note the difficulties in balancing 'disguise and distortion' (Lee, 1993: 187; Becker & Bryman, 2004: 345; British Sociological Association, 2017: 7; Social Research Association, 2021: 39; Saunders et al., 2015). Certainly such an approach needs careful consideration and justification. One researcher from a study on informed consent (Wiles, Crow et al., 2008: 423) noted:

> Some of the people I've interviewed have got very distinctive stories and you have to develop ways of ensuring their anonymity. [. . .] Sometimes when there's an issue that I want to get on the printed page but I need to preserve their anonymity then I might turn a him into a her or change the age or the part of the country. [. . .] You'd only do that if it doesn't make any difference to the message you're giving, and sometimes it does and sometimes it doesn't.

In situations where there are specific concerns about confidentiality, it is advisable to liaise closely with study participants about the ways in which data will be reported. This may involve sharing transcripts or other data (such as observational notes or photographs) with participants and getting consent for their use (see Mero-Jaffe, 2011; Rowlands, 2021). In the case of transcripts, this may involve inviting study participants to amend the transcript and agree to its use. It may also involve showing and getting agreement for the use of specific pieces of data (such as photographs or interview extracts) in outputs. Arguably, this is an approach that should always be adopted regardless of specific concerns about confidentiality. Certainly, people's concerns about confidentiality and the limits of confidentiality that can be provided are influenced by the form of dissemination. However, there can be negative consequences related to the sharing of notes from meetings or observational notes that relate to more than one person. Also, a public viewing, community presentation or an article in a local paper or organizational newsletter are likely to raise more concerns for individuals about confidentiality than a presentation at an academic conference or a paper in an academic journal. Researchers are best placed to explain to study participants the risks involved in particular forms of dissemination to enable participants to make informed decisions about how their data are used.

'Off the Record' Comments

Another form of confidential data that researchers sometimes have to deal with is comments which study participants make during the course of research which they don't want included in the research. Such comments are often prefaced with 'I wouldn't want this included', 'I wouldn't want anyone to know about this' or 'this is off the record'. Sometimes a participant may ask for a recording device to be turned off while they make the comment, but in other situations, the comments may be recorded. Managing these sorts of comments can be difficult. Clearly, once a researcher has been told something, albeit confidentially, they cannot be unaware of it. Indeed, study participants may want the researcher to know certain things so that the research is informed by these issues even though they do not want the comment to be ascribed to them personally. In general, comments made by individuals that they ask to be kept confidential cannot be used; it would be a breach of confidentiality to do so. However, it may be possible to negotiate with study participants the ways in which they would be willing for (and perhaps even want) the information they have provided to be used. Where a full transcript including the 'confidential' comments has been made, participants can be sent the transcript and asked if they would still like it excluded or whether they might be willing to reformulate the points in a way that would enable the information to form part of the research, if appropriate. Research exploring people's experiences of particular services, such as experiences of health care provision, can result in people complaining about poor levels of care. While they may not want to have their specific case identified, they may still want the research to reflect the concerns they have.

In the era of open access and 'big data', disclosures can also occur through the increasing sophistication of data linkage technology (see also Chapter 7). Even with direct identifiers removed, detailed narratives when combined with external data sources can lead to identification (e.g., a participant in an interview working in a rare profession in a small town could be linked to publicly available employment records to identify them). Linkage can be made between various data sets, such as health records, social media and administrative data. Researchers need to consider context-sensitive anonymization, differential privacy techniques to ensure that data linkage risks are clearly articulated to ethics committees and to potential participants (see Tsai et al., 2016)

Anonymization and Pseudonymization

The primary way that researchers seek to protect research participants from the accidental breaking of confidentiality is through the process of de-identification, either through anonymization or pseudonymization. De-identification of research participants is a central feature of ethical research practice which is written into the various guidelines to which social researchers work. Additionally, in the UK the Data Protection Act (2018), which is the UK's implementation of the GDPR, provides the legal framework for the de-identification of data. Differences between legislative governance frameworks for different countries have been explored by Scheibner et al. (2020). The GDPR and other frameworks distinguish between anonymized and pseudonymized personal data (Hintze & El Emam, 2018). In anonymization, personal data is processed in such a way that it would be impossible for anyone to identify the person from whom the data was collected. Pseudonymization refers to data that is processed in such a way that data cannot be attributed to a specific person without the use of additional information that is kept separately and subject to technical and organizational measures that protect the attribution of the personal data (European Union, 2016, 2019 see also Class et al., 2021). Under the GDPR, data controllers are mandated to provide notice to data subjects around the collection, use and disclosure of pseudonymized data, while anonymized data is no longer considered personal data, so disclosure requirements are not required. While complete anonymity may be difficult to achieve, it is recommended that all identifying data are removed prior to publication and, where an individual may be identifiable, explicit consent must be obtained before publication can proceed.

Pseudonyms are generally chosen by the researcher, but are sometimes given by a transcriber or suggested by participants (Lahman et al., 2023). When chosen by participants, pseudonyms can have important psychological meaning to both the participants and the content and process of the research (Allen & Wiles, 2016). The use of pseudonyms is not without its problems in relation to successful de-identification. Iphofen (2009: 94) notes that selecting pseudonyms that appear well-suited to the characteristics of a participant can pose confidentiality risks in that they may 'offer subtle or latent clues' to an individual's identity. Grinyer (2002), however, notes that using pseudonyms that are not 'equivalent' in some way to a participant's real name can seem inappropriate. Names can have specific social class, age and ethnic connotations and, arguably, their use can distort the meaning attributed to quotations. Providing people with the opportunity to choose their own pseudonym can also pose problems; Corden and Sainsbury (2006) note that researchers have found that participants sometimes choose the names of real people, such as their friends and Grinyer (2002) notes the difficulty of managing the situation if more than one participant wishes to choose the same pseudonym.

Pseudonyms are often given to locations; however, the descriptions and/or images provided, as noted above, make it relatively easy to identify, or at least make an educated guess, where a study is located (Clark, 2006). There are considerable examples of community research where people have been unhappy about the way they or their community have been characterized and of the ramifications this has had (see Crow & Wiles, 2008). This indicates a need to consider issues of anonymity and consent in relation to place as carefully as to people.

Identification

Some researchers have questioned the assumption that participants always want to be de-identified. There has been a growing trend to recognize that research participants often want to be identified in research outputs and that, in much social research, there is no good reason not to allow that to happen (Tilley & Woodthorpe, 2011). Anne Grinyer's (2002) important paper on this topic describes her experience conducting research with parents of young adults with cancer in which she sought her research participants' views about the de-identification of their accounts and the use of pseudonyms. Grinyer found that three quarters of her respondents wanted to have their own names used in the research rather than a pseudonym and, as a result, a mix of real names and pseudonyms were used in publications, reflecting participants' wishes. Researchers conducting research with children and young people as well as the bereaved have found that research participants often want their own names and/or the names of their deceased relatives to be used (see Wiles et al., 2011). In a study of research participants' views of the use of verbatim quotations in qualitative research, Corden and Sainsbury (2006) also found that research participants did not like the use of pseudonyms. Grinyer (2002: 4) notes the importance of providing research participants the opportunity to use their own names but notes that this must be balanced with protecting them from harm:

The balance of protecting respondents from harm by hiding their identity while at the same time preventing 'loss of ownership' is an issue that needs to be addressed by each researcher on an individual basis with each respondent.

A further difficulty arises in research being conducted within a specific group, network or organization in which some people opt for identification but others do not. The identification of some individuals can lead to the identification of others who wish to remain anonymous. In this situation, identification cannot be offered without breaching confidentiality for others. A similar situation occurs in relation to an organization; in cases where an institution wants to remain anonymous, it may not be possible to enable participants to opt for identification, at least not without the consent of the institution. One of the participants in a study on informed consent noted (Wiles, Crow et al., 2008: 425):

One of the intensive care units was bitterly disappointed that her unit wasn't named, but I had to explain that if I identified the unit then there would be a cascade of identification, you know, and people would be able to potentially identify all the staff and all the patients.

Visual Data and De-identification

'Visual methods' comprise a vast array of different types of approaches and data. Visual data include photographs, film, video, drawings, advertisements or media images, sketches, graphical representations and models created by a range of creative media. Prosser and Loxley (2008) identify four different types of visual data: 'found data' (e.g. family photograph albums); 'researcher created data' (such as images or film taken by researchers); 'respondent created data' (such as models or drawings created by respondents) and 'representations' (e.g. graphical representations of data).

Visual research, particularly where photographs and film are used as data, presents particular challenges for de-identification. Much of this type of visual material makes the de-identification of individuals or locations problematic if not impossible (Clark, 2006; Wiles, Prosser et al., 2008; Wiles et al., 2011). Challenges to de-identification may also arise with other forms of visual data, such as drawings, collage and other data visualization generation technologies (see Prosser & Loxley, 2008; Wiles et al., 2011; Lomax, 2020). The situation is complicated by the fact that individuals appear commonly to want to be identified in their visual images, a similar situation to that which emerges in some text-based research as discussed above. The association of image making with social media and digital technologies places further responsibilities on researchers (see Lomax, 2020).

Still and moving visual images that portray clearly identifiable individuals can be de-identified only by altering the image in some way so as to obscure an individual's identity. More commonly, visual researchers present these types of visual material in their entirety, thereby enabling individuals to be identified, with their consent (see Pink, 2007). Methods of obscuring people's identity include increasing the pixelation of facial features in order to blur them, the use of specific de-identification software that converts visual images into drawn images and blocking out eyes, faces or other distinguishing features (see Wiles, Prosser et al., 2008). Obscuring facial features alone may not be adequate to ensure anonymity in that there may be a range of other visual clues in the image that enable an individual to be identified. Obscuring facial features has been subject to criticism by some social researchers (Williams et al., (undated): 7; Sweetman, 2009; Nutbrown, 2011; Allen, 2015). Nevertheless, it is recognized that there are some individuals, groups or types of images that necessitate the identities of individuals being obscured. It is common practice, for example, for researchers working with children to use specialist software to de-identify children's images (Flewitt, 2005; Wiles, Prosser et al., 2008). The more common approach favoured by many social researchers is to present visual data in their entirety, with consent, and not to attempt to de-identify individuals (see e.g. Back, 2004; Holliday, 2004). In this mode of working, pseudonyms are not generally used. Many researchers who work with visual material have identified the importance of developing relationships of mutual trust with study participants so that the images that are taken emerge from collaborations between researcher and study participant and are jointly owned (Banks, 2001; Gold, 1989; Harper, 1998; Pink, 2007). This involves showing images to participants, and allowing them to comment on them, prior to publication or presentation, as well as consideration by researchers of the political, social and cultural contexts in which images will be viewed and interpreted. There may however be a tension between study participants' wishes about how images of them are used and researchers' responsibility to protect them from harm. Collaboration with research participants on issues around anonymity and dissemination involves more than simply meeting participants' wishes; researchers need to consider carefully and explain the various implications to individuals and in some cases, it may be necessary to override their wishes if this is viewed as being in study participants' best interests.

The longevity of visual and other data which can remain in the public domain through publication in books and articles for many years, if not indefinitely, also raises some issues that warrant consideration with research participants. While an individual may be happy for a specific image or expressed view to be made public at one point in their lives, they may be less so in the future as their circumstances change; yet once something enters the public domain, it may be difficult or impossible to remove it. The internet offers considerable opportunities for global dissemination but, without restricted access to sites, raises the possibilities that data can be copied and reproduced in contexts other than those for which they were obtained. This also raises specific issues in relation to the storage and archiving of research data (see Chapter 7). There is a need to ensure that all data are stored in ways that ensure confidentiality and that express consent is provided for their continued and subsequent use. Recent issues around data sharing of qualitative research data have been explored with results indicating that researchers have limited knowledge and experience with qualitative data repositories, how data should be shared responsibly and according to legal and regulatory guidelines. At the same time, repositories are generally not equipped to handle sensitive qualitative data and lack guidelines to protect confidentiality and provide restricted access (Mozersky et al., 2020).

Summary

Confidentiality and anonymity/pseudonymity are distinct but related concepts; confidentiality refers to the need to keep identifiable information about individuals private and anonymity and pseudonymity are two different ways in which data are kept confidential. Intentional disclosure of information may be necessary in certain circumstances if research participants are viewed as being at risk. Accidental disclosures of information also occur but care should be taken to avoid these where possible. There is an increasing trend in research towards research participants being identified rather than de-identified.

CHAPTER 5

Risk and Safety

Introduction

Ensuring the safety and well-being of research participants is an important element of ethical research practice. While much qualitative research may pose only minimal risks to participants it is important not to disregard the risks that can occur, particularly in research on topics which are in some way 'sensitive' because they focus on personal issues, taboo issues or issues which pose a threat for those participating in it (see Lee, 1993; Borgstrom et al., 2024). Such research also poses significant risks for researchers, which should not be overlooked. Consideration should also be given to wider risks to researchers' institutions, their disciplines and the field of study.

Risks for Research Participants

All activities pose some level of risk and research participation is no exception. It is generally accepted that participation in research should pose no more than minimal risk to participants, that researchers should assess the potential risks and that participants should be fully informed of these as well as the benefits of taking part in research. In response to the increased ethical regulation of social research, various authors have noted that the risks of harm arising from social research are minimal at most, if not non- existent (see, e.g., Atkinson, 2009; Dingwall, 2008; Mapedzahama & Dune,

2017). Certainly, in comparison with medical research, the risks from social research are slight. However, this does not mean that the risk of harm does not exist and authors such as Kent et al. (2002) and van Teijlingen (2006) have disputed the assumption that social research is risk-free.

Assessing Risk of Harm

Assessing risks that might arise as a result of taking part in a research project involves researchers reflecting on the nature of risk and harm and the ways in which their research might present risks to participants' well-being. Assessments of risk involve considerations of the potential for harm, both physical and psychological or emotional, as well as practical issues such as the costs participants might incur as a result of participating in research in terms of money, time and inconvenience. The range of risks that need consideration is discussed below.

The potential benefits of research also need to be considered, both to the research participants themselves and to the community or society more widely, so that research participants and researchers can assess whether the potential risks outweigh the benefits. Balancing possible risks of harm and the potential for benefit is far from straightforward. Risks of harm are generally (but not always) experienced by an individual, but benefits are often to groups, communities or society more generally. It is also the case that benefits arising from research, such as a change in policy or provision for a specific group, are often long-term and, if they occur at all, may do so some time after the research project has been completed. Smyth et al. (2016) make the important point that benefits need to be thought of, and articulated to participants as, 'hoped for' outcomes of research rather than those that are guaranteed, noting that this terminology is 'more honest about the uncertainty underlying all research'. Researchers may, for example, hope that their research brings about a change in the way groups are perceived, or the treatment or provision they receive, but these hoped-for benefits may not occur as a result of one specific research project; indeed, it may have no impact on the individual participant's experiences. It is certainly important not to raise participants' expectations about what the outcomes of the research may be. Some research ethics committees require that research explicitly describe how participants will be given access to the results; however, other committees do not require research to disclose study results either during or following a study (MacNeil & Fernandez, 2006)

Individuals may experience personal benefits as a result of taking part in research, such as feeling listened to, having an opportunity to express their views or feeling that their views will influence policy or practice. Some researchers have reported that their participants have gained considerable benefits as a result of being able to talk about issues or experiences with an independent person that they haven't been able to discuss with anyone else (Newton, 2017). However, it cannot be assumed that such benefits will occur. It is not the purpose of research to bring about such benefits; if they occur, they are perhaps best seen as a side effect of research participation. Clearly, if risks to participants are greater than minimal and the benefits not evident, then there is little justification for the research being conducted. However, who should make that decision? Arguably, participants are best placed to make decisions about the risks they are willing to take in relation to participating in research. Researchers, or indeed research ethics committees, who decide on participants' behalf that a project or method is too risky for participants, have been accused of paternalism (Hope, 2004, Pels, 2008). Nevertheless, researchers often experience a conflict between seeking to protect study participants on the one hand but allowing them the agency to make decisions about the risks they are willing to take on the other (Wiles et al., 2011).

Assessments of risk, harm and benefit are far from straightforward. It is not possible to identify all risks that an individual might encounter from participating in research. A researcher cannot know what an individual might find distressing and even fairly innocuous research topics can result in a research participant becoming distressed. In a study on private health care that Wiles undertook many years ago, one of the first interviews she undertook focused on a man's hospital stay for a minor routine operation and resulted in him crying as he recalled his wife's serious illness twenty years previously. Wiles could not have predicted this response and neither could the interviewee when he agreed to participate. In a study of the impact of death from natural causes on prisoners and prison regimes, Robinson reflects on the difficulties of predetermining who were likely to find the topic upsetting (a request made by the research ethics committee).

> On one occasion, a prisoner who seemed well-informed about the research came to sit with me by the entrance to his wing. He was keen to help and told me various things about how the prison responded after a death. He said, matter-of-factly, that there was a prisoner from the wing in the healthcare centre. This then sparked reminiscence about caring for his mother, who had died of a similar condition. His tone was sadder and his voice less confident, and after he'd finished he repeated what he'd said (Fieldnote, 20 September 2017). On another day, a prisoner I'd not met before approached and asked if I was doing the research about deaths in custody. He proceeded to tell me about two men he had known in the prison who committed suicide, one of whom was a friend, and about another man who he'd been helping, who had died of natural causes in the healthcare centre. He spoke quickly and quietly, but there were strong emotions in his voice and he talked about the need to hide emotions in prison (Fieldnote, 19 December 2017). (Robinson, 2020)

In Pascoe Leahy's (2022) life history interviews with women about motherhood, the participant Sybil introduced the topic of her broken marriage unexpectedly in response to a question about her first pregnancy:

> Sybil: We were both very excited about the whole thing. At that point I was very, I think innocent and naïve is the only way to describe me and I did not know that you could behave badly outside of marriage. I just didn't. I had no idea that people would do that to each other.
>
> Carla: Have an affair, for example?
>
> Sybil: Yeah. I didn't know that [crying].
>
> Carla: Do you want to take a minute or do you want to keep talking? Do you want me to stop the recording?
>
> Sybil: I'm okay. I'll be fine.
>
> Carla: It's very common that people feel affected in the interview. I always do, listening to people. It can be about all different things. If someone interviewed me about motherhood, I would cry just because I think it's so. . .

Sybil: Because of it, yes. It's a very emotional thing, yeah. Sorry, Carla.

Carla: That's all right. Do you want some more water?

Sybil: Yes, please. It's a good excuse to stop for a moment.

These examples illustrate the importance of emergent ethics, of thinking about and managing, ethical issues and risk throughout the lifetime of a research project. The important point to note is that while it is important that researchers think carefully about potential risks and benefits of participating in research and inform participants so that they can decide whether or not they want to take part, neither researchers nor participants necessarily know what issues might emerge in the process of the research and how they will be responded to by participants.

Types of Risk

A range of potential risks of taking part in qualitative research have been identified. Most risks of social research relate to participants' psychological or emotional well-being. Risks to participants' physical well-being are less likely but not unheard of (see Lee, 1993; Dempsey et al., 2016). Risks to well-being have been identified as arising from: an emotional response during data collection; an emotional response to ending involvement with a project; and the effect of the publication of research findings.

Perhaps the most common type of risk arises from a participant's response to a question asked or topic discussed during fieldwork. People becoming upset or distressed is probably a relatively common experience in qualitative research, particularly in research on so-called 'sensitive' topics (Lee, 1993). However, research can also engender other emotional responses in response to researchers' questions or activities. Embarrassment, humiliation or anxiety can occur in response to insensitive questions, questions or tasks that the research participant feels unable to answer or do, or topics or tasks that explore participants' underlying fears (see, e.g., Grinyer, 2001). Research participants can feel deceived if they were not, or feel that they were not, told the 'real' reasons for undertaking the research. They may also feel devalued if they feel their views are disregarded or not taken seriously. Qualitative researchers have proposed various strategies to protect research participants from harms caused by distress, such as the self-interview, post-interview follow-ups and adopting an ethics of reciprocity approach (see Pascoe Leahy, 2022).

It has been observed that research participants can feel used by researchers and that they may feel disregarded or devalued as a result of participating in research. Researchers sometimes do engage in various activities to 'manipulate' participants to participate in research and to provide rich data, a process referred to by Bengry-Howell and Griffin (2011) as 'methodological grooming'. Such activities may leave participants feeling used after the research is completed and the researcher has exited from their lives, particularly if their expectations of benefits are not met. This is particularly the case with longitudinal research when participants build up relationships with researchers over prolonged periods. As Iphofen (2009: 53) notes:

> In longer term encounters . . . the subject may need some 'closure' time and some opportunity to come to terms with a relationship that appeared to have friendship at its core but was, in effect, highly instrumental.

Considerable risks to participants can arise from the publication and dissemination of research; many of these issues have been discussed in Chapter 4 on anonymity and confidentiality. Despite de-identification, people may be upset at how they are portrayed in research reports (see Silverio et al., 2022). Crow and Wiles' (2008) review of community studies identified cases where some local residents were deeply unhappy about how they had been portrayed in publications. Such studies may also bring unwanted publicity, and media attention, to a research site given that the anonymization of specific communities is notoriously difficult. This is also the case for visual data and the way that images are constructed by researchers and consumed by those who view them (Rose, 2007: 255). This has drawn attention to the ethical implications, and consequences for individuals and their communities, of the ways in which researchers present images and the interpretations different audiences may make. Many established 'visual' researchers tend to adopt participatory or collaborative relationships with their study participants so that the materials created emerge from collaborations between them and are seen as jointly owned (Banks, 2001; Gold, 1989; Pink, 2007). Nevertheless, the potential remains for participants in studies that use visual material (as with all research) to be unhappy about the way they have been portrayed (Pink, 2003; Crow & Wiles, 2008).

The risk of unwanted media attention is not a risk only in community studies; it may also occur in research on specific groups or institutions or indeed in relation to categories of individuals. Research may result in negative publicity and the reinforcement of stereotypes about specific groups such as benefit claimants, young people, homeless people or ethnic minorities. The increasing pressure on researchers to provide evidence of the impact of their research and to get their research findings into the public domain may fuel these sorts of problems given the difficulties that researchers face in attempting to control how the media report their research findings. Publication may also pose other risks where an individual's identity is disclosed, such as censure from others which might in some cases result in loss of friendship or employment. In research on political activity or illegal activity, more extreme risks, including risk of physical harm or legal sanctions, might be present (see Lee, 1993). Other risks concern the costs incurred, both financial and personal, from participating in research. These issues are often overlooked but warrant consideration. Such costs might be a loss of earnings incurred by taking time out to participate in research. Participants might also experience inconvenience; the time spent in participating in a project means they have less time to do other things they might want or need to do. Some of these factors can be offset, to some degree, by offering payments to participants in recognition of their contribution.

Knowledge production itself can place participants at risk. In the field of migration studies, Zapata-Barrero (2020) explain that while scholars aim to improve the conditions and understanding of migration, their work can make sensitive knowledge available to governments and security agents. As Düvell et al. (2010: 231) describe with regard to their research on irregular transit migration in Ukraine, 'social knowledge' can easily be translated into 'investigative knowledge' and used to focus the priorities of state agencies. Düvell et al. (2010: 235) explain that researchers should focus less on the 'how' aspects of migration (contacts, travel routes *etc.*) and more on explaining the motivation and decision-making processes of irregular migrants. This supports social justice, rather than punitive and investigative approaches. In planning for the content and timing of their publications and dissemination, Düvell and colleagues (2010: 235) ask:

> Should all or only some results be published? Who is the audience? How will our results be received and discussed at a given time period (in the light of related political and public debates) and how may they be (ab)used? The question also arose as to what extent we can control and influence the (ab)use of our findings. We also considered whether the usual time delay between research and the publication of findings meant that publication would not have an immediate effect on the research subjects, and their locations or businesses.

The Risk of Exploitation and Harm

The use of qualitative approaches that collect in-depth and highly personal biographical and other information can bring specific risks around exploitation and harm (see Elliott, 2005; Squire, 2008; Livholts & Tamboukou, 2015; Goodson et al., 2016). This would include a range of methods such as ethnographic and narrative methods. Narrative methods encompass a wide range of approaches, including event-based narratives, narratives of experience and performative and cultural narratives; the first two of these focus on the content of people's narratives and the latter on the structure and form of narratives. Other forms of narrative approaches include biographical research, life history research and oral history (see Plummer, 2001) and can include Indigenous methodologies, such as 'yarning' (see Chapter 7). The methods employed in qualitative narrative research include the collection of data via interview and observation, generally over prolonged periods, as well as analysis of a range of documentary sources. Key elements of narrative approaches are that they involve researchers enabling research participants to tell stories about their lives, that researchers need to pay close attention to and value respondents' stories, that researchers develop close relationships with their study participants and that they form part of the narratives that are constructed. All these elements highlight the need for reflexivity in narrative research.

Numerous ethical issues have been identified as arising from narrative, life history and biographical approaches. Plummer (2001: 216) identifies seven ethical 'concerns' in life history approaches (see also Elliott, 2005; Squire, 2008). Primary among these are issues of exploitation, risk of harm, anonymity and confidentiality. Plummer (2001) identifies exploitation as perhaps the most crucial issue in that study participants are encouraged to provide their personal, and perhaps painful, stories but that it is the researcher that benefits, both professionally and materially, from the reporting of these stories in which the subject of the narrative is anonymized and generally receives no credit or reimbursement. While this may be more evident in narrative research as individuals are sharing a great depth about their life experiences, ethical frameworks ask us to consider the benefits of the research both to participants and the wider community and that there is both fair distribution and access to those benefits. The risk of harm is also significant in narrative research. As Elliott (2005: 137) notes, people's narratives are bound up with their sense of identity and the process of data collection and the interpretation and dissemination of these narratives can, if done insensitively, cause harm to individuals and their relatives, friends and communities. Plummer develops this theme by arguing that (2001: 224):

Telling their stories could literally destroy them – bring them to suicidal edges, murderous thoughts, danger. More modestly, they may be severely traumatised. The telling of a story of life is a deeply problematic and ethical process in which researchers are fully implicated.

In addition to potentially impacting a participant's personal integrity when revealing 'too much' and suffering distress by following the narrative method, Thunberg (2022) writing about their own work with young victims of crime, notes that researchers may need to adapt the method in response to both verbal and non-verbal cues indicating personal distress. Other researchers such as Ellis (2016), in her narrative research with a Jewish Holocaust survivor, discuss the importance of developing a relational ethics of care, a compassionate approach that emphasizes the development of compassionate relationality between researcher and participants with both justice and care perspectives (see Chapters 31–47 in Goodson et al., 2016 for a range of perspectives and accounts around ethics in narrative research).

Issues of confidentiality and anonymity are also particularly problematic in narrative and biographical research in that these methods often render participants identifiable, or at least potentially so. Often participants are identified in the publication of material, with their consent, but this is not without the sorts of problems discussed in Chapter 3. This then raises issues about what can, or should, be confidential in such studies and how such material should be managed. While there are risks associated with methods such as narrative life histories, we would also like to emphasize that these approaches have been used in research that prioritizes epistemic justice. Researchers have developed ethical codes for narrative inquiry based on relational ethics and ethics of care, which support core values such as social justice, human rights, integrity and the dignity and worth of the individual (see Denzin, 2016: 605 and also 'Part 4: Ethical Approaches' in Goodson et al., 2016).

Minimizing Risks of Harm

A number of ways have been identified to minimize and manage risks of harm from participating in research. Careful thought needs to be given prior to a study commencing of the possible risks of harm that the research might pose to individuals and/or the communities of which they are part. Research participants should have the risks and benefits of research participation explained to them as part of the consent process and make their own decisions about whether or not they want to participate. As discussed above, risks or harm should also be assessed throughout a research project as they emerge; the publication and dissemination of research are particular points when considerations of risks of harm need to be addressed. Research participants should also be informed, as part of the consent process, about who they can contact should they have a complaint about any aspect of their involvement in a study. Such complaints need to be reviewed and the research changed to take into account complaints as appropriate.

Strategies also need to be in place to manage any distress or discomfort that participants may experience during fieldwork. Research on a wide range of topics can generate emotional responses and researchers need to be sensitive to research participants' feelings. This may mean monitoring participants' body language for signs of fatigue or distress and responding to such signs by suggesting that data collection be suspended or stopped. It may also mean enabling people to decline to answer particular questions or discuss specific issues. For some groups, such as children or people in institutional settings, active encouragement for them to refuse to discuss particular issues may be necessary. In a research project on informed consent, researchers working with children reported providing participants with red cards that they could hold up if they didn't want to answer a particular question or didn't want to continue with the interview (Wiles et al., 2005). They also noted the importance of researchers spending time with participants prior to the research commencing to enable them to 'rehearse' this so that they felt confident enough to do it. Another strategy identified was training participants to say 'pass' if they did not want to discuss specific topics (Wiles et al., 2005).

Involvement in research should mean that participants leave the research process feeling no more unhappy or distressed than they did when they began it. Of course, it is not always in a researcher's power to ensure this is the case, but debriefing after an interview or other data collection activity is an important means of researchers assessing participants' response to the research. It is often appropriate to provide information or resources about support that people can access if the research has, or might, raise issues that an individual finds distressing. Such support might, for example, be contact numbers for Citizens Advice organizations, a counselling service or support groups relevant to the topic of the research (see Whitney & Evered, 2002 for details related to developing a qualitative research distress protocol, guided by a dynamic of participant centredness).

Risks to Researchers

Managing risks to researchers throughout a research project is an important and often neglected, consideration (Mitchell & Irvine, 2008; Lee-Treweek & Linkogle, 2000). Bloor et al.'s (2007) inquiry into the risk to well-being of researchers in qualitative research provides an extremely useful exploration of the issues. They note that:

> While research-related harm thankfully remains comparatively rare, the evidence . . . suggests that it is a more common phenomenon than the absence of formal complaints would suggest. (Bloor et al., 2007: 5)

It is often more junior researchers and PhD students who are at greater risk of harm (Bloor et al., 2010; Schneider, 2020; Tolich et al., 2020; Orr et al., 2021). There are a number of different potential risks to researchers including physical, professional and emotional, with the latter seeming to be the more common.

Physical Risks

'Physical' risks comprise actual physical harm or threat of physical harm. Bloor et al. (2007) note that cases of serious injury and death are rare in social research and that fear of harm is greater than actual cases of injury. Nevertheless, some deaths, sexual assaults and serious harms of researchers have been reported (see Lee-Treweek & Linkogle, 2000; Das, 2015; Bloor et al., 2007: 18) and, as Kenyon and Hawker (1999) note, 'once would be enough', in other words, the fact that it is rare is little consolation if you are the rare case who experiences physical harm. While it is important not to overstate the risks, it is crucial that researchers carefully assess what potential risks might arise and make attempts to minimize them. However, it is also important to note that risks are culturally constructed and that particular risk environments are context dependent and fluid as Ghosh (2018) has described for her ethnographic project about the loss of land and livelihood experienced by villagers living in close proximity to a coal mine in a rapidly developing State in Central India. Risks of physical harm arise from three aspects of a research project: the location, the topic and the participants, all of which may be interlinked. In terms of location, risk of physical harm can occur when conducting research in some locations or settings. Considerations of physical harm generally focus on risks from others 'in the field'. However, the risk of illness and disease, particularly when working in developing countries, should not be overlooked. Lee's (1995) distinction between 'ambient' and 'situational' danger is a useful one when considering physical risks to researchers; ambient danger refers to research conducted in dangerous environments or locations and situational danger refers to risks arising from the presence of a researcher in a setting which may provoke aggression or hostility from members of the group being researched (Lee, 1993: 10, 1995: 3). In many cases both ambient and situational dangers may be present. Ambient danger is present in volatile research environments or settings, such as research conducted in war zones or areas in which there is political or social unrest. Risks may arise simply by being in a dangerous environment and the everyday risks of such an environment (such as being injured by gunfire or in an anti-Government demonstration). Dangers may also exist when conducting research in unfamiliar settings and cultures which do not, on the face of it, present obvious dangers, particularly when researchers are working overseas. Such dangers may arise from not understanding safe ways of conducting oneself in a different culture, such as the areas in which it is safe for a woman to walk alone at night. They may also arise from reacting to cultural practices which a researcher deems as disturbing. Iphofen (2009: 86) notes that researchers can expose themselves to physical danger if they record or try to intervene in particular occurrences, such as the mistreatment of individuals. These risks are not confined to research being conducted in countries with which the researcher is not familiar. Similar risks also occur in researching various subcultures in a researcher's 'home' country. It has been noted that it is anthropological fieldwork that poses the greatest dangers to researchers in terms of physical harm (Iphofen, 2009: 86).

The risks associated with particular topics are closely linked with the location of research. Research focusing on activities defined as illegal or deviant in some way, such as drug use, football hooliganism and a range of criminal activities, may raise a number of risks of physical harm to researchers. Risk of harm may come from members of the group being studied who take a dislike to the focus of the research or the questions asked by the researcher or it may come from people who are external to the group who pose a threat to the group as a whole, which may include the researcher.

Risk of physical harm is greater in covert research with such groups and may result if the researcher's true identity is disclosed. Physical harm is also a risk if participant observer roles are adopted to such an extent that the researcher 'goes native' and takes on the identity of the group being studied. In such cases, the researcher may find themselves embroiled in activities that place them in physical danger. Other types of topics that may engender risk of physical harm for researchers who adopt some form of participative ethnographic approach are those that focus on 'dangerous' recreational activities, such as speedway or rally driving, or types of employment, such as roofers or security 'bouncers' (see Bloor et al., 2007: 19). Here the physical risk is not necessarily from research participants but from the activity itself. Griffin and Bengry-Howell (2008), for example, in an ethnographic study of young working-class men who modify their cars, reflect on the decision taken by Bengry-Howell to have a ride in the car of one of the study participants:

> [He] willingly put his life at risk in pursuance of research goals, by getting into a car that belonged to a person he vaguely knew who had admitted during interview that he had a penchant for driving at high speeds. On the other hand, the opportunity to actually sit alongside Jonno in his car, whilst he demonstrated what his car could do, had enabled [him] ... to directly experience the way in which the cultural practice of driving at high speeds operated within the context of the car modifier's world. (Griffin & Bengry-Howell, 2008: 28)

Individuals can pose risks to researchers in the contexts and ways outlined above but there are potentially additional risks that an individual may pose to a researcher's physical well-being unrelated to the geographical location or topic of the research. The context of much qualitative research involves researchers collecting data with individuals in private places, often study participants' homes. This often involves interviewing individuals that are unknown to them. The risk of the lone researcher coming into contact with someone who poses a physical threat to them is unlikely, but nevertheless possible, and it appears to be something about which researchers experience great unease (Kenyon & Hawker, 1999). It is certainly the case that being alone in a stranger's home does place researchers in a potentially vulnerable situation. Participants in Kenyon and Hawker's (1999) study report cases of serious harm and considerable anxiety about the potential for such harm. This issue is one which organizations have taken seriously as part of risk assessment procedures. There are several strategies which researchers can, and should, adopt to maximize their safety.

Organizations that employ researchers, and support research students, have a responsibility to protect them from harm. However, while there are generally formal structures in place, such as risk assessment procedures, insurance and lone working policies, these do not appear to be universally used by those who manage research and, in some cases, may offer inadequate safeguards even where they are used (Bloor et al., 2007: 4). Various recommendations, guidelines and protocols aimed at maintaining researchers' physical safety have been made (Bloor et al., 2007; Kenyon & Hawker, 1999; McCosker et al., 2001; Social Research Association, 2001). These include making careful assessments of risk in relation to the physical location of the fieldwork site, such as whether there are local tensions, political unrest or general safety issues for an individual in being located in and moving around the area. Assessments of risk in relation to data collection are also necessary and care is advised particularly in relation to individual interviews conducted in private places. Protocols for managing safety in such contexts, including leaving details of the interview location with a colleague with a plan for action if the researcher does not return at the expected time, are important. In some contexts, it may be that it is more appropriate to use pairs of researchers to conduct interviews or to arrange interviews in public places. The Social Research Association's Code of Practice on Safety (2001) provides comprehensive advice on a range of issues relating to researcher safety (see also Iphofen, 2009: 88).

Emotional Risks

The greater risk to researchers in undertaking qualitative research has been identified to be to their emotional well-being (Stahlke, 2018). This can include emotional trauma and, more commonly, emotional distress. Qualitative research generally necessitates researchers empathizing with their participants in the process of collecting data. In much research, particularly research on 'sensitive' topics such as sexual abuse, suicide, terminal illness, bereavement and family breakdown, this involves researchers listening to people's experiences of hardship, grief, loss or fear. Such research can leave researchers feeling emotionally distressed and there is considerable evidence that this is widespread among qualitative researchers (Bloor et al., 2007: 44). Bloor et al. (2007) describe research on emotionally demanding topics as a form of what Hochschild (1983) has termed 'emotional labour' in that researchers have to manage their emotions in the process of hearing about or observing the emotions, feelings and experiences of their research participants in the interest of obtaining 'good data' and managing the research process. Watts (2008) describes the feelings generated in her ethnographic study of a cancer drop-in centre:

> The emotion that has dominated participants' narratives in this study is fear . . . the seeking of reassurance is emotionally distressing because whatever response I give, it will not be the one they covet, which is the promise of cure and the certainty of a longer life.
>
> Whilst they continue to hope I am sometimes laid low in my spirit. (Watts, 2008: 7)

Of course, some researchers view it as important to engage emotionally with their research participants and to 'give something back' to them not only by revealing information about themselves and their experiences but by developing longer-term relationships with them (Oakley, 1981). However, this does not necessarily protect them from experiencing emotional distress and indeed may result in increased levels of distress as well as raising ethical dilemmas inherent in maintaining what may in effect be unequal relationships. In the face of emotional distress, a desire to help research participants is often provoked by observing or hearing about distressing events or experiences in the process of fieldwork. Brannen (1988) notes that such a response may have more to do with helping the researcher come to terms with the emotions evoked by the interview rather than helping the respondent (see Lee, 1993: 106). Adopting a position of 'proxy counsellor' or 'emotional helper' to research participants is certainly replete with problems; researchers do not necessarily have the skills to manage their respondents' emotional responses, and it is, arguably, unethical to adopt such a role (Bloor et al., 2007: 26; Watts, 2008).

Emotional trauma can result from distressing memories on the part of the researcher being generated by the research. Emotional difficulties can also result from the process of observing practices or hearing about experiences or views to which a researcher is morally opposed but to which they are obliged to 'go along with' in order to avoid jeopardizing the research. Other emotional difficulties that researchers have reported while in the field are feelings of isolation and lack of support. This is a particular issue for PhD students who, despite supervision, tend to work alone while in the field. It is also an issue for researchers working overseas in unfamiliar surroundings, a particular issue for many anthropologists. Conducting research on sensitive topics can have a cumulative impact as Williamson et al. (2020: 63) describe in their study of researchers working in the field of gender-based violence

> You think it would get easier over the years, but it doesn't. The fact that we keep having to have these conversations is in itself depressing on top of the nature of the issues we are dealing with.

Researchers who identify as 'insiders', for example researchers who share the same migration experience with research participants, have also discussed the unique inter-relationship between ethics and the emotions (see Romocea, 2014). As a Romanian migrant researcher conducting research with Romanian migrants settled in the UK, Romocea found that her relationship to the topic of the research, the terminologies used and language choice during the interviews and the legal aspects of their migration status required reflexive emotional engagement and ethical commitment during the research.

A number of strategies have been identified to manage risks of emotional distress arising from the research process. Good preparation prior to entering the field is obviously important and often overlooked (see Johnson & Macleod Clark, 2003). Placing limits on the amount of time spent in the field and/or interspersing data collection with time spent with other members of the research team or with research supervisors is one important management strategy. Counselling from a professional counsellor independent of the research team has been identified as potentially useful if specific problems occur, although this does not appear to be a widely used strategy (see Corden et al., 2005). Most useful, and commonly used, appears to be a range of self-care strategies including opportunities for debriefing in research teams or with peers and using such groups as a source of support (Corden et al., 2005; Watts, 2008). Other qualitative researchers have noted healthy (taking time out, exercise, counselling) and less healthy (comfort eating, alcohol) coping strategies that researchers may use in the short and long-term (Williamson et al., 2020). Where procedures for debriefing are not set up as part of a research project, researchers may turn to informal support networks to 'offload', but this can raise issues of data confidentiality if clear understandings of confidentiality are not established as part of the process (Wiles, Crow et al., 2008). The use of a reflective diary or journal has been identified as another strategy for managing emotional distress (Bloor et al., 2007: 35).

While managing emotional distress is important, some writers have criticized research ethics guidelines as presenting a risk-averse pathologizing view of emotion (Olson, 2021). In a study of human ethics guidelines across four countries, Olson (2021) argues that the way in which emotions are constructed by research ethics guidelines is either superfluous, harmful or risky and overly simplistic. Often, emotions on the research participant's side are constructed as potentially harmful and to be avoided or managed, and on the researcher's side as potentially hazardous to sound decision-making. This undermines expressions of dignity and respect and ' . . . by casting emotions as risks, guidelines designed to protect participants from harm may be preventing the cathartic benefits of shared and emotion-rich research interactions, and silencing participants' emotionally charged narratives' (Olson, 2021: 539). Instead, research ethics guidelines should attend to the complexity of emotion and 'cultural and socially saturated aspects of everyday life', encouraging researchers to adopt embodied, caring and emotionally reflexive approaches to research (Olson, 2021: 539).

Professional Risks

Other risks that researchers might encounter are reputational risks, to themselves as individuals, to their discipline and/or to their institution. Research governance procedures are likely to be in place in most institutions where researchers work to assess these risks prior to a study commencing, although problems may of course arise throughout a research project. Particular issues may arise in the process of publication of a study, particularly through engagement with the media or collaboration with journalists (see Baser & Martin 2020). A degree of conflation, distortion and misinformation can occur which can have negative consequences for researchers and their institutions as well as their research participants (see Beasley & Walker, 2014 for a discussion of research ethics and journalism). Reputational risk is also a factor in data archiving in that researchers form part of the data archived and feature in transcripts, field notes and detailed information about study design, data collection and analysis. The availability and scrutiny of these data by researchers for the purposes of secondary analysis may have particular reputational implications for early career researchers (see Neale & Bishop, 2012b). This issue is explored further in Chapter 7.

Qualitative researchers sometimes hold dual researcher and professional roles and have experienced professional scrutiny by regulatory bodies as a consequence of their research. Sarah Stahlke is a qualitative researcher with a nursing background. In her research project examining nurses working experiences and change efforts, Stahlke has felt exposed and vulnerable because of the ways in which her research has attracted the attention of regulatory leaders and threatened her professional licence. Stahlke notes

> Along with emotions and threat of professional and political sanction, I also experienced a profound challenge to my values in several of my research interactions. Displays of power and passive aggression, adherence to dominant ideologies, and struggles with ethics in practice were disturbing to me. (2018: 7)

Such threats when 'studying up' (potentially threatening the power of elites or those in power) have been experienced by other qualitative researchers (see Aguiar & Schneider, 2016), including insider researchers (Toy-Cronin, 2018). Stahlke (2018) encourages researchers to be fully prepared for professional risks through careful planning at the outset, ongoing monitoring and building in opportunities for informal debriefing and support.

Summary

Despite some researchers' claims that social research is relatively risk-free, there is evidence that it poses a range of potential risks for both research participants and researchers. The greatest risk in social research is to researchers' and their participants' emotional and psychological well-being. This is especially the case for students and early career researchers prompting researchers to urge universities and other institutions to ensure research ethics submissions include evidence of: adequate and detailed supervision plans; staff having the necessary research training and skills; plans being in place for critical incidents, such as disclosure; data collection and research completion processes being well planned (see Lenton et al., 2021).

Ethical Dilemmas

Introduction

This chapter outlines some of the everyday ethical dilemmas that researchers experience in the conduct of research. All research generates ethical issues of one type or another. Some of these can be predicted before the research commences, but many have to be managed 'in the field' as the research proceeds. The dilemmas that emerge and the way that they are managed are inevitably specific to the research context and the researcher's moral and ethical framework. While there have been some ethical 'horror stories' in the social sciences, these are few and far between. For the most part, researchers manage the ethical issues that emerge in considered and reflexive ways that enable them to conduct research which will produce valid findings while at the same time treating research participants with respect. The need for careful consideration, evaluation and justification of ethical decisions is central to good ethical decision-making.

Ethical Dilemmas

There are some celebrated 'horror stories' about unethical research in the social sciences. The most commonly cited ones are two psychology experiments, Milgram's obedience to authority experiments which began in 1961 and Zimbardo's Stanford Prison experiment conducted in 1971. Milgram's experiment involved research participants in the role of 'teacher' being told to administer what they thought was an electric shock to another person in the role of 'learner' if they failed a word test. Some study participants continued to administer what they thought were electric shocks when told to do so, despite the apparent distress experienced by those receiving the shocks. Study participants were debriefed at the end of the experiment to explain the nature of the experiment and that the electric shocks were not real.

However, concerns have been raised about the anxiety generated among participants. Zimbardo's experiment was a study of the psychological effects of being a prisoner or prison guard. Students were allocated the role of 'prisoner' or 'prison guard' in a simulated prison. The experiment was stopped after six days due to the abusive behaviour of the 'guards' and the stress and anxiety experienced by the 'prisoners'. These two studies were behavioural experiments rather than qualitative studies.

A less commonly cited study and one that is clearly qualitative is Laud Humphreys' ethnographic study of the 'Tearoom trade' conducted in 1970. Humphreys studied anonymous sexual encounters between men in public toilets in the park of a large US city. Humphreys acted as a 'lookout' in the toilets in order to observe the activity of the men. Most of this research was conducted covertly as he argued this was the only way this study could be conducted. In order to collect demographic information on the men he observed, Humphreys traced their home addresses via their car licence plates. He then approached them at home, disguised as a researcher conducting research on men's health and asked them questions which enabled him to collect data on their race, marital status and occupation. Humphreys' study has been widely criticized as being unethical in virtually all aspects: his study involved deceit of participants both in the initial observation and follow-up interviews and he violated privacy. Nevertheless, the findings of the study did generate important insights and Humphreys has argued, from a consequentialist position, that this justifies the research design (see Warwick, 1982).

Tolich (2014) criticized the first edition of this book and other authors for demonizing these classic studies as 'celebrated horror stories', justifying the need for ethical review processes. Tolich argues that we should look more critically at these studies and think about how they might have been undertaken differently (see also

Perlstadt's (2024a) book *Assessing Social Science: Research Ethics and Integrity* for a critical review of these high-profile case studies). For example, Tolich explains that in Zimbardo's case it was the Stanford University Institutional Review Board (IRB) that failed to acknowledge the conflict of interest in Zimbardo's role as both Chief Investigator and main prison warden in the role-play experiment. With Zimbardo in this dual role, he was unable to recognize the possible harm to his participants as the violence escalated. Tolich encourages us to view the specificities in how the IRB should have recognized this conflict of interest, rather than blindly condemning them retrospectively. In the Milgram experiment, Tolich notes that Milgram was proactive in attempting to minimize harm by debriefing participants following the experiment to support their mental health. He used a follow-up survey to assess the impact of the study on participants and had an informal reference group who followed the results of his study. Tolich (2014) argues that the learnings for a contemporary project of this kind today are around the need for following up appropriately with support from independent counselling services for those participants who required further support, identified either after the experiment or following the post-survey.

Instead of uncritically referring to these celebrated ethical stories, Tolich points to contemporary examples of qualitative research that require further ethical consideration. This includes Carolyn Ellis' (1986, 1995) study of a Chesapeake fishing community, where some of her informants were upset at her research publication because of the ease with which they were able to identify themselves, the representation of their lives (particularly around issues related to sexuality) and a perception that Carolyn had made money from the book at the community's expense (see Tolich, 2004). Tolich also encourages us to read Sudhir Venkatesh's (2008) *Gang Leader for a Day* as an example of a study that received no ethical approval and which brought participants into direct harm. Tolich contrasts this study alongside Mitch Duneier's *Streetwalk Society*, which demonstrates strict adherence to ethical considerations. Tolich (2014) is critical of some autoethnographer's claims that because the focus of their study is the self, their research does not require prior ethical review. Autoethnography is a research method that draws on autobiographical techniques and examines the lived experience of the author. However, as the self is embedded in social relationships with others, Tolich argues that autoethnographers need to respect the autonomy of others and seek their consent to be involved in the research. In response, autoethnographers, such as Ellis (2007), emphasize a 'relational' ethical framework that largely situates itself outside of traditional ethical concepts of informed consent and personal autonomy. More recently, there have been attempts at writing about forms of ethical autoethnography (Lapadat, 2017; Edwards, 2021).

These examples in which problematic practice is central to the research design are relatively few and far between in qualitative research in the social sciences. This, of course, does not mean that serious ethical breaches do not continue to occur in qualitative social research. Examples from other qualitative studies include: Ngozwana's (2018) discussion of issues related to participant withdrawal, confidentiality and anonymity in a study of civic education in Lesotho, Africa; Chenhall, Senior and Belton's (2011) presentation of three case studies in Indigenous Australia raising issues related to informed consent and perceived conflicts of interest associated with participatory research approaches; and Ribenfors and Blood's (2023) discussion of the ethical complexities related to situations where adult participants with intellectual disabilities disclosed experiences of harm and illegal activity. In a critical literature review that included forty-two qualitative studies, Taquette and Borges da Matta Souza (2022) found that ethical dilemmas commonly centred around key issues. Breaches of confidentiality and anonymity were a key concern for qualitative researchers, especially in research settings in small community or organizational contexts (Damianakis & Woodford, 2012), in online communities (Zimmer, 2010; Gerrard, 2021), when working with couples (Braybrook et al., 2017) or with participants with public or highly specialized profiles, making their identities easily recognizable (Ellersgaard et al., 2022). A related issue is the increasing capacity for third parties to link different data sets to enable the identification of individuals. With very limited information collected during a qualitative interview, such as gender, local area code and date of birth, Sweeney et al. (2013), have shown how easy it can be to link qualitative data with other kinds of data sets with information about medical history, procedures and names (see also Chapter 7).

Other dilemmas in the literature include situations where participants autonomy to consent is unclear. This often occurs in research contexts where there are marked power differentials or in the utilization of methodologies such as autoethnography, where participants become unwitting (often non-consenting) interlocutors. Situations where there is confusion around the roles of researcher and participant, whereby researchers inappropriately take on therapeutic roles, have also been cited. This can be especially difficult with researchers who have dual professional roles as researcher and caregiver/therapist/social worker (see Landau, 2008). In their review, Taquette et al. (2022) found that the most commonly cited ethical dilemmas were around the risks associated with causing 'damages' to participants and researchers. This included raising strong emotions related to a projects' subject matter for both research participants and researchers, the impact of researchers' own ideology and emotions about a topic unduly influencing data interpretation and potential risks associated with member checking (see Goldblatt et al., 2011).

Below are some further ethical dilemmas based on experiences reported by researchers. Rather than outlining how these ethical challenges were resolved, these are presented as illustrations of the types of ethical challenges that emerge in research and as prompts for readers to reflect on ethical challenges.

Dilemma 1: In a study exploring people's experiences of recovery from a heart attack, an interviewee expressed extreme feelings of worthlessness resulting from his health condition, which meant he was unable to work or to undertake activities he viewed as part of his male identity. Feeling he might be depressed and at risk, the interviewer suggested that he talk to his doctor about his feelings, but he said he didn't want to do that as all the doctor would do would be to give him more medication. He also commented that he didn't want his wife to know or she would worry. The researcher promised confidentiality but was concerned about his mental health. Should she tell someone about him and, if so, who?

Dilemma 2: In a study in an educational context exploring school-based friendships and using participatory and child-friendly research methods, the process for consent for children to participate in the study was that consent was needed from both the child and his/her parents. On the day the research was to take place, one child gave in her consent form on which the parent's signature had clearly been forged. The child denied they had forged it and was desperate to take part in the research project and expressed anxiety about feeling excluded if she was unable to participate. Should the researcher overlook the forged consent given the research does not pose any risks to the child and indeed excluding them might be judged as more harmful?

Dilemma 3: A physiotherapist who is undertaking an ethnographic case study project in a school for children with special needs for her PhD observed that a teaching assistant was encouraging a child to write rather than use a computer. The physiotherapist was aware that the child's physical condition was such that they will not have the dexterity to use a pen long-term and will need to develop computing skills in order to keep up with their work. However, her role in the school as a researcher who is observing interaction meant that if she intervened, the staff and the child would see her in a different light and this would be likely to impact on the relationships she had with them and the quality of data collected. However, if she did not intervene then she would not be acting in the best interests of the child, which she was professionally obliged to do. Should she intervene in the interests of the child's well-being even if that does pose a risk to the research, or should she continue to observe what is happening in the setting without affecting it?

These three dilemmas encompass the common broad ethical issues that researchers encounter in their research: issues of consent, anonymity, confidentiality, risk and role conflict. While these broad issues are common themes that emerge in research, the specific ethical dilemmas researchers experience within them are inevitably unique to the research project being undertaken. Consequently, the way that dilemmas are managed is, to some degree, unique in that it must be the most appropriate decision in the light of the research topic, the participants and the context. As has been noted in Chapter 2, ethical frameworks are important in helping researchers to address ethical dilemmas, but these do not provide an immediate answer. Rather, each issue must be carefully considered, drawing on ethical frameworks, in order to decide how it can be resolved.

Five detailed case studies are now presented. These draw on accounts of research in which ethical issues are described in some detail. They provide an exploration of five different types of dilemmas and how they were resolved in the context of the specific research project. These explore dilemmas of consent (Lawton, 2001), dilemmas of disclosure (Rowe, 2007), dilemmas of confidentiality (Edwards & Weller, 2009), dilemmas of representation (Scheper-Highes, 2000) and dilemmas of data governance (Boulton et al., 2004).

CASE STUDY

Dilemmas of Consent: Julia Lawton

Julia Lawton's (2001) research was conducted in an in-patient hospice in the UK and explored the experiences of dying patients. The study aimed to explore the phenomenon of social death, that is the loss of identity and personhood that has been identified as occurring during the course of terminal illness, and the effects of a patient's death on other patients. Research in palliative care had, at the time the study was conducted, largely excluded dying people from research because of their assumed vulnerability and the considerable ethical and practical considerations such research raises. Lawton sought to address these concerns by conducting a participant observation approach in which she took on the role of an in-patient volunteer in order to unobtrusively observe patients and day-to-day life, and death, in the hospice. This observation was conducted with consent both from the hospice staff and patients. Patients were informed about the study by senior medical staff at the time that they were admitted to the hospice and were given the opportunity to opt out of any observations that were made. Despite the plans in place to manage the informed consent of hospice patients, several dilemmas in relation to consent were raised. A full discussion of the issues discussed here can be found in Lawton (2001).

The first dilemma concerned the difficulties in the process of gaining informed consent among a very fluid and ever-changing population. Large numbers of patients were admitted to the hospice and on some occasions, several patients were admitted at the same time in situations that were often chaotic because of patients' competing needs or the nature of an individual's medical condition. The admission of patients to the hospice was not necessarily a situation in which gaining informed consent for a study was a primary concern. As Lawton (2001: 698) notes:

> A fairly significant proportion of patients was admitted on an emergency basis . . . it was not unusual for patients to be admitted in a state of extreme anxiety, experiencing very distressing symptoms, the consequences being that some were in no state to be informed of, let alone take in, the details of the research. A small proportion actually reached the hospice in a coma and died within a matter of hours of their admission.

So this first set of dilemmas about informed consent concerned whether it was always possible to assume that informed consent had been achieved prior to observation taking place. In such a busy and stressful environment patients clearly were not able to give lengthy consideration to whether or not they were willing to participate in a research project. It may also have been the case that not all patients would remember consenting to the study. The difficulty also emerged in relation to people who were comatose when they were admitted. In these cases, their family members were consulted for consent on their behalf but this raises a number of ethical dilemmas concerning whether or not relatives should be able to give consent for another person.

The second set of dilemmas concerned issues of ongoing consent. Consent was obtained at the time of admission to the hospice but this did not necessarily mean that patients remembered that the research was taking place in subsequent encounters with the researcher. This is a particularly problematic issue in participant observation. In this case,

Lawton's role as a volunteer could have meant that patients viewed her primarily in this role rather than as a researcher. This led her to question whether information provided to her during interactions with patients, particularly that of a personal nature, could legitimately be used for research purposes. This could have been resolved by giving patients frequent reminders that the research was taking place.

However, she felt that constantly highlighting the research would have adversely affected the unobtrusive nature of the research and ultimately the quality of the findings.

A related dilemma concerned the extent to which a patient's consent could be assumed to remain valid when their medical condition deteriorated such that they ceased to be the person they were when they gave initial consent. Lawton refers to a case of someone she calls 'Annie' who changed from being 'lively and talkative' when she first came into the hospice to being 'withdrawn and disengaged' as her condition deteriorated, so much so that she requested heavy sedation with the result that she was unable to communicate in the last two weeks of her life (Lawton, 2001: 700). Annie had given consent to the study on her admission to the hospice and was supportive of it. However, the fact that she was sedated meant that it was impossible to ascertain whether she wished to remain in the study once her condition deteriorated. Including people in the last stage of their life was important for the study because one of the study aims was to explore the impact of patients' deaths on other hospice patients. This case, and others like it, were important in informing the study findings which had organizational implications for the hospice. However, as Lawton (2001: 700) notes it is important to consider how Annie and others like her might have felt if they had known how their data were to be used.

The third set of dilemmas concerns a different aspect of consent which relates to the ways in which, in qualitative research, the specific outcomes of research cannot be predicted. At the outset of a study, a general research focus and research question or set of research questions will generally have been designed, but the number of study participants, the period of data collection, and the specific direction the research will take are often dependent on the data collected and the emerging analysis. This has particular implications for consent. In common with other qualitative studies, Lawton's study evolved into something other than that for which participants originally gave their consent, and her findings ended up critiquing the hospice movement. This left Lawton to pose the question of whether patients would have consented to participate, and indeed whether hospice staff would have granted her access, had they known what the outcome of the research would be.

The dilemmas identified by Lawton centre around the need to conduct high-quality research that can provide answers to important research questions which will have the ability to impact policy and practice but to do so in ways that respect research participants' wishes as well as their dignity. Lawton managed these dilemmas, not by continual checking of consent in relation to the data collected and used, but by careful and selective use of the data collected. She notes (Lawton, 2001: 699):

> Researchers who employ this methodology have a responsibility to use the data they collect in a sensitive, ethical and reflexive manner. In this project, every effort was made to quote patients and to use specific case studies in a highly selective fashion. The experiences of many patients were only drawn on in abstract ways, for example, in developing the generalized themes and trends that were highlighted in the study.

The key issue here is that Lawton produced these findings through a rigorous and ethical research process that repsected the autonomy of participants, and the critical findings were not based on a subjective evaluation based on her own values, which would be unethical.

CASE STUDY

Dilemmas of Disclosure: Michael Rowe

Michael Rowe's research was a study of British policing (Rowe, 2007). Using ethnographic methods, he accompanied uniformed police officers as they went about their normal duties in three areas within one police service. The aims of this study were to explore the factors that shape officers' decision-making and their exercise of discretion. His research involved accompanying and observing police in their day-to-day activities over a period of eighteen weeks and taking field notes of his observations. Rowe (2007) identifies a number of ethical issues that emerged from his research but the focus here is on two specific incidents which presented him with ethical dilemmas. These two incidents centre around issues of role conflict, namely if and when a researcher should report an incident they are concerned with which will result in breaking confidentiality and/or affecting the very thing a researcher has set out to observe. Rowe noted that his reading of ethnographic studies of policing led him to expect to find malpractice that would lead to serious ethical dilemmas. In fact, the situations he observed were comparatively minor but nevertheless did cause concern. A full discussion of the issues outlined below can be found in Rowe (2007).

The most significant incident that Rowe observed concerned an incident in which a police officer lied to a victim of crime. The 'victim' was a woman with learning difficulties who reported the theft of a mobile phone by a young man known to her. The officer said that he would go and talk to the person she had accused of stealing her phone. However, the officer told the researcher that he thought that the mobile phone may not have been stolen at all and that the woman may have lent it to the person she accused of stealing it and he had simply not returned it as agreed. Even if this were not the case, he thought that the young man would probably lie and say that it was. Either way, it was felt that the woman would not be a 'credible witness' due to her learning disability and, given the incident was minor, it was not likely to lead to any criminal proceedings. The officer decided that he would tell the woman that he had spoken to the young man's mother and that she would get him to return the phone to her once he arrived home even though this was not the case. The officer noted:

> There's no point making a crime report, or a statement. We would get the same result after two hours' paperwork, so why bother? (Rowe, 2007: 46)

Rowe was very surprised by this incident, both the fact that the officer had lied and also that he had been open to the researcher about it. The incident was viewed as particularly troubling because the victim of the crime had learning difficulties. He decided that three options were available to him: to do nothing; to discuss the matter with the officer; or to report it to a more senior officer. The first of these would protect his position as a researcher because he was not intervening but would mean he was colluding with the officer's behaviour, which fell short of officially stated police standards. The second might impact negatively on the relationship developed by the researcher with the officers he was studying and might result in officers limiting the activities that he was able to observe or censoring their behaviour while he was observing. The third option would be likely to result in significant consequences in relation to the ongoing research and relationships with officers as well as the additional problem that he would be breaching confidentiality and also run the risk of spoiling the field for other researchers. Rowe decided not to report the incident primarily because he felt the seriousness of the officer's behaviour did not outweigh the likely consequences of reporting it. He notes that if an officer had committed an offence of a more serious nature a different decision might have to be taken.

A second incident, which did not involve criticism of an officer, was managed in rather a different way. In this incident, the researcher observed a suspect put something in his mouth and swallow it.

This occurred outside of the view of an officer. The researcher was concerned that the suspect may have swallowed drugs, an action that might have a detrimental impact on them and the officer. At the same time, however, from a methodological point of view, he did not want to interfere with the situation and influence events but rather to observe what would naturally unfold if he was not present. However, he decided that the potential impact on the suspect and the officer was primary and so he told the officer what he had seen.

The dilemmas identified by Rowe centre around a similar issue to that identified by Lawton, that of how to manage ethical issues that emerge in the context of naturalistic enquiry that seeks to minimize the researcher's impact on the field. For Rowe, moral questions about whether to intervene and the consequences of such interventions for the research and those involved with it are dilemmas which have to be considered situationally, according to the severity of the incident. He notes (Rowe, 2007: 47, 48):

> This response was based on a calculation of outcome rather than the content of the action – and so reflects broader debates about the status of ethics in a postmodern era . . . Since policing is unpredictable, the ethical dilemmas police researchers might face cannot be easily anticipated. Given this, Norris's conclusion that ethics are inevitably situational (Norris, 1993) was borne out in this study. If an absolute code of ethics is not feasible, researchers must be prepared to be reflexive in terms of ethical dilemmas.

CASE STUDY

Dilemmas of Confidentiality: Timescapes

A research project on young people's lives conducted by Edwards and Weller raised significant, and perhaps unusual, ethical dilemmas relating to confidentiality. The project was conducted as part of Timescapes, a UK programme of qualitative longitudinal research projects. The focus of the project was on the meanings, experiences and changes over time in young people's relationships with siblings and friends. The study involved repeated interviews with young people born between 1989 and 1996. During the course of the final set of interviews, conducted during 2009, an ethical issue relating to confidentiality emerged following the unexpected death of one of the study participants. This raised some issues and dilemmas about consent but more importantly about confidentiality. The project researchers invited researchers involved in other Timescapes projects to contribute their thoughts about how these ethical dilemmas might be resolved.

Details about these deliberations and the project more generally can be found here: https://timescapes-archive.leeds.ac.uk/

The sudden death of the research participant, Dan, raised ethical and legal issues concerning the data collected. While he had verbally agreed to all the data collected being archived, it had been intended to provide participants with more detailed information about archiving and asking them to sign 'consent to archiving' forms in the round of interviews that were due to take place at the time of his death. Edwards and Weller raised the question as to whether they could archive the data from Dan that they had already collected on the basis of his verbal consent given two years previously. They considered asking his parents to give consent, but this raised further issues, such as whether this would mean that his parents had ownership over the data and what to do if they demanded their own copies of Dan's data, thereby overriding the promises of confidentiality given to Dan. Another issue was what to do if they refused permission despite Dan's verbal consent at an earlier stage, which could be seen as overriding Dan's wishes. The researchers also identified a further moral issue relating to confidentiality. They felt that, given Dan's sudden and unexpected death, his parents would like to have, and perhaps should be provided with, some of the non-sensitive audio material they had collected from Dan during interviews. While making such an offer would go against promises of confidentiality made at the time of the interviews, this might be seen as acceptable given the circumstances, as long as the data provided were of a non-sensitive nature.

Edwards and Weller received eleven responses from fellow researchers within the Timescapes programme to the issues they raised, representing a range of views. Some researchers felt that there was no justification for overriding the promise of confidentiality given to Dan, while others felt the situation warranted the disclosure of non-sensitive data. The range of responses illustrates the lack of consensus about these issues among the social sciences community.

Edwards and Weller note that there was no single solution to these ethical dilemmas. Drawing on an ethics of care perspective, they took what they felt to be the morally caring course of action. They decided that Dan's former verbal consent was adequate to enable them to archive Dan's data without consent from his parents. However, they offered his parents the opportunity to archive any personal memories they had of Dan alongside this. They also offered Dan's parents a sample of Dan's voice. Dan's parents wanted to take up this offer and were provided with a DVD of extracts from Dan's interview where he discussed his likes and his career aims. The dilemmas identified by Edwards and Weller centre around the contexts in which agreements made, such as for consent, confidentiality and anonymity, might be breached. Their experience was relatively unusual, but not unheard of or without parallel. In their case, their views about what was the 'morally caring' course of action for all concerned, which would, as far as they could be aware, not go against the wishes of their study participant, defined the action they took.

CASE STUDY

Dilemmas of Confidentiality and Representation: Nancy Scheper-Hughes

First published in 1979, Nancy Scheper-Hughes (2001) *Saints, Scholars and Schizophrenics* involved ethnographic research in a small rural village fictitiously called Ballybran on the west coast of Ireland. In a period marked by social and economic upheaval, Scheper-Hughes provides an account of the gradual decline of community cohesion due to factors such as declining birth rates and emigration, as well as the breakdown of traditional values and familial bonds. This erosion was accompanied by a reduction in social activities and village institutions, compounded by national policies aimed at encouraging young farmers to retire. Issues related to alcoholism, sexual apathy and mental illness are depicted as symptoms of this social anomie. Scheper-Hughes proposed that the complexities of mental health issues, such as schizophrenia, extend beyond merely strained family dynamics to encompass what she termed as 'bad faith relations'. In her observations of Ballybran, she noted an implicit expectation for parents to retain at least one child, typically the youngest son, to remain in the village while supporting the eldest child's pursuit of education and a better life elsewhere. Through collaboration with various community figures, such as teachers, shopkeepers and the parish priest, farming parents tended to designate a 'sacrificial child', one destined to remain within the village's limited prospects indefinitely. This child would internalize their role, feeling both indispensable yet insufficient for opportunities beyond the village's confines. While the book was met with positive reviews from anthropological journals (Gallaher, 1980; Loudon, 1980), reviewers from the field of psychiatry were less enthusiastic, critiquing her argument and use of data that Irish socialization practices were producing higher rates of schizophrenia (Kelly, 2022). Critiques also focused on the inaccurate representation of Irish society (Murphy, 1979).

At the same time that Scheper-Hughes was notified that she was going to be awarded the Margaret Mead Award from the Society for Applied Anthropology, the book became embroiled in a trans-Atlantic controversy (see Scheper-Hughes, 2000 and in the Preface to newer editions of the book). Michael Viney (1980, 1983), a journalist, embarked on a journey to uncover the pseudonymous town, initiating the controversy. In subsequent reviews, Scheper-Hughes faced criticism for her perceived bias and ethnocentrism in her examination of the community's issues and conflicts. Furthermore, she was accused of ethical breaches for exposing community secrets and violating their privacy. When Scheper-Hughes returned to Ballybran, she found that her presence was not welcomed, and she was urged to leave. She found that residents had various complaints about her book. The first was about representation and the portrayal of the village, best summed up by the schoolmaster:

> It's not your science [i.e., your accuracy] I'm questioning, but this: don't we have the right to lead unexamined lives, the right not to be analyzed? Don't we have a right to hold on to an image of ourselves as 'different' to be sure, but as innocent and unblemished all the same? (Scheper-Hughes, 2001: xvi)

While the community member expressed anger at the representation of their village (and sharing of community secrets) to the outside world, they also discussed the impact of the exposure of their internal struggles and pain to one another. Scheper-Hughes carefully de-identified her participants by forming composite stories and individuals. However, when Scheper-Hughes discussed this issue with villages, the reply indicates the problems of such an approach.

> Nonsense! You know us for better than that. You think we didn't, each of us, sit down poring over every page until we had recognized the bits and pieces of ourselves strewn about here and there. You

turned us into amputees with hooks for fingers and some other blackguard's heart beating inside our own chest. How do you think I felt reading my words come out of some Tom-O or Pat-O or some publican's mouth? Recognize ourselves, indeed! I've gone on to memorize some of my best lines (Scheper-Hughes, 2001: xix)

Scheper-Hughes (2000) reflects that if she were writing the book again, she would have avoided the use of pseudonyms and composite stories that can be easily decoded by participants and persistent investigators or journalists. She writes about anonymity, stating that 'the practice makes rogues of us all – too free with our pens, with the government of our tongues, and with our loose translations and interpretation of village life' (2000: 128). Scheper-Hughes reflects that she could have included descriptions of the many positive aspects of village life, including the deeply egalitarian aspects of gender and social relations. Ethnographies are always deeply subjective and partial, often reflecting the discourses in the academy and beyond at the time of writing. What this case study points to is the central role that relationality and transparency play in conducting research that seeks to understand sensitive topics that are acknowledged but perhaps go unsaid in particular communities. Ensuring there are adequate processes to discuss the possible impacts of making the invisible 'visible' with the community is important. However, this can have very real impacts on the anonymity of individuals. Recent discussions have focused on developing a rights-informed approach in the sharing of research findings with research participants (see George et al., 2023).

CASE STUDY

Dilemmas of Data Governance: Amohia Boulton, Jennifer Tamehana and Tula Brannelly

The dilemmas presented in this case study occurred during a Māori-led research project funded by New Zealand's main health funding research body called the Health Research Council of New Zealand (Boulton et al., 2013). The project was hosted by an *iwi* (tribal) owned research centre and the researchers sought to understand the practice *vs* service focused approaches associated with a health service that uses traditional *rongoā* (traditional Māori healing) approaches to care. The researchers conducted in-depth interviews with a range of key informants (healers, policy-makers, funders of *rongoā* Māori); a survey of healers, clinicians and rongoā practitioners; and an in-depth case study with three health services currently providing rongoā services. The key ethical issues for the project were around the issue of enacting *Kaitiakitanga*, which translates as stewardship or guardianship and wider concerns related to the legal and ethical aspect of cultural and intellectual property related to the research data collected.

While negotiating data ownership for the project, the appropriate organization to govern data collected was identified as the peak body created under a ministerial directive in 2010 called Te Kāhui Rongoā (TKR). The TKR's role was to ensure proper governance of rongoā (traditional medicine) and to provide a guardianship role (*kaitiakitanga*) over knowledge and research data to protect, grow, nurture and develop Māori traditional healing practices. TKR was in the position of being able to act as a collective voice for Indigenous rights and to provide an ethical and moral mandate for rongoā Maori.

While the Ministry of Health supported TKR as the national body for rongoā Māori practitioners with establishment funding, TKR did not have the further resources to establish a sustainable governance body and repository database. Subsequently, the researchers felt that they were unable to burden TKR with the responsibilities associated with data governance without the proper resourcing. Boulton et al. (2013) claim that governments should take responsibility to support traditional knowledge based on the United Nations (2007) Declaration on the Rights of Indigenous Peoples and the Waitangi tribunal (2011). However, movements to recognize Indigenous guardianship of traditional knowledge (which are increasingly being played out in the international arena) do not always align with legal and ethical policies around definitions of ownership, control and intellectual property. The dilemmas discussed here focus on the complex issues at the interface between Indigenous knowledge systems and Western legal and ethical frameworks (Tikly & Bond, 2013). Nevertheless, the basic principle that the researcher has a duty to ensure that the benefits that arise from research are directed back to communities is vital to Indigenous social justice concerns.

Making Ethical Decisions

These case studies drawn from published research provide interesting and detailed descriptions of ethical dilemmas raised by research in different contexts. They demonstrate that, in making ethical decisions, researchers frequently have to balance the quality of their research with the ethical treatment of their research participants and that at times there can be a conflict between these two aims. They illustrate how there is often not one clear solution to the ethical dilemmas that emerge in research but rather that decisions are situational and contextual. They also illustrate how other researchers, drawing on different moral frameworks, might resolve ethical dilemmas in different ways to the researchers in these case studies. In short, they illustrate that specific ethical issues may be viewed and justified differently according to the specific issue, the context and the researcher. Importantly, however, they illustrate the careful consideration and reflexivity that these researchers have employed in resolving their ethical dilemmas.

Summary

There have been various ethical dilemmas described in the social sciences. For the most part, researchers manage the ethical issues that emerge in considered and reflexive ways that enable them to conduct research which will produce valid findings while at the same time treating research participants with respect. The need for careful consideration, evaluation and justification of ethical decisions is central to good ethical decision-making.

CHAPTER 7

Where Next for Research Ethics?

Introduction

There have been several developments in research methods over the last decade or so which have, arguably, significantly changed the nature of the way in which many social scientists conduct research and consequently the ethical issues with which they engage. In this chapter, trends and developments in qualitative research methods and the ethical issues that they raise are outlined. The chapter concludes by discussing whether these ethical issues demand new approaches to research ethics or involve the reworking of familiar issues in new contexts. It also outlines some ideas about the direction for research ethics in the future.

Developments in Research Methods

The last decade or so has seen a rapid growth in the development and use of a number of specific methodological approaches in qualitative research. These include: decolonizing methods; visual and creative methods; participatory methods; digital and e-research and data sharing. Some of these developments reflect what has been termed the 'cultural turn' in the social sciences and the interest in identity, while others reflect what has been referred to as the democratization of research and the moves to the involvement and empowerment of research participants. The rapid growth in digital technology and Artificial Intelligence (AI), changes in the ways that people interact online and the scope that online communications provide for understanding aspects of the social world are another factor involved in some of these developments. A further factor is the need to ensure data sharing in the interests of maximizing value from research and providing datasets and resources of value to future researchers. It has been observed that the developments outlined here have been driven by a number of factors, such as advances in technology, cross-fertilization across disciplines and demands for accountability (Xenitidou & Gilbert, 2009; Druckman & Donohue, 2020). Some of the developments in each of these methods and approaches and the major corresponding ethical issues they raise are explored below. In this brief outline to each of these methodological areas it is possible to identify only very general issues. It is of course the case that the ethical issues that arise within each of these methodological approaches are contextual and will vary according to the nature of the project.

Decolonizing Methods: Yarning

In countries where populations are disproportionately impacted by specific inequities, there have been criticisms of research as reinforcing continued forms of domination, subjectification, observation, disempowerment and continued colonization. In Linda Tuhawai-Smith's book, *Decolonising Methodologies: Storytelling and Indigenous Peoples* (1999) she states:

> The intellectual project of decolonizing has to set out ways to proceed through a colonizing world. It needs a radical compassion that reaches out, that seeks collaboration, and that is open to possibilities that can only be imagined as other things fall into place. Decolonizing Methodologies is not a method for revolution in a political sense but provokes some revolutionary thinking about the roles that knowledge, knowledge production, knowledge hierarchies and knowledge institutions play in decolonization and social transformation.

Much of the history of research in the western European world has been a narrative of extraction and discovery at the expense of others, often in less powerful positions. For qualitative research, methodologies that do not involve participant communities in the creation, collection, analysis and dissemination of data can be ethically problematic for those who have experienced systematic oppression and discrimination. Members from these communities question the right of scientists, representing powerful institutions, to extract and speak for them, when they continue to be oppressed and disempowered by those societies wishing to study them. This has led to the development of various qualitative research methods that privilege community-specific knowledge systems and attempt to shift power hierarchies implicit in researcher-participant relationships (see also discussion of epistemic injustice in Chapter 3). While some researchers have used participatory action approaches to transform research approaches (Cornish et al., 2023; Mertens, 2021), others have articulated critical and Indigenous methodological approaches (see Denzin et al., 2008; Kapā'anaokalāokeola Nākoa Oliveira & Kahunawaika'ala Wright, 2016; Anderson & O'Brien, 2016). A recent focus has been on the development of approaches with story as method (Kovach, 2021), including 'yarning' (Bessarab & Ng'andu, 2010), Kapati time (Ober, 2017), talking circles (Lowe & Wimbish-Cirilo, 2016), story work (Archibald, 2008) and other approaches (see Rieger et al., 2023), such as 'Dadirri' and 'Engoori' (Waller, 2018) and Talanoa (McGrath & Ka'ili, 2010).

Yarning is being used in Australia and internationally reflecting Indigenous 'ways of being' and as a way to decolonize research practice (see Bessarab & Ng'andu, 2010 and Kennedy et al., 2022). Grounded in two-way knowledge sharing and relationality, it provides a culturally safe and sensitive approach that allows for flexibility, co-creation and Indigenous-led discussion. While having a researcher who identifies as Indigenous to lead yarning sessions is viewed as preferable, where this is not possible, the yarning approach can assist in avoiding the impact of not having an Indigenous person collect the data.

Where an Indigenous researcher leads a yarning session and participates in the subsequent stages of research, there are some specific ethical issues. Issues around confidentiality are important to consider with yarning research, especially if the researcher is from or has familial links within the community. Other more implicit ethical issues are related to the cultural relationships that the researcher may have with participants. In Indigenous Australia, it is important to note that there are certain responsibilities, roles and relationships depending on a person's position in their kinship network, their age and gender (Healy et al., 1985; Gray et al., 1991). Different types of avoidance relationships have been described between certain relatives (often between certain in-laws), such as prescriptions around speech styles and modes of interaction (see Merlan, 1997). Following a specific topic of conversation or talking directly to specific participants in a yarn may be breaking specific cultural protocols, so Indigenous frameworks need to be applied in these contexts.

Kovach, an Indigenous scholar from Saskatchewan, Canada, discusses how the relational aspects of Indigenous-centred methods are a form of ethics in itself. Kovach (2021: 147) discusses that an Indigenous research ethics should be one where the researcher conducts themselves in a way that reflects *miyo*, meaning 'good, well and valuable'. Such Indigenous ethics frameworks can help guide Indigenous researchers who are working in other Indigenous settings, for example in Summers's (2013) description of conducting a research project as a First Nations Oji-Cree nation woman from the 'first world' with an Indigenous community in the 'third world', among a Patachancha community in Peru. Other Indigenous scholars have discussed the importance of Indigenous researchers being critically reflexive and accountable and not relying on their identity as the only ethical basis of their engagement (Menzies, 2001). Other Indigenous writers such as Jacobs-Huey (2002), Jankie (2004) and Madison (2005) discuss the need to problematize positionalities, as Indigenous experiences intersect with various identities and realities, all of which are relevant for considering ethical responsibility. These discussions echo those of the insider-outsider literature, which has reflected on ethical issues related to role conflict, consent, and confidentiality (Voloder & Kirpitchenko, 2016; Toy-Cronin, 2018).

Visual and Creative Methods

There has been a rapid growth in interest in visual research methods over the last decade or so across a range of social science disciplines and research settings (Clark et al., 2010). 'Visual methods' comprise a vast array of different types of approaches and data. Visual data include photographs, film, video, drawings, advertisements or media images, sketches, graphical representations and models created by a range of creative media. Prosser & Loxley (2008) identify four different types of visual data: 'found data' (e.g. family photograph albums); 'researcher created data' (such as images or film taken by researchers); 'respondent created data' (such as models or drawings created by respondents) and 'representations' (e.g. graphical representations of data).

Visual methods raise a number of ethical issues. Perhaps the primary issue centres around the use of material in which individuals are recognizable or potentially recognizable, and the challenges this raises in relation to issues of anonymity, confidentiality and consent (see Chapter 4). Consent should be obtained for taking and using such images. However, this in itself is not always straightforward in that it may not be possible to obtain consent for all people in images and, even if consent is obtained, respondents may not be able to fully appreciate what the implications of being identified may be. The fact that it is increasingly the preference of both researchers and respondents that study participants are *not* anonymized in visual research findings raises a further set of ethical considerations, not least that this presents a challenge to established ethical practice. Wider ethical issues have also been identified concerning the way that images are constructed by researchers and consumed by those who view them (Rose, 2007: 255). This has drawn attention to the ethical implications, and consequences for individuals and their communities, of the ways in which researchers present images and the interpretations different audiences may make. Many established 'visual' researchers tend to adopt participatory or collaborative relationships with their study participants so that the materials created emerge from collaborations between them and are seen as jointly owned (Banks, 2001; Gold, 1989; Pink, 2009; Spencer, 2021). Nevertheless, the potential remains for participants in studies that use visual material (as with all research) to be unhappy about the way they have been portrayed (Pink, 2003; Crow & Wiles, 2008). Various researchers have emphasized the importance of reflexive praxis in designing ethical visual research that engages with the 'multivoicedness' of the research process (see LaMarre

& Chamberlain, 2022; Williamson et al., 2021; Dare et al., 2021; Lenton et al., 2021).

Prosser has argued that visual research methods sit uneasily within conventional ethical practice and regulation in social research and that this poses problems in relation to the review of visual research by research ethics committees or boards (Prosser, 2000; Wiles et al., 2011). Proponents of visual research have noted the importance of visual researchers developing ethical practice and becoming members of the committees or boards which conduct ethical review to improve the ethical review and decision-making processes in relation to visual research (Pauwels, 2008).

Participatory Methods

Interest in participatory research approaches has grown significantly in the last twenty years. This has been fuelled, in part, by pressure from particular groups of 'service users' for involvement in the research that informs their treatment, care and experiences, as well as from researchers working in specific fields such as gender studies, childhood studies, ethnic studies and disability studies, who have identified the importance of empowering participants. The resulting insistence by some grant-giving bodies for 'user involvement' in research has meant that most researchers working in health and social care have to have at least some element of involvement from members of the population they are researching in the design and/ or conduct of their research. Participatory approaches are most commonly used in research with children and young people (see, e.g. Renold et al., 2008; Bradbury-Jones et al., 2018; Water, 2024), research with a range of 'service users', including people with physical and learning disabilities (see, e.g. Tarleton et al., 2004; Kuper et al., 2021), Indigenous/First Nation communities (Funnell et al., 2020; Kendall et al., 2011) and research on community and/ or community development (see, e.g. Lassiter et al., 2004; Brush et al., 2020). There are various participatory research methodologies including participatory action research, human centred design, community based participatory research (CBPR), participatory rural appraisal, participatory mapping and participatory video, but in the main, participatory research is distinguished by the level of collaboration between researcher and participants. The levels of involvement that research participants might have with a research project range from consultation, through to collaboration and full control by research participants (Involve, 2004; Frankham, 2009; Spears Johnson et al., 2016). Participatory research is characterized by the involvement of research participants across all stages of a research project. However, research has demonstrated that the nature of community participation can vary, and projects with the most amount of participation often have a more egalitarian distribution of research rights and responsibilities (Spears Johnson et al., 2016)

Researchers using participatory approaches foreground ethical issues as part of their approach (Banks & Brydon-Miller, 2018). The key ethical issues identified focus primarily on the power differentials between participants and researchers. Frankham (2009) identifies the key ethical issues for researchers attempting to involve service users in research as being tensions around the ownership and authorship of research and the related issues of accountability and remuneration. Similar issues are reflected on by Tarleton et al. (2004) in relation to research with people with learning disabilities and by Heath et al. (2009: 73) in relation to research with children and young people. Informed consent has also been identified as a particular challenge in relation to research with children and young people because of the often longitudinal nature of participatory research and the fluid nature of the interactions between researcher and participant. Renold et al. (2008), for example, found that in their longitudinal project on children and young people in the care of the local authority they had to devise various strategies to render participation visible throughout the project.

One of the challenges of participatory approaches is that researchers' interactions with their participants can vary over time and across situations. This is true for all qualitative research but more markedly so in relation to participatory approaches, when the direction of a study, the specific methods used and the dissemination strategy are always in a state of negotiation. This can create tensions in relation to processes of ethical review which operate on the basis of anticipated ethical issues. As Renold et al. (2008: 443) note in relation to their research on 'looked-after children', participatory research ethics is not so much about 'multiple negotiated dilemmas';

rather it involves an 'ongoing dialogue in the micro-complexities inherent in everyday fieldwork relations'.

Digital and E-research

Possibly the most significant developments in research methods in the last decade relate to various forms of digital, online and e-research. This includes the ever-expanding internet of things (IoT), a phrase used to explain the growing number of networked interrelated devices that connect and exchange data with other IoT devices and the cloud (Greengard, 2021). The majority of the population in the Western world use the internet and increasingly a significant part of social interaction occurs online, particularly for some social groups (Dutton & Blank, 2011). The scope for making use of the internet in research has been widely recognized; Eynon et al. (2017) note that the internet can be seen as a huge 'research laboratory'. The ability to collect and combine various types of online and offline digital qualitative and quantitative data is a further development which has generated considerable research activity. This has seen the exponential growth of disciplines such as the 'digital humanities', which has engaged with both descriptive and normative ethics (see Schuster & Dunn, 2020). The development of software tools to analyse activity on the internet, across sites or on specific sites has resulted in a growth in 'webometric' research (see e.g. Thelwall & Sud, 2002; Thelwall, 2022). Research has also been conducted in virtual environments such as 'Second Life' where behavioural experiments have been conducted (Eynon et al., 2017) in addition to ethnographic research (Boellstorf, 2015). The possibilities for future qualitative researchers are potentially limitless in the era of IoT when the devices in our households and that we carry with us have the potential to record our conversations and link to other forms of data, such as biometric, shopping and travel information. This has led researchers to think through embedding ethical frameworks in the design of technological IoT systems (Ustek-Spilda et al., 2019).

Online, digital and e-research have significant ethical implications. There have been challenges arising from what has been referred to as 'Web 2.0', and more recently 'Web 3.0', primarily focusing on data from social networking sites and other user-generated content such as blogs (Snee, 2008). Research on social networking and blogging has used ethnographic methods or 'netnography' (Kozinets, 2019) within sites, often in combination with quantitative methods such as social network analysis (see Eynon et al., 2017; Snee, 2008). The primary ethical issue arising from these developments and online research in general relates to the issues of privacy and consent (see also Chapter 3). It was noted in Chapter 3 that distinguishing between what is public and private on the web is problematic. Snee (2008) notes the nature of the Web 2.0/3.0 environment complicates this further in that social networking sites encourage the sharing of personal and even intimate information. The extent to which such information is viewed by the author as being in the public domain is not necessarily easy to gauge (see Schultze & Mason, 2012; Kozinets, 2019). There are also issues relating to anonymity because, even if people or institutions are de-identified in research reports, information collected from the internet is often easily traceable via a search engine. Identifying when anonymity should be used and when it is appropriate to cite an internet user as an author by name is again not straightforward. It is certainly the case that not all internet users want to remain anonymous; this may apply particularly to authors of blogs, and to de-identify people in such circumstances could be seen as infringing copyright and raise issues of intellectual property. In the case of netnography, researchers have suggested that where information shared between the members of an online community might be harmful to them, this information should not be included as direct quotes in research outputs because of the ease with which this information can be traced back to individuals (see Anne-Marie et al., 2017).

Issues of consent are also potentially problematic, as has been discussed in Chapter 3. Lehner-Mear (2020), in a study of mother perspectives about primary school homework from open-access parenting websites in the UK, argued that gaining consent from forum users would have undermined the intentions of the project to understand new perspectives that potentially counter dominant discourses. In this study, the disclosure of the research project could have influenced mothers to provide socially accepted views rather than counter discourses and perspectives. This was especially pertinent given the strong moral pressures on mothers to comply with school tasks. Lehner-Mear (2020) suggests that consent should be negotiated within the context of the methodology, the research questions and the culture of the online communities. This 'negotiated ethics' approach should also include an assessment of the vulnerability, harm and respect required for each project and an understanding of the nature of the data collected. Research should also determine if the data is public or private and participants' perception of their anonymity. This should be continuously monitored. All these issues are complicated by the fact that in online research, geographical boundaries do not exist and thus different legal and ethical regulations apply to the data collected. How data is stored becomes more challenging in Web 3.0 environments, such as the 'Metaverse', where digital data is decentralized, potentially removing ethical and legal regulations that have protected users in the past. While this requires new approaches to data safety (Yu et al., 2023), proponents of Web 3.0 would argue that dencentraliZed networks and blockchain technology is more secure giving more control to users.

In common with the concerns raised by researchers using visual methods, it has been noted that ethical review committees lack knowledge about Web 2.0/3.0 and that researchers may need to educate committee members as well as the wider research community. Eynon et al. (2017: 26) note that despite concerns that online research raises specific ethical challenges, there has more recently been a convergence in the view that research ethics for online research can be drawn from existing frameworks for offline settings. Similarly, Snee (2008: 20) found that most internet researchers did not feel that a specific 'Web 2.0' ethics is needed. Nevertheless, it is recognized that some special considerations are necessary when researching online and that issues of confidentiality, anonymity, disclosure, informed consent and privacy are cast in a different light in online research. Ann-Marie et al. (2017: 9) call for ethical guidelines in online environments and point to three overarching questions that might assist researchers in choosing an ethically justified approach:

- Do you need to ask the informed consent of the members of the online community in question?

- Do you need to protect the anonymity of the members of the online community in question?

- How important is the accountability of your research?

In better understanding ethical procedures in new methodologies, such as netnography, authors such as Kozinets (2019) have produced useful flowcharts and concepts to assist researchers in making decisions about ethical procedures. These can be supplemented by resources developed by the Association for Internet Researchers (Franzke et al., 2020)

Data Sharing and Big Data

In the last decade or so there has been a marked increase in the development of policies to promote or recommend data sharing; this is increasingly a requirement on the part of research funders (Van den Eynden et al., 2009). In the UK, the ESRC Qualitative Data Archival Resource Centre (QUALIDATA) is regarded as one of the centres for archiving qualitative data on a national scale and similar developments have occurred in the United States, Europe and Australia to enable the sharing and reuse of data from qualitative research (see Corti & Thompson, 2007; Corti, 2019, 2000). In Australia, under the National Health and Medical Research Council's (NHMRC) Open Access Policy, researchers who receive NHMRC funding are strongly encouraged to open accessible data licensed repositories to share research data (NHMRC, 2023). Metadata associated with any publication is required to be open access in an institutional repository no later than three months following publication and there are now repositories such as the Australian Data Archive to collect, preserve and make accessible digital research data. The National Institute of Health in the US has also enhanced its current policies requiring the sharing of scientific data and accompanying metadata through established data repositories. DuBois and colleagues (2023) discuss the implications for qualitative researchers and provide important guidance on how to de-identify qualitative data, support high-quality secondary use, budget for data sharing, obtain the necessary permissions and assess the current state of US data repositories and their preparedness for sharing qualitative data.

Often there is a tension between the management of open research data platforms that share qualitative data inclusive of meaningful metadata to contextualize the information (such as gender, location, race) and privacy regulations that emphasize that data should not contain personal or sensitive information that would make it possible to identify participants in a study (Class et al., 2021). Anonymization and pseudonymization of large qualitative data sets has seen the development of various automated techniques, such as Named Entity Recognition (Sedkaoui & Simian, 2020), Natural Language Processing (Kleinberg et al., 2017) and other tailor-made software (Class et al., 2021). One critique of such autonomous and connected systems is that it can be difficult to identify responsibilities and liabilities (Jasanoff, 2017).

Data sharing and archiving has become even more relevant with researchers increasingly utilizing mixed methods approaches (Poth & Shannon-Baker, 2022), undertaking 'big qual' projects (Brower et al., 2019) working with large data sets (Mauthner, 2019), and extending qualitative evidence synthesis methods to open access qualitative data sets (Flemming & Noyes, 2021; see Mills (2019) for a discussion on big data for qualitative research). In part, this development reflects a financial imperative for data sharing in order to achieve better value for money for research funders and avoid duplication of research effort. However, data sharing also provides researchers with opportunities to gain methodological and substantive insights from existing research data. Corti and Thompson (2007) identify six approaches to reusing data: description; comparative research, re-study or follow-up study; re-analysis or secondary analysis; research design or methodological advancement; verification; and teaching and learning. It has been noted that archiving for the purposes of data sharing raises significant ethical challenges. Neale and Bishop (2012a) argue that these occur because the priorities and interests of the various parties involved do not necessarily coincide. Balancing the rights and responsibilities of the primary researcher, the research team, secondary researchers who want to make use of the data, the data archivist, research participants, research funders and the general public may present significant challenges. The central issues revolve around informed consent, confidentiality and anonymity.

To ensure that research participants give consent for data archiving and reuse, it is essential that this explicitly forms part of the consent process. Gaining informed consent for data sharing and reuse is particularly problematic in that researchers and their participants do not know what future uses will be made of these data; it is impossible to know what questions researchers will ask of the dataset and how long in the future such secondary analysis may take place. It is possible that secondary research may be conducted in ways that the primary researcher and the research participants might object to on ethical or methodological grounds. While these concerns may be responded to by restricting access arrangements for data so that researchers have to register for access to the data and to comply with specific arrangements for viewing the data (such as having to register for its use and to use it only in non-public environments), it is far harder to justify limiting the ways in which secondary researchers analyse these data. Arguably it is not in the interests of the research community, research funders and the general public to limit the uses that can be made of research, especially where it is publicly funded. Neale and Bishop (2012b) argue that researchers have a duty to protect their research participants but they have to balance this with a wider responsibility to the research community and the public and that they need to work closely with their participants to make this explicit in the case of data sharing.

Researchers themselves are also vulnerable to criticism from other researchers as a result of archiving their research data. Neale and Bishop (2012b) note that researchers undertaking secondary analysis may criticize a primary researcher's ways of working or not take account of the different cultural and intellectual environments in which these data were produced. They argue that both secondary and primary researchers have ethical responsibilities to adopt an ethics of care approach in their dealings with each other so that the primary researcher acknowledges the rights of the secondary researcher to analyse their data as they see fit, but that this should occur in ways that respect the integrity of the primary researcher's original work. Irwin (2013) discusses the ethical challenges related to secondary analysts, who are often removed from the context and cultural specificities in which the original research was generated. This is particularly problematic for secondary analyses of data that employed participatory action research approaches where the building of knowledge and empowerment are embedded in culturally specific social arrangements (Irwin, 2013). Rigour in secondary analysis of qualitative data has been discussed by researchers with various practices adopted, such as member checking, memoing, triangulation, peer debriefing, inter-rater agreement, and maintaining audit trails (Ruggiano & Perry et al.,

2019). Thomson and McGeeney (2018) have discussed new ethical approaches when conducting research with children in building longitudinal data sets for archiving and reuse (see also Thomson et al., 2024). They developed a set of principles formulated around possibility, shareability, co-production and posterity to assist in data collection and managing informed consent (see also Crivello & Morrow, 2021 for description of the ethical issues related to data archiving related to the *Young Lives study*, a four-country longitudinal study of children growing up in poverty).

Issues of de-identification and confidentiality are also prominent in relation to archiving and data sharing. Ensuring confidentiality through processes of de-identification is important, but at the same time, the integrity of the data needs to be protected to ensure its utility. The usefulness of data can be undermined if relational information, geographical references or alterations to aural or visual data are made such that their value to secondary researchers is minimal. Neale and Bishop (2012b) note that while researchers have a duty to protect participants, they also have a responsibility to get their accounts heard as widely as possible. Managing this issue involves balancing these competing responsibilities.

Ethical concerns around the archiving and subsequent reuse of qualitative data have become even more topical in the light of what has become known as the 'big data era' and in new approaches around open science (Hesse et al., 2019; Bechmann and Kim in Iphopen, 2020; Mozersky et al., 2020; Class et al., 2021). Although still somewhat opaque, big data refers to large data sets with increasing volume, variety and velocity (Favaretto et al., 2020). Key ethical concerns have often centred around discussions related to privacy implications (Herschel & Miori, 2017) and more recently with issues related to broader requirements set out by new laws, such as the European GDPR and local country regulations (Vlahou et al., 2021). While big data related to qualitative research often refers to information on social media related to Facebook and Instagram posts and Twitter/X feeds, new technologies in data archiving are making it possible to deposit and access a range of qualitative data from interviews to participant observation (see Mills, 2017; Hesse et al., 2018). This compliments new innovations, such as wearable and mobile technologies, that generate qualitative data about people's lives. This has seen the growth of 'citizen science' associated with research utilizing IoT devices (Scheibner et al., 2020). Privacy concerns are immediate ethical challenges particularly when data flows become automated and users are unaware of the level of metadata that is being made available (Hesse et al., 2019). De-identification is problematic where datasets can be drawn together to identify individuals (Metclaf & Crawford, 2016). Increasingly this has led to the proliferation of a new generation of qualitative researchers with skills in data science and computation (Hesse et al., 2019). Researchers working in the field of IoT emphasize the importance of privacy (the need for protocols to comply with local privacy legislation, including data portability), data quality (the need for the design of IoT devices to be appropriate for the environment in which they are used and to be representative and unbiased in their collection strategies) and intellectual property (the need for a case by case decision about the use of commercial or open sourced hardware) as key ethical concerns (Scheibner et al., 2020).

There are other ethical concerns for qualitative researchers in this area. While big data has meant increasing opportunity to gain access to data to what previously may have been difficult to access groups, such as young people or activists, the perspectives of individuals and groups who do not engage with social media or the internet are largely absent. This question of representativeness is an ethical issue when data mistakenly represents certain groups. The positivist context in which such data is harvested and analysed is also very specific to the metadata collected (location, shopping preferences etc.), rather than the type of interpretative contextual issues traditional qualitative researchers account for, such as the nature of social interactions, the role of the researcher's own positionality, and the context in which the data originated. Concerns have also been raised about the emphasis that the big data movement gives to 'bigger is better' (Hesse et al., 2019). In-depth reflexive qualitative studies with small sample sizes that capture the depth of experiences on a specific topic are what makes qualitative research distinctive, contributing to a more nuanced theoretically informed understanding of the human world. The data associated with such studies are contextual and reflexive, and so possibilities for misinterpretation and misrepresentations are more likely when conducting secondary analyses or when combining datasets. This is important when considering the curation and safeguarding of data in future archive and repository sites.

Data Sovereignty

The term data sovereignty has gained significance as governments and organizations have sought to frame laws on data governance, in an era where data is increasingly becoming commodified and used for various market and research interests (see Singi et al., 2020). The EU GDPR is just one example of legislation that seeks to regulate the use of personal data and protect citizen rights (see Goddard, 2017). Referring to regulatory and data security contexts, data sovereignty refers to the jurisdictional control and legal authority that can be asserted over data through its physical location (Hummel et al., 2021b). Recently, Indigenous data sovereignty has become part of international calls for the need to protect against the misuse of data related to Indigenous people and to ensure that Indigenous communities are the primary beneficiaries of their data (Global Indigenous Data Alliance, 2019; United States Indigenous Data Sovereignty, 2020). Responding to histories of injustice and ongoing colonialism, where data has been extracted by non-Indigenous people and institutions for their own gain, Indigenous leaders and scholars recognize data as a cultural and economic asset over which Indigenous people have sovereign rights that govern the collection, ownership and application of that data (Walter et al., 2020). Indigenous data sovereignty has seen the formulation of new research methodologies and practices that place Indigenous peoples, their worldviews, governance and knowledge systems into their own control (Foxworth & Ellenwood, 2022; Kukutai & Taylor, 2006; Walter et al., 2020). For qualitative researchers, this has seen the development of various storytelling methods, such as yarning, kaupapa and other Indigenous-led methodologies (see Ward & Fredericks, 2021; Wilson et al., 2022).

For research ethics, various Indigenous ethical guidelines have been formulated to guide the research community (see Further Reading and Resources for specific guidelines; Carroll et al., 2020; Patterson et al., 2006; Wright et al., 2016; McGuffog et al., 2023). Internationally, these ethical guidelines share common principles around the need for research projects to engage with and be assessed by communities so that both project design and outcomes align with community priorities and respect and include Indigenous knowledges and methodologies. Participants in research should have the opportunity to be involved in all aspects of the research from project design to knowledge dissemination and representation. Research agreements that include clear recommendations about the ownership and use of data should be formulated so that Indigenous data sovereignty is respected. The Global Indigenous Data Alliance (2019) has produced the CARE principles to empower communities in the decision-making process around the collection, use and curation of data. They stand for Collective benefits, Authority to control, Responsibility, and Ethics (GIDA, 2019).

While many of the ethical issues raised earlier for participatory research apply here, there are specific concerns in Indigenous contexts. University and other institutions/bodies often have intellectual property rights over data generated through research, but Indigenous data sovereignty principles place emphasis on Indigenous control of intellectual property (see Cocq, 2022 for a discussion of this among the Sámi of Norway, Sweden and Finland). Recent discussions have urged for the development of legal recognition of Indigenous data rights through country specific laws/ treatises/agreements (Hudson et al., 2023). Where governments do recognize Indigenous sovereignty on tribal lands, such as in the United States and Canada, Indigenous communities have specific rights over how their data is used by researchers (Haozous et al., 2021). However, how data is used within communities is often not within the scope for human research ethics committees and can lead to breaches in anonymity and confidentiality, where participants themselves may share cultural information with others that may not be intended for publication (Tsosie, 2020). Also, sovereign rights in the United States and Canada are often geographically specific, so Indigenous peoples who live outside their tribal lands and participate in research are not afforded the same protections as when they are living on tribal lands (Haozous et al., 2021).

Artificial Intelligence

Artificial Intelligence (AI) is now being integrated into the research of qualitative researchers (Anis & French, 2023; Marshall & Naff, 2023). While the use of AI in audio transcription is ubiquitous, AI is now being used to code and sort data, with programmes such as ATLAS.ti and NVivo introducing 'intentional AI coding' into their platforms. Anis and French (2023) have argued that AI can make qualitative research more efficient (in highlighting patterns with large volumes of data), explicatory (in identifying complex or ambiguous data that may not fit with a coding scheme) and equitable (in overcoming limitations in language abilities, styles and academic conventions for underprivileged scholars). However, they also warn that AI will never replace a researcher. AI is limited in interpreting and bringing meaning to the data and in engaging with theoretical constructs and reflexivity. Various authors have urged for caution with AI analysis often leading to an oversimplification of complex qualitative data that involves emotional subtleties, cultural contexts and individual idiosyncrasies, such as humour and sarcasm (see Lupton & Watson 2021). Furthermore, AI carries with it the implicit biases prevalent in society; AI is trained on data that contains bias (gender, race and class), which can carry into qualitative analysis and skew interpretations and perpetuate structural inequalities (see Binns, 2018; Adib-Moghaddam, 2023). Marshall and Naff (2024) have described the ethical concerns of researchers and their perspectives on AI, noting ethical concerns around the use of generating and publishing content that is AI generated and the potential future issues where research participants might be interacting with AI chatbots for online synchronous interviews. Issues around consent processes, data security and the ability of a chatbot to respond to participant distress are of concern.

While qualitative researchers have been outsourcing transcription of their primary data sources, such as recorded interviews, for some time, prior to AI, these were completed by humans. During this process, data which is identifiable either in the form of direct names or specific events can be de-identified before the transcript is finalized. This de-identification process does not occur with AI, with potentially identifying information remaining in transcripts. These transcripts are then stored on cloud-based servers, which can be accessed either through breaches/hacks or government subpoenas. One journalist tells the story of using a popular transcription to speech service that uses AI and machine learning to record an interview with a human rights activist (Kine, 2022). The reporter received correspondence the following day from the service. The service provided the AI transcription and inquired into the purpose of the interview, using the interviewee's real name. The reporter entered into an extended dialogue with the transcription service about the purpose of the email, fearing that the information had been shared or accessed by interested authorities. The reporter finally discovered that the correspondence was simply a follow-up evaluation question about the service and not related to the content or identity of the interviewee. They were identified because the journalist had named the transcription file with the interviewees first name. A simple mistake, but the journalist points to the potential threats and risks in using AI services. Researchers are increasingly being required by human research ethics committees to inform their participants that AI-based transcription services will be used. Various organizations (such as the European Commission) have started to develop and implement research processes for AI projects (see Resseguier & Ufert, 2024).

Where Next for Research Ethics?

Researchers working in each of the methodological approaches outlined above have identified the specific ethical challenges raised. The topics relate, broadly, to the general issues identified in traditional qualitative approaches and discussed in the various ethical and moral research ethics frameworks presented in Chapter 2; those of anonymity and confidentiality, informed consent and risk of harm. This is perhaps not surprising given that this is the framework by which ethical questions in social research are addressed. Nevertheless, some of the specific issues identified within these broad ethical topics imply, to a greater or lesser extent, a re-framing of traditional approaches to ethics. This is perhaps particularly pertinent in relation to the issue of anonymity. In all the approaches discussed above, some challenges to the need for anonymity are raised. This is a view supported by many researchers, particularly visual and participatory researchers, who argue that research participants often want to be identified and should have the right to be, providing this does not pose risks to their or other participants' well-being (Grinyer, 2002; Wiles et al., 2011). Tilley & Woodthorpe (2011) argue that the concept of anonymity may be inappropriate in the context of twenty-first-century qualitative research activity. They note that anonymity can conflict with demands to disseminate widely, particularly on the internet, which poses various threats to anonymity. They also note that anonymity can conflict with the wishes of funding bodies and with knowledge transfer to policy-makers and practitioners.

Nduna and colleagues (2022: 561) further this argument explaining that in research with communities who have experienced oppression and structural inequities, anonymity can be viewed as deeply unethical and representative of colonizing Western-oriented ethical principles. Discussing their work as Black (South) African scholars conducting research in their own communities, Nduna and colleagues argue that ethical requirements for anonymity restrict 'colloboration, empowerment, ownership, contextualization, targeted dissemination, intervention and policy influence' (2022: 561). They state that research ethics committees should be looking for the ways in which researchers make collaborative decisions with the communities concerned, supported by relevant ethical guidelines (Nduna et al., 2022: 561). In a commentary piece, Singh and Engel-Hills (2022) note that while Nduna and colleagues remind us that ethics systems must be more responsive to and aligned with local socio-cultural practices and belief systems, it is also important to consider additional ethical issues—particularly the legal dimensions of privacy and the unintended consequences of naming communities, such as the potential for stigma and discrimination. Singh and Engel-Hills (2022) point to the ongoing opportunities for education and sharing through various networks and groups, such as the Global Forum for Bioethics in Research (GFBR, 2025, see resource list).

A further important issue raised by the review of the above approaches is that research ethics committees and regulation more broadly are viewed by many people as curtailing or limiting research using these approaches. It is argued that members of ethics committees lack an understanding of non-traditional methods and that researchers using, for example, visual and online approaches need to educate them to ensure that this does not pose a challenge to such research being conducted. These criticisms form part of a wider critique of the ethical governance and regulation of the social sciences (Atkinson, 2009; Hammersley, 2009; Sieber, 2012; Kohn & Shore 2017; Bell & Wynn 2021). Criticisms of the regulation of research in the UK, North America, Australia and New Zealand have thus far had limited impact on what has been referred to as 'ethics creep'. It seems probable that debates about the merits of regulation, and perhaps also resistance to it, will remain a feature of social science research into the foreseeable future (see Stanley &

Wise, 2010; Gunsalus et al., 2007). More recently researchers from humanities and social science (HASS) disciplines have highlighted the potential value of ethics review processes and possibilities for greater collaboration between HASS researchers and ethics review boards (Carniel et al., 2022)

One of the key issues that researchers using the approaches outlined above identify is the need for situational relativist approaches to be adopted in managing the ethical issues that emerge in research rather than adherence to a set of principles or rules. Adherence to principle and rule-based ethical frameworks appears to be identified as particularly challenging in relation to these developing and emerging research approaches. This is a key debate in the research ethics literature and one which, arguably, lies at the heart of concerns about regulation. Plummer (2001: 226) regards the distinction between ethical absolutists (who view ethical principles as important in driving ethical decision-making) and situational relativists (who view ethical decision-making as emerging from an individual researcher's moral framework) as an unhelpful dichotomy. In a conversational piece on research ethics in childhood research, Hanson and colleagues (2023) discuss the tension between situated ethics prevalent in much childhood research and institutionalized approaches to research through protocols and regulations. They note that dominating childhood research is a conceptual framework that 'primarily sees children as passive objects of protection, indelibly marked by their legal status as minors' (2023: 344). This is in contrast with approaches to issues such as consent, anonymity and privacy that are child centric and organized round children's rights framework. While research involving children needs to be of a high standard, reinforced by a regulatory framework that protects them from harm, it also needs to respect their autonomy and engage their opinions and perspectives through methods that are appropriate and enabling. However, Hanson and colleagues (2023: 355) describe future challenges in research with children around the following issues:

- Tensions between procedural ethics and ethics in practice

- Negotiating and advocating for children's rights and ethical processes with gatekeepers

- Decolonizing children's rights, research ethics and research

- Negotiating ethical approaches across international contexts

- Balancing research integrity and participatory processes (finding/redefining/reconsidering the researcher role)

- Tensions between children's anonymity and recognition; and

- Research in the digital, online space

Returning to Plummer (2001), his argument, is consistent with the one which we have put forward in this book (see Chapter 2), that ethical decision-making needs to be guided by an ethical framework. Such frameworks do not *determine* decision-making but rather provide researchers with a means of thinking systematically about moral behaviour in research.

A key issue alongside the exponential growth of participatory research is the ethics of knowledge production itself. As different communities who have traditionally been the subject of research seek to redress the power imbalances often inherent in research relationships, the issue of who produces knowledges about what and how that knowledge is produced has become prominent (Josephides & Grønseth, 2017). This has become an important movement for Indigenous communities (Latulippe & Klenk, 2020), migrant and refugee groups (Grønseth, 2017; Krawczyk & Dieudonné, 2023) and writers in mad studies and critical disability studies (see LeFrançois & Voronka, 2022). In their edited volume, Josephides and Grønseth (2017) discuss that in the ethics of knowledge creation there are significant tensions between 'state' and 'social' practices. State practices are those regulations, laws and guidelines that define and influence ethical knowledge production, determining how and by whom knowledge is created, who has access and the rights to disseminate it and who is excluded from this process. Social practices are those situations where knowledge production is created through relationships and engagement with communities and individuals and regulated through 'empathy, imagination, affinity and solidarity' (Josephides & Grønseth, 2017: 4). In understanding the relationships between the two, Josephides and Grønseth (2017) find that state practices do not have adequate ethical relations to the community and so ignore how knowledge is attached to individuals and communities who are directly connected to that knowledge. Further, state knowledge is often used for politically defined purposes, producing problem-focused constructions of particular communities that justify intervention. Josephides and Grønseth (2017: 8) ask qualitative researchers to justify how their process of knowledge production is different to that of 'state practices'. They argue for research practices that support an 'ethics of regard' that is attuned to the concerns and lives of research participants and actively works against oppression, degradation and sovereign powers. In assessing the viability of knowledge creation, their volume investigates the following questions:

What are the practical implications of the knowledge created, and for whom? How does the new knowledge make everyone more capable of dealing with their life concerns? What possibilities does the new knowledge add to everyone's life-course and well-being? (Josephides & Grønseth, 2017: 9)

In 2009, Pacific Islander leaders came together at the *Regional Pacific Ethics of Knowledge Production workshop in Apria* (13–15 November 2007) where they discussed ethical issues related to the preservation, production, exchange and use of knowledge (see Du Plessis & Fairburn-Dunlop, 2009 for the introduction to the special issue). A key issue for the contributors was the challenges between Indigenous and Western knowledge systems. In their view, ethical research practice should be a negotiated space with local knowledge informing a post-colonial space that bridges different knowledge systems. Du Plessis and Fairbairn-Dunlop (2009: 113) conclude with some of the following questions echoing those of (Josephides & Grønseth, 2017)

How can knowledge arising out of different epistemologies be appropriately incorporated into Western science?

How are traditional types of knowledge and customary rights over certain flora and fauna to be recognized in national and global systems of knowledge production, commodification and exchange?

Who should decide whether certain forms of scientific activity should be undertaken and under what conditions?

What is the relationship between the passions scientists bring to the pursuit of greater knowledge and the Samoan concept of tofa sa'ili, or the pursuit of wisdom?

Are there scientists who pursue what Tamasese Ta'isi Efi refers to in his article as faautago loloto or the deep view of the here and now, while other scientists seek tofa mamao, or the long view?

Summary

The last decade or so has seen a rapid growth in the development and use of a number of specific methodological approaches in qualitative research. These include: visual and creative methods; participatory methods; Indigenous methodologies; digital and e-research, and the use of big data and data sharing. The ethics of issues related to the intellectual property of qualitative data has also become an important topic in discussions related to data sovereignty and ethical knowledge creation. Some of the ethical issues raised by these approaches imply a re-framing of traditional approaches to ethics. This is perhaps particularly pertinent in relation to the issue of anonymity. Research ethics committees and regulation more broadly are viewed as curtailing or limiting research using these approaches. It seems likely that debates about the merits and form of regulation will remain a feature of social science research in the foreseeable future.

FURTHER READING AND RESOURCES

General Guidance on Research Ethics

There are a number of useful books which provide an introduction to research ethics, discussion of the key issues that need consideration and guidance on the process of gaining ethical approval for a research project.

Bos, J., Hoeneveld, F., van Steenbergen, N., Abma, R., van Meijl, T., & Lepianka, D. (2021). *Research ethics for students in the social sciences*. Cham: Springer International Publishing.

Iltis, A. S., & MacKay, D. (2024). *The Oxford handbook of research ethics*. Oxford: Oxford University Press.

Iphofen, R. (2009). *Ethical decision making in social research*. Basingstoke: Palgrave Macmillan.

Iphofen, R., & Tolich, M. (Eds.). (2018). *The SAGE handbook of qualitative research ethics*. London: SAGE Reference

Israel, M., & Hay, I. (2006). *Research ethics for social scientists*. London: Sage.

Gregory, I. (2003). *Ethics in research*. London: Continuum.

Mertens, D., & Ginsberg, P. (Eds.). (2009). *The* handbook *of* social research ethics. Thousand Oaks: Sage.

Smyth, B. M., Downing, M., & Martin, M. M. (2025). *The Routledge handbook of human research ethics and integrity in Australia*. London: Routledge.

van den Hoonaard, W. C., & van den Hoonaard, D. K. (2016). *Essentials of thinking ethically in qualitative research*. New York: Routledge.

Most of the above books and resources discuss the various moral and ethical frameworks for thinking about research ethics. The following books explore some of the specific ethical positions or frameworks:

Alderson, P., & Morrow, V. (2020). *The ethics of research with children and young people: A practical handbook*. London: SAGE Publications.

Beauchamp, T., & Childress, J. (2001). *Principles of biomedical ethics*. Oxford: Oxford University Press. This book is the key handbook for principlist approaches. While it was developed primarily for medical ethics, it is widely used as the basis for social science ethics.

Demircloğlu, A. (2024). *Methodologies and ethics for social sciences research*. Hershey, Pennsylvania: IGI Global.

George, L., Tauri, J., & MacDonald, L. T. A. O. T. (Eds.). (2020). *Indigenous research ethics: Claiming research sovereignty beyond deficit and the colonial legacy*. Bingley Emerald Publishing Limited.

Giardina, M. D., & Denzin, N. K. (2016). *Ethical futures in qualitative research: Decolonizing the politics of knowledge*. New York: Routledge.

Hammersley, M., & Traianou, A. (2012). *Ethics in qualitative research: Controversies and contexts*. London: SAGE Publications.

Iphofen, R. (2020). *Handbook of research ethics and scientific inquiry*. Cham: Springer.

Israel, M. (2014). *Research ethics and integrity for social scientists: Beyond regulatory compliance*. London: SAGE Publications.

Jeesop J., Birch., M., Mauthner, M., & Miller, T. (2012). *Ethics in qualitative research*. London: SAGE Publications.

Kara, H. (2018). *Research ethics in the real world: Euro-Western and indigenous perspectives*. University of Bristol: Policy Press.

Lahman, M. K. E. (2017). *Ethics in social science research: Becoming culturally responsive*. Thousand Oaks: SAGE Publications.

Macfarlane, B. (2009). *Researching with integrity*. New York: Routledge. This book provides a detailed exploration of virtue ethics and identifies the moral virtues, and corresponding vices, that the virtuous researcher should ideally adopt at different stages of the research process.

Mauthner, M., Birch, M., Jessop, J., & Miller, T. (Eds.) (2002). *Ethics in qualitative research*. London: Sage. This book explores ethical issues from a feminist ethics of care approach.

Nakray, K. (2015). Social science research ethics for a globalizing world: A critical overview of interdisciplinary and cross-cultural perspectives. In K. Nakray, M. Alston, & K. Ehittenbury (Eds.), *Social science research ethics for a globalizing world* (pp. 5–28). New York: Routledge.

Pasquale, F., Dubber, M., & Das, S. (2020). *The Oxford handbook of ethics of AI*. Oxford: Oxford University Press.

Tolich, M. (2016). *Qualitative ethics in practice*. London: Taylor & Francis.

van den Hoonaard, W. C. (2023). *Seeking a research-ethics covenant in the social sciences*. Alberta: University of Alberta Press.

Welland, T., & Pugsley, L. (2018). *Ethical dilemmas in qualitative research*. London: Taylor & Francis.

Zion, D., Briskman, L., & Bagheri, A. (Eds.). (2021). *Indigenous health ethics: An appeal to human rights* (Vol. 3). Singapore World Scientific.

Risks and Safety

Useful publications relating to risk and safety of research participants and researchers are:

Bloor, M., Fincham, B., & Sampson, H. (2007). *Qualiti (NCRM) commissioned inquiry into the risk to well-being of researchers in qualitative research*. Cardiff: Cardiff University. http://www.cardiff.ac.uk/socsi/qualiti/publications.html

Federman, D. D., Hanna, K. E., & Rodriguez, L. L. (2003). *Responsible research: A systems approach to protecting research participants*. Washington (DC): National Academies Press.

Grimm, J. J., Koehler, K., Lust, E. M., Saliba, I., & Schierenbeck, I. (2020). *Safer field research in the social sciences: A guide to human and digital security in hostile environments*. Los Angeles: SAGE Publications.

Lee, R. (1993). *Doing research on sensitive topics*. London: Sage Publications.

Lee-Treweek, G., & Linkogle, S. (Eds.). (2000). *Danger in the field*. London: Taylor & Francis.

Mulligan, D. L., & Danaher, P. A. (2021). *Researchers at risk: Precarity, jeopardy and uncertainty in academia*. Cham, Germany: Springer International Publishing.

Sieber, J. E., & Tolich, M. B. (2013). *Planning ethically responsible research*. London: SAGE Publications.

Social Research Association. (2003). *A code of practice for the safety of social researchers*. Available from: https://the-sra.org.uk/SRA/SRA/Resources/Good-Practice.aspx

Consent

General books on ethics all discuss issues of consent; the following books and resources focus specifically on this issue.

Corrigan, O., McMillan, J., Liddell, K., Richards, M., & Weijer, C. (Eds.). (2009). *The limits of consent: a socio-ethical approach to human subject research in medicine*. Oxford: OUP Oxford.

Kirchhoffer, D. G., & Richards, B. J. (Eds.). (2019). *Beyond autonomy: Limits and alternatives to informed consent in research ethics and law.* Cambrdige: Cambridge University Press.

Marshall, P. A., & Marshall, P. L. (2007). *Ethical challenges in study design and informed consent for health research in resource-poor settings.* Switzerland: World Health Organization.

Müller, A., & Schaber, P. (2020). *The Routledge handbook of the ethics of consent.* London: Taylor & Francis.

Smyth, M., & Williamson, E. (Eds.). (2004). *Researchers and their 'subjects': Ethics, power, knowledge and consent.* Bristol: Policy Press.

Wiles, R., Health, S., Crow, G., & Charles, V. (2008). *Informed* consent *in* social research: *A* literature review. NCRM Methods Review Papers NCRM/001 (Unpublished). http://eprints.ncrm.ac.uk/85/

Ethical Issues in Relation to Specific Methods

There are a number of resources that focus on ethical issues in relation to specific methods. Particularly useful are the following:

Anderson, E. E. (Ed.). (2023). *Ethical issues in community and patient stakeholder–engaged health research* (Vol. 146). New York: Springer Nature.

Banks, S., & Brydon-Miller, M. (2018). *Ethics in participatory research for health and social well-being.* London: Routledge.

Coeckelbergh, M. (2020). *AI ethics.* Cambridge, Massachusetts: MIT Press.

Hasselbalch, G. (2021). *Data ethics of power: A human approach in the big data and AI era.* Cheltenham: Edward Elgar Publishing.

LeCompte, M. D., & Schensul, J. J. (2015). *Ethics in ethnography: A mixed methods approach.* Walnut Creek: AltaMira Press.

Lenette, C. (2022). *Participatory action research: Ethics and decolonization.* Oxford: Oxford University Press.

McKee, H. A., & Porter, J. E. (2009). *The ethics of internet research: A rhetorical, case-based process.* Lausanne: Peter Lang.

Restore. (n.d.). *Online research ethics resources.* http://www.restore.ac.uk/orm/site/home.htm This website has an extensive section on online research ethics which includes resources, reading lists and training materials.

Stahl, B. C., Schroeder, D., & Rodrigues, R. (2022). *Ethics of artificial intelligence: Case studies and options for addressing ethical challenges.* Cham: Springer International Publishing.

Whiteford, L. M., & Trotter II, R. T. (2008). *Ethics for anthropological research and practice*. Long Grove, Illinois: Waveland Press.

Whiteman, N. (2012). *Undoing ethics: Rethinking practice in online research*. New York: Springer .

Wilson, H. F., & Darling, J. (Eds.). (2020). *Research ethics for human geography: A handbook for students*. Los Angeles: Sage Publications.

Woodfield, K. (Ed.). (2017). *The ethics of online research*. Leeds: Emerald Publishing Limited.

Zimmer, M., & Kinder-Kurlanda, K. (2017). *Internet research ethics for the social age: New challenges, cases, and contexts*. Lausanne: Peter Lang International Academic Publishers.

There are also resources relating to ethical issues in visual methods, for example:

Dodd, S. (Ed.). (2020). *Ethics and integrity in visual research methods*. Leeds: Emerald Publishing Limited.

Mannay, D., & Pauwels, L. (2019). *The SAGE handbook of visual research methods*. London: SAGE Publications.

Warr, D., Guillemin, M., Cox, S., & Waycott, J. (2016). *Ethics and visual research methods*. New York: Palgrave Macmillan

Wiles, R., Prosser, J., Bagnoli, A., Clark, A., Davies, K., Holland, S., & Renold, E. (2008). *Visual ethics: Ethical* issues *in* visual research. NCRM Working Paper. http:// eprints.ncrm.ac.uk/421/

There are also numerous resources relating to the archiving of qualitative data and the ethical issues in archiving and the re-use of data available from the UK Qualitative data archive at: https://www.data-archive.ac .uk/

The UK Timescapes projects has also produced various guidelines relating to the ethics of archiving and reusing qualitative longitudinal data, for example: Neale, B., & Bishop, L. (2012). The ethics of archiving and re-using qualitative longitudinal data: A stakeholder approach. *Timescapes Methods Guides Series. Guide no 18.* Available at: https:// timescapes-archive.leeds.ac.uk/timescapes/research/

See also the following books:

Corti, L. (2020). *Archiving qualitative data*. London: SAGE Publications Limited.

Corti, L., Van den Eynden, V., Bishop, L., & Woollard, M. (2019). *Managing and sharing research data: A guide to good practice*. London: SAGE Publications.

Roulston, K., & deMarrais, K. (2021). *Exploring the archives: A beginner's guide for qualitative researchers*. Gorham, ME: Myers Education Press.

Professional Guidelines and Codes

All the social science discipline-specific organizations have guidelines or codes of ethical conduct which can be accessed from their websites. In the UK, the Social Research Association has produced ethical guidelines for social researchers that are relevant across sectors of work and disci- plines. These are accessible via their website (www.the-sra.org.uk). The EU Code of ethics for socio-economic research under the RESPECT project (https://www.employment-studies.co.uk/resource/eu-code-ethics-socio-economic-research) are relevant for social and economic researchers working in EU countries. These are a synthesis of professional and ethical codes of practice and legal requirements across the EU.

The Economic and Social Research Council (ESRC) Framework for Research Ethics (http://www.esrc.ac.uk/about-esrc/information/research- ethics.aspx) provides a code of conduct for social research. Compliance with this is mandatory for research funded by the ESRC and recommended for research funded by other bodies.

In Australia the key guideline for research activity is the *National Statement on ethical conduct in human research 2025* (https://www.nhmrc.gov.au/about-us/publications/national-statement-ethical-conduct-human-research-2025). There are specific guidelines for research with Aboriginal and Torres Strait Islanders peoples including the NHMRC's *Ethical conduct in research with Aboriginal and Torres Strait Islander peoples and communities: Guidelines for researchers and stakeholders 2018, Keeping research on track II 2018* (https://www.nhmrc.gov.au/research-policy/ethics/ethical-guidelines-research-aboriginal-and-torres-strait-islander-peoples) and the Australian Institute of Aboriginal and Torres Strait Islander Studies *for Aboriginal and Torres Strait Islander Ethics 2020* (https://aiatsis.gov.au/research/ethical-research)

In New Zealand, guidelines for research are provided by the Health Research Council of New Zealand with the *HRC Research Ethics Guidelines 2021* (https://gateway.hrc.govt.nz/). These standards are founded on the Te Tiriti o Waitangi/The Treaty of Waitangi, which sets the foundation for the enduring relationship between Māori and the Crown as equal partners. The National Ethics Advisory Committee – Kāhui Matatika o te Motu (NEAC) is an independent advisor to the Minister of Health on ethical issues related to health and disability research and services (https://neac.health.govt.nz/).

In Canada, research is guided by the *Tri-Council Policy Statement: Ethical Conduct for Research involving humans* (TCPS 2 2022) (https://www.canada.ca/en/health-canada/services/science-research/science-advice

-decision-making/research-ethics-board/policy-guidelines-resources
.html). TCPS 2 is a joint policy of Canada's three federal research
agencies – the Canadian Institutes of Health Research (CIHR), the
Natural Sciences and Engineering Research Council of Canada
(NSERC), and the Social Sciences and Humanities Research Council of
Canada (SSHRC)

In America, the US Department of Health and Humanities in the
Office for Human Protections publishes a variety of policy and
regulatory guidance documents to assist researchers comply with
HSS regulations on conducting ethical research (https://www.hhs
.gov/ohrp/international/ethical-codes-and-research-standards/index
.html). These include ethical codes, such as the Belmont Report and
Research Standards as outlined in the 45 Code of Federal Regulations
46, 21 CFR 50 (Protection of Human Subjects) and the 21 CFR 56
(Institutional Review Boards).

Outside of the United Kingdom, United States, Canada, Australia and
New Zealand, researchers have documented guidelines, ethics systems
and specific issues for qualitative research (select publications in
English only):

Europe

Froud, R., Meza, T. J., Ernes, K. O., & Slowther, A. M. (2019). Research
ethics oversight in Norway: Structure, function, and challenges. *BMC
Health Services Research*, *19*, 1–6.

Gallagher, B., Berman, A. H., Bieganski, J., Jones, A. D., Foca, L.,
Raikes, B., & Ullman, S. (2016). National human research ethics:
A preliminary comparative case study of Germany, Great Britain,
Romania, and Sweden. *Ethics & Behavior*, *26*(7), 586–606.

Griffin, G., & Leibetseder, D. (2019). "Only applies to research conducted
in Sweden…": Dilemmas in gaining ethics approval in transnational
qualitative research. *International Journal of Qualitative Methods*, *18*,
1609406919869444.

Niedbalski, J., & Ślęzak, I. (2018). Ethical aspects of dissemination and
archiving qualitative data in Poland. In A. Morais, P. C. Campos, &
L. A. Vicente (Eds.), *Computer supported qualitative research: Second
International Symposium on Qualitative Research (ISQR 2017)* (pp.
250–259). Cham: Springer International Publishing.

Slavnic, Z. (2013). Towards qualitative data preservation and re-use—
Policy trends and academic controversies in UK and Sweden. *Forum
Qualitative Sozialforschung/Forum: Qualitative Social Research*,
14(2), 10.

von Unger, H. (2016). Reflexivity beyond regulations: Teaching research ethics and qualitative methods in Germany. *Qualitative Inquiry*, 22(2), 87–98.

Latin America and the Caribbean

Aguilera, B., Carracedo, S., & Saenz, C. (2022). Research ethics systems in Latin America and the Caribbean: A systemic assessment using indicators. *The Lancet Global Health*, 10(8), e1204–e1208.

Armijo, M., & Willatt, C. (2024). Ethics committees and shaping of children's participation in qualitative educational research in Chile. *Children & Society*, 38(1), 1–15.

Canario Guzmán, J. A., Espinal, R., Báez, J., Melgen, R. E., Rosario, P. A. P., & Mendoza, E. R. (2017). Ethical challenges for international collaborative research partnerships in the context of the Zika outbreak in the Dominican Republic: a qualitative case study. *Health Research Policy and Systems*, 15, 1–13.

Israel, M. (2017). Ethical imperialism? Exporting research ethics to the global south. In R. Iphofen & M. Tolich (Eds.), *The SAGE Handbook of Qualitative Research Ethics*. London: Sage Publications.

Mercado-Martínez, F. J. (2002). Qualitative research in latin America: Critical perspectives on health. *International Journal of Qualitative Methods*, 1(1), 61–73.

Ortiz-Prado, E., Simbaña-Rivera, K., Gómez-Barreno, L., Tamariz, L., Lister, A., Baca, J. C., Norris, A., & Adana-Diaz, L. (2020). Potential research ethics violations against an indigenous tribe in Ecuador: a mixed methods approach. *BMC Med Ethics,* 21(1), 100.

Valdez-Martinez, E., Turnbull, B., Garduno-Espinosa, J., & Porter, J. D. (2006). Descriptive ethics: a qualitative study of local research ethics committees in Mexico. *Developing World Bioethics*, 6(2), 95–105.

Pacific Countries

Anae, M. (2016). Teu le va: Samoan relational ethics. *Knowledge Cultures*, 4(03), 117–130.

Anae, M. (2019). Pacific research methodologies and relational ethics. In *Oxford research encyclopedia of education*. Retrieved 2 Oct. 2025, from https://oxfordre.com/education/view/10.1093/acrefore /9780190264093.001.0001/acrefore-9780190264093-e-529.

Czymoniewicz-Klippel, M. T., Brijnath, B., & Crockett, B. (2010). Ethics and the promotion of inclusiveness within qualitative research: Case examples from Asia and the Pacific. *Qualitative Inquiry*, *16*(5): 332–341.

Denholm, J. T., Bissell, K., Viney, K., Durand, A. M., Cash, H. L., Roseveare, C., & Biribo, S. (2017). Research ethics committees in the Pacific Islands: Gaps and opportunities for health sector strengthening. *Public Health Action*, 7(1), 6–9.

Heard, E. (2023). Ethical challenges in participatory action research: Experiences and insights from an arts-based study in the pacific. *Qualitative research*, *23*(4), 1112–1132.

Vaioleti, T. M. (2006). Talanoa research methodology: A developing position on Pacific research. *Waikato Journal of Education*, *12*, 20–31.

The Research for Development Impact Network provides important information about ethics processes and practices for the Pacific and Asia. https://rdinetwork.org.au/resources/skills-for-development -impact/ethics-ethical-research/ethicals-approvals/ethical-practices-in -the-pacific-and-asia-2/

Asia and SE Asia

General

Berekeyeva, A., Sharplin, E., Courtney, M., & Sagitova, R. (2024). Ethical human participant research in Central Asia: A quantitative analysis of attitudes and practices among social science researchers based in the region. *Research Ethics*, *20*(2), 304–330.

Chou, C., Lee, I. J., & Fudano, J. (2023). The present situation of and challenges in research ethics and integrity promotion: Experiences in East Asia. *Accountability in Research*, 1–24.

Dahal, B. (2020). Research ethics: A perspective of South Asian context. *Edukacja*, *152*(1), 9–20.

Ditton, M., & Lehane, L. (2011). Research ethics: Cross cultural perspective of research ethics in Southeast Asia. In *Transmission of academic values in Asian Studies workshop (2009: Australian National University, Canberra, ACT)*. The Australia-Netherlands Research Collaboration.

Sagitova, R., Ramazanova, M., Sharplin, E., Berekeyeva, A., & Parmenter, L. (2024). Understanding human participant research ethics: The perspectives of social scientists in Central Asia. *International Journal of Educational Research*, *124*, 102303.

Tolich, M., & Anito Jr, J. (2022). Asian qualitative research ethics: Lessons for the West. In Safary Wa-Mbaleka & Arceli H. Rosario (Eds.), *The SAGE handbook of qualitative research in the Asian context* (pp. 51–63). London: Sage Publications.

China

Alpermann, B. (2022, June 27). Ethics in social science research on China. *Made in China Journal.* https://madeinchinajournal.com/2022/06/27/ethics-in-social-science-research-on-china/

Huang, J., Zhou, Y., & Sheeran, T. (2021). Educational researchers' ethical responsibilities and human subjects' ethical awareness: Implications for research ethics education in China. *Ethics & Behavior, 31*(5), 321–34.

Li, D. (2024). Ethical governance in Chinese universities: an overview of research ethics committees. *Ethics & Behavior, 35*(1), 1–12.

Wang, Y., Wu, S., He, L., Li, L., & Wang, Z. (2023). Social work research ethics in China: A scoping review of research involving human subjects during COVID-19. *International Social Work, 66*(1), 233–253.

Zeng, W., & Resnik, D. (2010). Research integrity in China: problems and prospects. *Developing World Bioethics, 10*(3), 164–171.

Zhou, J. (2021). Problems and development strategies for research ethics committees in China's higher education institutions. *Journal of Medical Ethics, 47*, e56.

East Timor

Martins, N., Gusmao, C., Soares, D., Laot, M., Amaral, S., Messner, J., & Francis, J. R. (2023). Strengthening Health Research and Ethics Systems in Timor-Leste. *WHO South-East Asia Journal of Public Health, 12*(1), 63–70.

Indonesia

Fourianalistyawati, E., Uswatunnisa, A., Mahdiannur, M. A., Saleky, A. P., Soebandhi, S., Reni, A., & Kurniasih, N. (2018). Research development in Indonesia: Ethics committee in open science and collaboration era. *Journal of Physics: Conference Series, 1114*(1), 012069.

Oey-Gardiner, M., & Rahardi, F. (2021). *Ethics in social science research in Indonesia.* Jakarta: Yayasan Pustaka Obor Indonesia.

Rachmawaty, R. (2017). Ethical issues in action-oriented research in Indonesia. *Nursing Ethics*, 24(6), 686–693.

Resosudarmo, B. (2022). Ethics in social research in Indonesia. *Bulletin of Indonesian Economic Studies*, 58(2), 233–235.

Japan

Asai, A., Okita, T., & Enzo, A. (2016). Conflicting messages concerning current strategies against research misconduct in Japan: A call for ethical spontaneity *Journal of Medical Ethics*, 42, 524–527.

Iijima, Y., Ogasawara, K., Toda, S., & Takano, T. (2019). An overview of ethical review committees in Japan: Examining the certification applications of ethical review committees. *Nagoya Journal of Medical Science*, 81(3), 501–509.

Lee, K. W., & Kim, O. J. (2021). Trends in japanese research ethics in the 21st century: Research misconduct and related policies. *Korean Journal of Medical Ethics*, 24(4), 461–481.

Macfarlane, B., & Saitoh, Y. (2008). Research ethics in japanese higher education: Faculty attitudes and cultural mediation. *Journal of Academic Ethics*, 6, 181–195.

Nochi, M. (2020). Research ethics from the viewpoint of a Japanese qualitative researcher. In R. Barnard & Y. Wang (Eds.), *Research ethics in second language education* (pp. 128–39). London: Routledge.

Suzuki, M., & Sato, K. (2016). Description and evaluation of the research ethics review process in Japan: Proposed measures for improvement. *Journal of Empirical Research on Human Research Ethics*, 11(3), 256–66.

Tsuchiya, T. (2003). In the shadow of the past atrocities: Research ethics with human subjects in contemporary Japan. *Eubios Journal of Asian and International Bioethics*, 13(3), 100–102.

Yanagawa, H., Katashima, R., & Takeda, N. (2015). Research ethics committees in Japan: A perspective from thirty years of experience at Tokushima University. *The Journal of Medical Investigation*, 62(3.4), 114–118.

Korea

Kim, O. J., Park, B. J., Sohn, D. R., Lee, S. M., & Shin, S. G. (2003). Current status of the institutional review boards in Korea: Constitution, operation, and policy for protection of human research participants. *Journal of Korean medical science*, 18(1), 3.

Nho, Hwan-Jin. (2016). Research ethics education in Korea for overcoming culture and value system differences. *Journal of Open Innovation: Technology, Market, and Complexity*, 2(1), 4.

Malaysia

Olesen, A. P., Amin, L., & Mahadi, Z. (2018). Researchers experience of misconduct in research in Malaysian higher education institutions. *Accountability in Research*, 25(3), 125–141.

Olesen, A. P., Amin, L., & Mahadi, Z. (2019). Research ethics: Researchers consider how best to prevent misconduct in research in malaysian higher learning institutions through ethics education. *Science Engineering Ethics*, 25, 1111–1124.

Poon, J. M. L., & Ainuddin, R. A. (2011). Selected ethical issues in the analysis and reporting of research: Survey of business school faculty in malaysia. *Journal of Academic Ethics*, 9, 307–322.

Kyrgyzstan

Sagitova, R., Syrgak kyzy, Z., & Parmenter, L. (2024). Negotiating local and global: Developing Social Science research ethics policy in a Central Asian context. *Research Ethics*, 21(1), 161–179.

Taiwan

Chou, C., Pan, S. J., & Hsueh, M. L. (2022). Assessment criteria for research misconduct: Taiwanese researchers' perceptions. *Accountability in Research*, 30(8), 613–632.

Tansikian, T., & Huang, Y. C. (2016). The development of research ethics involving indigenous people in taiwan: A brief introduction. *Hu Li Za Zhi*, 63(3), 25.

甘 Zhen-Rong Gan偵蓉, & Israel, M. (2020). Transnational policy migration, interdisciplinary policy transfer and decolonization: Tracing the patterns of research ethics regulation in Taiwan. *Developing World Bioethics*, 20(1), 5–15.

India

Contractor, Q. (2008). Fieldwork and social science research ethics. *Indian Journal of Medical Ethics, 5*(1), 22–23.

Kulkarni, R., & Saraiya, U. (2015). Accreditation of ethics committees in India: Experience of an ethics committee. *Indian Journal of Medical Ethics, 12*, 241–245.

Kumar, A., & Mahapatro, M. (2018). Community based qualitative health research: Negotiating ethics in India. *Quality & Quantity, 52*, 1437–1446.

Morrow, V. (2013). Practical ethics in social research with children and families in young lives: A longitudinal study of childhood poverty in Ethiopia, Andhra Pradesh (India), Peru and Vietnam. *Methodological Innovations Online, 8*(2), 21–35.

Parker, M. (2017). CBPR principles and research ethics in Indian Country. *Community-based Participatory Research for Health: Advancing Social and Health Equity*, 207–214.

Riessman, C. K. (2005). Exporting ethics: A narrative about narrative research in South India. *Health, 9*(4), 473–90.

Sarrett, J. C. (2014). Ethics and ethnography: Lessons from researching autism in India. *Journal of Ethnographic & Qualitative Research, 8*(4), 239–250.

Schrag, Z. M. (2010). *Ethical imperialism: Institutional review boards and the social sciences, 1965–2009*. Baltimore: Johns Hopkins University Press.

International guidelines can also be found at:

The International Compilation of Human Research Standards documents more than 1,000 laws, regulations, and guidelines—referred to as "standards"—that regulate the protection of human subjects across 131 countries. Additionally, it includes standards from international and regional organizations. Originally published in 2005, this Compilation is designed to be utilized by researchers, Institutional Review Boards (IRBs)/Research Ethics Committees, sponsors, and other stakeholders engaged in human subjects research protection worldwide. https://www.hhs.gov/sites/default/files/ohrp-international -compilation-2021-asia.pdf

The World Health Organisations provides various guidelines and information on various aspects of human research ethics in a global context https://www.who.int/activities/ensuring-ethical-standards-and -procedures-for-research-with-human-beings

REFERENCES

Adib-Moghaddam, A. (2023). *Is artificial intelligence racist?: The ethics of AI and the future of humanity*. London: Bloomsbury Publishing.

Adler, P. A., & Adler, P. (2002). The reluctant respondent. In J. F. Gubrium & J. A. Holstein (Eds.), *Handbook of interview research: Context and method* (pp. 515–535). Thousand Oaks: Sage.

Aguiar, L. L., & Schneider, C. J. (Eds.). (2016). *Researching amongst elites: Challenges and opportunities in studying up*. London: Routledge.

Aguilera, B., Carracedo, S., & Saenz, C. (2022). Research ethics systems in Latin America and the Caribbean: A systemic assessment using indicators. The Lancet Global Health, 10(8), e1204–e1208.

AIFS. (2024). *Mandatory reporting of child abuse and neglect*. Australian Insititute of Family Studies, Canberra: Australian Government.

Akpa-Inyang, F., & Chima, S. C. (2021). South African traditional values and beliefs regarding informed consent and limitations of the principle of respect for autonomy in African communities: A cross-cultural qualitative study. *BMC Med Ethics*, 22, 111.

Alderson, P. (2004). Ethics. In S. Fraser, V. Lewis, S. Ding, M. Kellett, & C. Robinson (Eds.), *Doing research with children and young people*. London: Sage.

Alderson, P., & Morrow, V. (2020). *The ethics of research with children and young people: A practical handbook*. London: Sage.

Allen, B. (2009). Are researchers ethically obligated to report suspected child maltreatment? A critical analysis of opposing perspectives. Ethics & Behavior, 19(1), 15–24.

Allen, L. (2015). Losing face? Photo-anonymisation and visual research integrity. *Visual Studies*, 30(3), 295–308.

Allen, R. E. S., & Wiles, J. L. (2016). A rose by any other name: Participants choosing research pseudonyms. *Qualitative Research in Psychology*, 13(2), 149–165.

Anne-Marie, T., Chau, N., & Kimppa Kai, K. (2017). Ethical questions related to using netnography as research method. *The ORBIT Journal*, 1(2), 1–11.

Allmark, P. (2002). The ethics of research with children. *Nurse Researcher*, December 2002.

American Anthropological Association. (2025). *AAA statement on ethics: Principles of professional responsibility*. Arlington: AAA. https://americananthro.org/about/policies/statement-on-ethics/

American Psychological Association. (2016). *Ethical principles of psychologists and code of conduct*. Washington: APA.

American Sociological Association. (2018). *Code of Ethics*. Washington, DC: American Sociological Association. https://www.asanet.org/about/ethics/

Anis, S., & French, J. A. (2023). Efficient, explicatory, and equitable: Why qualitative researchers should embrace AI, but cautiously. *Business & Society*, 62(6), 1139–1144.

Andersen, C., & O'Brien, J. M. (2016). *Sources and methods in indigenous studies*. London: Taylor and Francis.

Archibald, Jo-Ann. (2008). *Indigenous storywork: Educating the heart, mind, body, and spirit*. Vancouver: UBC Press.

Association of Social Anthropologists of the UK and the Commonwealth. (2021). *ASA Ethical Guidelines 2021 for good research practice*. Available from: https://www.theasa.org/ethics/

Atkinson, P. (2009). Ethics and ethnography. *21st Century Society: Journal of the Academy of Social Sciences*, 4(1), 17–30.

Australian Anthropological Society. (2012). *AAS Code of ethics*. Canberra: Australian Anthropological Society.

Australian Government. (2024). *The privacy act*. Canberra: Officer of the Australian Information Commissioner, Australian Government.

Australian Psychological Society. (2007). *APS Code of ethics*. Melbourne: The Australian Psychological Society Limited.

Babb, S. (2021). The privatization of human research ethics: An american story. *European Journal for the History of Medicine and Health*, 78(2), 392–411.

Back, L. (2004). Listening with our eyes: Portraiture as urban encounter. In C. Knowles & P. Sweetman (Eds.), *Picturing the social landscape: Visual methods and the sociological imagination* (pp. 132–146). London: Routledge.

Banks, M. (2001). *Visual methods in social research*. London: Sage.

Banks, S., & Brydon-Miller, M. (Eds.). (2018). *Ethics in participatory research for health and social well-being: Cases and commentaries* (1st ed.). London: Routledge.

Baser, B., & Martin, N. (2020). Collaboration between academics and journalists: Methodological considerations, challenges and ethics. *Journal of Conflict Transformation and Security*, 8(1), 114–126.

Beasley, C., & Walker, L. (2014). Research ethics and journalism in the academy: Identifying and resolving a conflict of culture. Research Ethics, 10(3), 129–140.

Beauchamp, T., & Childress, J. (1979). *Principles of biomedical ethics*. New York: Oxford University Press.

Beauchamp, T., & Childress, J. (2001). *Principles of* biomedical *ethics. 5th Edition*. New York: Oxford University Press.

Beck, K. B., MacKenziem, K. T., Kirby, A. V., McDonald, K., Moura, I., Breitenfeldt, K., … & Working to Increase Inclusivity in Research Ethics (WIRE) Consortium. (2025). Guidelines for the creation of accessible consent materials and procedures: Lessons from research with autistic people and people with intellectual disability. Autism in Adulthood.

Becker, S., & Bryman, A. (2004). *Understanding* research *for* social policy *and* practice: *Themes,* methods *and approaches*. Bristol: Policy Press.

Behera, S. K., Das, S., Xavier, A. S., Selvarajan, S., & Anandabaskar, N. (2019). Indian Council of Medical Research's National Ethical Guidelines for biomedical and health research involving human participants: The way forward from 2006 to 2017. *Perspectives in Clinical Research*, 10(3), 108–114.

Bell, K., & Wynn, L. (2021). Research ethics committees, ethnographers and imaginations of risk. *Ethnography*, 24(4), 537–558.

Bell, K., & Wynn, L. (2023). Research ethics committees, ethnographers and imaginations of risk. *Ethnography*, 24(4), 537–558.

Bengry-Howell, A., & Griffin, C. (2011). Negotiating access in ethnographic research with "hard to reach" young people: Establishing common ground or a process of methodological grooming? *International Journal of Social Research Methodology*, 15(5), 403–416. https://doi.org/10.1080/13645579.2011.600115

Bessarab, D., & Ng'Andu, B. (2010). Yarning about yarning as a legitimate method in Indigenous research. International Journal of Critical Indigenous Studies, 3(1), 37–50.

Binns, R. (2018). Fairness in machine learning: Lessons from political philosophy. In *Proceedings of the 2018 Conference on Fairness, Accountability, and Transparency* (pp. 149–159). New York: PMLR.

Blank, R. (2025). Legal dimensions of human research ethics. In B. M. Smyth, M. Downing, & M. M. Martin (Eds.), *The Routledge handbook of human research ethics and integrity in Australia*. London: Taylor & Francis.

Bloor, M., Fincham, B., & Sampson, H. (2007). *Qualiti (NCRM)* commissioned inquiry *into the* risk *to* well-being *of* researchers *in* qualitative research. Cardiff: Cardiff University. http://www.cardiff.ac.uk/socsi/qualiti/ publications.html

Bloor, M., Fincham, B., & Sampson, H. (2010). Unprepared for the worst: Risks of harm for qualitative researchers. *Methodological Innovations Online, 5*(1), 45–55.

Boceta, R., Martínez-Casares, O., & Albert, M. (2021). The informed consent in the mature minor: Understanding and decision-making capacity. *Anales de Pediatría (English Edition), 95*(6): 413–422.

Boddy, J., Hanrahan, F., & Wheeler, B. (2023). *Thinking through family: Narratives of care experienced lives.* Forlag: Bristol University Press.

Boellstorf, M. (2015). *Coming of age in second life: An anthrolpologist explores the virtually human.* Princeton: Princeton University Press.

Borgstrom, E., Mallon, S., & Murphy, S. (Eds.) (2024). *Unpacking sensitive research: Epistemological and methodological implication.* Abingdon: Routledge.

Bostock, L. (2002). "God, she's gonna report me": The ethics of child protection in poverty research. *Children and Society, 16*(4), 273–283.

Boulton, A., Tamehana, J., & Brannelly, T. (2013). Whänau-centred health and social service delivery in New Zealand: The challenges to and opportunities for innovation. MAI Journal, 2(1), 18–32.

Boulton, M., Brown, N., Lewis, G., & Webster, A. (2004). *Implementing the ESRC research ethics framework: The case for research ethics committees.* ESRC Research Ethics Framework: Discussion Paper 4 (Working paper). York and Oxford: University of York and School of Social Studies and Law. http://www.york.ac.uk/res/ref/docs/REFpaper4 _v2.pdf

Bradbury-Jones, C., Isham, L., & Taylor, J. (2018). The complexities and contradictions in participatory research with vulnerable children and young people: A qualitative systematic review. *Social Science & Medicine, 215,* 80–91.

Brannen, J. (1988). The study of sensitive subjects. *Sociological Review, 36*(3), 352–363.

Braybrook, D. E., Mróz, L. W., Robertson, S., White, A., & Milnes, K. (2017). Holistic experiences and strategies for conducting research with couples. *Qualitative Health Research, 27*(4), 584–590.

British Educational Research Association. (2004). *Revised ethical guidelines for educational research.* http://www.bera.ac.uk/publications /ethical-guidelines

British Psychological Society. (2007). *Report of the working party on conducting research on the internet: guidelines for ethical practice in psychological research online.* https://www.gla.ac.uk/media/Media _326705_smxx.pdf

British Psychological Society. (2021). *Code of ethics and conduct.* Leicester: British Psychological Society.

British Sociological Association. (2017). *Statement of ethical practice for the British Sociological Association.* https://www.britsoc.co.uk/ethics

British Sociological Association – Visual Sociology Group. (2006). Statement of ethical practice. https://visualsociology.org/code-of-research-ethics/.

Brower, R. L., Jones, T. B., Osborne-Lampkin, L., Hu, S., & Park-Gaghan, T. J. (2019). Big Qual: Defining and debating qualitative inquiry for large data sets. *International Journal of Qualitative Methods, 18,* 160940691988069.

Brush, B. L., Mentz, G., Jensen, M., et al. (2020). Success in long-standing community-based participatory research (CBPR) partnerships: A scoping literature review. *Health Education & Behavior, 47*(4), 556–568.

Burr, J., & Reynolds, P. (2010). The wrong paradigm? Social research and the predicates of ethical scrutiny. *Research Ethics, 6*(4), 128–133.

Cameron, A., Lloyd, L., Kent, N., & Anderson, P. (2004). Researching end of life in old age: Ethical challenges. In M. Smyth & E. Williamson (Eds.), *Researchers and* their subjects: *Ethics,* power, knowledge *and consent* (pp. 105–118). Bristol: Policy Press.

Campbell, R., Goodman-Williams, R., & Javorka, M. (2019). A trauma-informed approach to sexual violence research ethics and open science. *Journal of Interpersonal Violence, 34*(23–24), 4765–4793.

Canadian Institutes of Health Research. (2022). *Tri-Council Policy Statement: Ethical conduct for research involving humans.* Canada: Natural Sciences and Engineering Research Council of Canada, and Social Sciences and Humanities Research Council.

Calvey, D. (2018). Covert: The fear and fascination of a methodological pariah. In R. Iphofen & M. Tolich (Eds.), *The SAGE handbook of qualitative research ethics* (pp. 470–484). London: Sage.

Carniel, J., Hickey, A., Southey, K., Brömdal, A., Crowley-Cyr, L., Eacersall, D., Farmer, W., Gehrmann, R., Machin, T., & Pillay, Y. (2022). The ethics review and the humanities and social sciences: Disciplinary distinctions in ethics review processes. *Research Ethics, 19*(2), 139–156.

Carroll, S. R., Garba, I., Figueroa-Rodríguez, O. L., Holbrook, J., Lovett, R., Materechera, S., & Hudson, M. (2020). The CARE principles for indigenous data governance. *Data Science Journal, 19,* 43–43.

Chenhall, R. D. (2007). *Benelong's Haven: Recovery from alcohol and drug misuse in a residential treatment centre.* Melbourne: Melbourne University Press.

Chenhall, R., Senior, K., & Belton, S. (2011). Negotiating human research ethics: Case notes from anthropologists in the field. *Anthropology Today, 27*(5), 13–17.

Christian, K., Johnstone, C., Larkins, J. A., & Wright, W. (2022). Seeking approval from universities to research the views of their staff: Do gatekeepers provide a barrier to ethical research? *Journal of Empirical Research on Human Research Ethics*, 17(3), 317–328.

Chojnicka, J. (2024). Transitioning (on the) internet: Shifting challenges and contradictions of ethics of studying online gender transition narratives. *Qualitative Sociology review*, 20(1), 60–80.

Clark, A. (2006). *Anonymising research data*. ESRC National Centre for Research Methods. Real Life Methods Node. Manchester: University of Manchester (Working Paper). http://www.reallifemethods.ac.uk/publications/workingpapers/

Clark, A., Prosser, J., & Wiles, R. (2010). Ethical issues in image-based research. *Arts and Health*, 2(1), 81–93.

Clarke, G., Boorman, G., & Nind, M. (2011). "If they don't listen I shout, and when I shout they listen": Hearing the voices of girls with behavioural, emotional and social difficulties. *British Educational Research Journal*, 37(5), 765–780.

Class, B., de Bruyne, M., Wuillemin, C., Donzé, D., & Claivaz, J. B. (2021). Towards open science for the qualitative researcher: From a positivist to an open interpretation. *International Journal of Qualitative Methods*, 20(6), 160940692110346.

Cocq, C. (2022). Data colonialism and data sovereignty in indigenous spaces. AoIR Selected Papers of Internet Research. https://spir.aoir.org/ojs/index.php/spir/article/view/12990

Coomber, R. (2002). Signing your life away?: Why Research Ethics Committees (REC) shouldn't always require written confirmation that participants in research have been informed of the aims of a study and their rights – the case of criminal populations (Commentary). *Sociological Research Online*, 7(1). http://www.socresonline.org.uk/7/1/ coomber.html

Corden, A., & Sainsbury, R. (2006). *Using* verbatim quotations *in* reporting qualitative social research: *The views of research users*. York: Social Policy Research Unit, University of York.

Corden, A., Sainsbury, R., Sloper, P., & Ward, B. (2005). Using a model of group psychotherapy to support social research on sensitive topics. *International Journal of Social Research Methodology*, 8(2), 151–160.

Cornish, F., Breton, N., Moreno-Tabarez, U., Delgado, J., Rua, M., de-Graft Aikins, A., & Hodgetts, D. (2023). Participatory action research. Nature Reviews Methods Primers, 3(1), 34.

Corti, L. (2000). Progress and problems of preserving and providing access to qualitative data for social research—The international picture of an emerging culture. *Forum Qualitative Sozialforschung Forum: Qualitative Social Research*, 1(3).

Corti, L. (2019). Archiving qualitative data. In P. Atkinson, S. Delamont, A. Cernat, J. W. Sakshaug, & R. A. Williams (Eds.), *SAGE research methods foundations*. London: Sage.

Corti, L., & Thompson, P. (2007). Secondary analysis of archived data. In C. Seale, G. Gobo, J. Gubrium, & D. Silverman (Eds.), Qualitative research practice. London: Sage.

Crow, G., & Wiles, R. (2008). *Managing anonymity and confidentiality in social research: The case of visual data in community research*. ESRC National Centre for Research Methods (NCRM Working Paper). http:// eprints.ncrm.ac.uk/459

Crivello, G., & Morrow, V. (2021). Ethics learning from Young Lives: 20 years on. London: Young Lives.

Cutliffe, J., & Ramcharan, P. (2002). Levelling the playing field? Exploring the merits of the ethics-as-process approach for judging qualitative research proposals. *Qualitative Health Research*, 12(7), 1000–1010.

Damianakis, T., & Woodford, M. R. (2012). Qualitative research with small connected communities: Generating new knowledge while upholding research ethics. *Qualitative Health Research*, 22(5), 708–718.

Dare, J., Seiver, H., Andrew, L., Coall, D. A., Karthigesu, S., Sim, M., & Boxall, K. (2021). Co-creating visual representations of safe spaces with mental health service users using photovoice and zoom. *Methods in Psychology*, 5, 100059.

Das, D. (2015). Dangers in fieldwork: Research ethics and the predicament of self-harm in anthropological research. In *Social science research ethics for a globalizing world* (pp. 187–207). London: Routledge.

Dempsey, L., Dowling, M., Larkin, P., & Murphy, K. (2016). Sensitive interviewing in qualitative research. *Research in Nursing & Health*, 39, 480–490.

Denzin, N. K. (2016). A relational ethic for narrative inquiry, or in the forest but lost in the trees, or a one-act play with many endings. In *The Routledge international handbook on narrative and life history* (pp. 615–627). London: Routledge.

Denzin, N. K., Lincoln, Y. S., & Smith, L. T. (Eds.). (2008). Handbook of critical and indigenous methodologies. London: Sage.

Dingwall, R. (2008). The ethical case against ethical regulation in humanities and social science research. *21st Century Society: Journal of the Academy of Social Sciences*, 3(1), 1–12.

Druckman, D., & Donohue, W. (2020). Innovations in social science methodologies: An overview. *American Behavioral Scientist*, 64(1), 3–18.

DuBois, J. M., Mozersky, J., Parsons, M., Walsh, H. A., Friedrich, A., & Pienta, A. (2023). Exchanging words: Engaging the challenges of sharing qualitative research data. Proceedings of the National Academy of Sciences of the United States of America, 120(43), e2206981120.

Dudi-Venkata, N. N., Cox, D. R., Marson, N., Tan, L., Pockney, P., Muralidharan, V., ... & Clinical Trials Network Australia New Zealand (CTANZ). (2021). Variation in human research ethics committee and governance processes throughout Australia: A need for a uniform approach. ANZ Journal of Surgery, 91(11), 2263–2268.

Du Plessis, R., & Fairbairn-Dunlop, P. (2009). The ethics of knowledge production–Pacific challenges. *International Social Science Journal*, 60(195), 109–114.

Dutton, W. H., & Blank, G. (2011). *Next* generation users: *The internet in Britain, Oxford Internet Survey 2011*. Oxford: University of Oxford.

Düvell, F., Triandafyllidou, A., & Vollmer, B. (2010). Ethical issues in irregular migration research in Europe. *Population, Space and Place*, 16(3), 227–239.

DVRG (2004). Domestic violence and research ethics. In M. Smyth & E. Williamson (Eds.), *Researchers and their subjects: Ethics, power, knowledge and consent*. Bristol: Policy Press.

Edwards, J. (2021). Ethical autoethnography: Is it possible? *International Journal of Qualitative Methods*, 20.

Edwards, R., & Mauthner, M. (2012). Ethics and feminist research: Theory and practice. In *Ethics in Qualitative Research* (2nd ed., pp. 14–28). London: Sage.

Edwards, R., & Weller, S. (2009). *Timescapes project one: Ethical dilemma correspondence*. http://www.timescapes.leeds.ac.uk/assets/files /PROJECT-1-ethical-dilemma-correspondence-2.pdf

Edwards, S., Ashcroft, R., & Kirchin, S. (2004). Research ethics committees: Differences and moral judgement. *Bioethics*, 18, 408–427.

El Emam, K., Buckeridge, D., Tamblyn, R., et al. (2011). The re-identification risk of Canadians from longitudinal demographics. *BMC Medical Informatics and Decision Making*, 11(46), 1–12.

Ellersgaard, C. H., Ditlevsen., K., & Larsen, A. G. (2022). Say my name? Anonymity or not in elite interviewing. *International Journal of Social Research Methodology*, 25(5), 673–686.

Elliott, J. (2005). *Using* narrative *in* social research: *Qualitative and* quantitative *approaches*. London: Sage.

Ellis, C. (1986). *Fisher folk: Two communities on Chesapeake Bay*. Kentucky: University Press of Kentucky.

Ellis, C. (1995). Emotional and ethical quagmires in returning to the field. *Journal of Contemporary Ethnography*, 24(1), 68–98.

Ellis, C. (2007). Telling secrets, revealing lives: Relational ethics in research with intimate others. *Qualitative Inquiry*, *13*(1), 3–29.

Ellis, C. (2016). Compassionate research: Interviewing and storytelling from a relational ethics of care. In *The Routledge international handbook on narrative and life history* (pp. 441–455). London: Routledge.

Ellsberg, M., & Heise, L. (2002). Bearing witness: ethics in domestic violence research. *The Lancet*, *359*(9317), 1599–1604.

ESRC. (2025). *Research ethics framework*. Economic and Social Research Council. https://www.ukri.org/councils/esrc/guidance-for-applicants/research-ethics-guidance/framework-for-research-ethics/

Ess, C., & The AOIR Ethics Working Committee. (2002). *Ethical decision-making and internet research: Recommendations from the AoIR Ethics Working Committee*. https://aoir.org/reports/ethics.pdf

Estalella, A., & Ardèvol, E. (2007). Field ethics: Towards situated ethics for ethnographic research on the internet. *Forum Qualitative Sozialforschung Forum: Qualitative Social Research*, *8*(3), 1–25.

Estalella, A., & Ardévol, E. (2011). E-research: Challenges and opportunities for social sciences. Convergencia, 18(55), 87–111.

European Science Foundation. (2023). The European code of conduct for research integrity. Retrieved from https://allea.org/portfolio-item/european-code-of-conduct-2023/

European Union. (2016). *General data protection regulation (GDPR)*. https://gdprinfo.eu/

European Union. (2019). *Pseudonymisation techniques and best practices. Recommendations on shaping technology according to data protection and privacy provisions*. European Union Agency for Cybersecurity. https://www.enisa.europa.eu/publications/pseudonymisation-techniques-and-best-practices

European Union Agency for Fundamental Rights. (2019). *The General Data Protection Regulation – One year on – Civil society: Awareness, opportunities and challenges*. Publications Office. https://data.europa.eu/doi/10.2811/538633

Eynon, R., Fry, J., & Schroeder, R. (2017). The ethics of internet research. In N. Fielding, R. Lee, & G. Blank (Eds.), The Sage handbook of online research methods. London: Sage.

Eynon, R., Schroeder, R., & Fry, J. (2009). New techniques in online research: Challenges for research ethics. Twenty-First Century Society, 4(2), 187–199.

Favaretto, M., De Clercq, E., Schneble, C. O., & Elger, B. S. (2020). What is your definition of Big Data? Researchers' understanding of the phenomenon of the decade. PLoS ONE, 15(2), e0228987.

Fine, M. (2016). Just methods in revolting times. Qualitative Research in Psychology, 13(4), 347–365.

Flemming, K., & Noyes, J. (2021). Qualitative evidence synthesis: Where are we at? International Journal of Qualitative Methods, 20.

Flewitt, R. (2005). Conducting research with young children: Some ethical considerations. Early Child Development and Care, 175(6), 553–565.

Fox, N. J., & Alldred, P. (2015). New materialist social inquiry: Designs, methods and the research-assemblage. International Journal of Social Research Methodology, 18(4), 399–414.

Foxworth, R., & Ellenwood, C. (2022). Indigenous peoples and third sector research: Indigenous data sovereignty as a framework to improve research practices. Voluntas, 34, 100–107.

Frankham, J. (2009). Partnership research: A review of approaches and challenges in conducting research in partnership with service users. Southampton: ESRC National Centre for Research Methods Review Paper. Retrieved from http://eprints.ncrm.ac.uk/778/

Franzke, A. S., Bechmann, A., Zimmer, M., Ess, C., & the Association of Internet Researchers. (2020). *Internet Research: Ethical Guidelines 3.0.* https://aoir.org/reports/ethics3.pdf

Funnell, S., Tanuseputro, P., Letendre, A., Bearskin, L. B., & Walker, J. (2020). "Nothing about us, without us." How community-based participatory research methods were adapted in an Indigenous end-of-life study using previously collected data. Canadian Journal on Aging / La Revue canadienne du vieillissement, 39(2), 145–155.

Gabbidon, K., & Chenneville, T. (2021). Strategies to minimize further stigmatization of communities experiencing stigma: A guide for qualitative researchers. Stigma and Health, 6(1), 32.

Gallaher, Jr., A. (1980). Schizophrenia, Irish style. Reviews in Anthropology, 7(2), 155–163.

George, M. S., Gaitonde, R., Davey, R., Mohanty, I., & Upton, P. (2023). Engaging participants with research findings: A rights-informed approach. Health Expectations, 26(2), 765–773.

Gerrard, Y. (2021). What's in a (pseudo)name? Ethical conundrums for the principles of anonymisation in social media research. Qualitative Research, 21(5), 686–702.

GFBR. (2025). Global Forum on Bioethics in Research. https://www.gfbr .global/

Ghosh, D. (2018). Risky fieldwork: The problems of ethics in the field. *Energy Research & Social Science*, 45, 348–354.

Gibson S., Benson O., & Brand S. L. (2012). Talking about suicide: Confidentiality and anonymity in qualitative research. Nursing Ethics, 20(1), 18–29.

Giles, F. C., McKenzie, M., Kyei-Nimakoh, M., Satyen, L., Tarzia, L., & Hegarty, K. (2025). Management of imposter participants when conducting online research with victim-survivors and perpetrators of violence. *Methodological Innovations, 18*(2), 79–88.

Gilligan, C. (1982). In a different voice: Psychological theory and women's development. Cambridge, MA: Harvard University Press.

Glasdam, S., Ó Cathaoir, K., & Stjernswärd, S. (2024). Balancing different legal and ethical requirements in the construction of informed consents in qualitative international collaborative research across continents: Reflections from a Scandinavian perspective. *Journal of Academic Ethics, 23*, 349–362.

Gold, S. (1989). Ethical issues in visual fieldwork. In G. Blank, J. McCartney, & E. Brent. (Eds.), *New technology in sociology: Practical applications in research and work* (pp. 99–109). New Brunswick, NJ, Transaction.

Goodenough, T., Williamson, E., Kent, J., & Ashcroft, R. (2004). Ethical protection in research: Including children in the debate. In M. Smyth & E. Williamson (Eds.), *Researchers and their subjects: Ethics, power, knowledge and consent*. Bristol: Policy Press.

Goodyear-Smith, F., Lobb, B., Davies, G., Nachson, I., & Seelau, S. M. (2002). International variation in ethics committee requirements: Comparisons across five Westernised nations. BMC Medical Ethics, 3(1), 2.

Global Indigenous Data Alliance. (2019). History of Indigenous data sovereignty. *Global Indigenous Data Alliance*, https://www.gida-global.org/

Goddard, M. (2017). The EU General Data Protection Regulation (GDPR): European regulation that has a global impact. International Journal of Market Research, 59(6), 703–705.

Goffman, A. (2009). On the run: Wanted men in a Philadelphia ghetto. *American Sociological Review, 74*, 339–357.

Goldblatt, H., Karnieli-Miller, O., & Neumann, M. (2011). Sharing qualitative research findings with participants: Study experiences of methodological and ethical dilemmas. Patient Education & Counseling, 82(3), 389–395.

Goodson, I., Antikainen, A., Sikes, P., Andrews, M., & Sikes, P. J. (Eds.). (2016). The Routledge international handbook on narrative and life history. New York: Routledge.

Gorman, S. M. (2011). Ethics creep or governance creep? Monash Bioethics Review, 29, 23–38.

Gray, A., Trompf, P., & Houston, S. (1991). The decline and rise of Aboriginal families. In J. Reid & P. Trompf (Eds.), *The health of Aboriginal Australia*. Sydney: Harcourt Brace and Company.

Gregory, I. (2003). *Ethics in research*. London: Continuum.

Greengard, S. (2021). *The internet of things*. Cambridge, MA: MIT Press.

Griffin, C., & Bengry-Howell, A. (2008). Ethnography. In C. Willig & W. Stainton-Rogers (Eds.), The Sage handbook of qualitative research in psychology. London: Sage.

Griffith, R. (2016). What is Gillick competence? *Human Vaccines & Immunotherapeutics, 12*(1), 244–247.

Grinyer, A. (2001). Ethical dilemmas in nonclinical health research from a UK perspective. Nursing Ethics, 8(2), 123–131.

Grinyer, A. (2002). The anonymity of research participants: Assumptions, ethics and practicalities. Social Research Update, Issue 36.

Grønseth, A. S. (2017). Empathic relation with Tamil refugees: Challenging morality and calling for ethics of knowledge creation. In A. S. Grønseth & L. Josephides (Eds.), The ethics of knowledge creation: Transactions, relations, and persons (1st ed., Vol. 31, pp. 29–48). London: Berghahn Books.

Guillemin, M., & Gillam, L. (2004). Ethics, reflexivity, and "ethically important moments" in research. Qualitative Inquiry, 10(2), 261–280.

Guillemin, M., Gillam, L., Rosenthal, D., & Bolitho, A. (2012). Human research ethics committees: Examining their roles and practices. *Journal of Empirical Research on Human Research Ethics, 7*(3), 38–49.

Guishard, M. A., Halkovic, A., Galletta, A., & Li, P. (2018). Toward epistemological ethics: Centering communities and social justice in qualitative research [43 paragraphs]. Forum Qualitative Sozialforschung / Forum: Qualitative Social Research, 19(3), 27.

Gunsalus, C. K., Bruner, E. M., Burbules, N. C., Dash, L., Finkin, M., Goldberg, J. P., Greenough, W. T., Miller, G. A., Pratt, M. G., Iriye, M., & Aronson, D. (2007). The Illinois White Paper: Improving the system for protecting human subjects: Counteracting IRB "mission creep". Qualitative Inquiry, 13(5), 617–649.

Guta, A., Nixon, S. A., & Wilson, M. G. (2013). Resisting the seduction of "ethics creep": Using Foucault to surface complexity and contradiction in research ethics review. Social Science & Medicine, 98, 301–310.

Haggerty, K. (2004). Ethics creep: Governing social science research in the name of ethics. Qualitative Sociology, 27(4), 391–414.

Haggerty, K. (2016). Ethics creep*: Governing social science research in the name of ethics. In M. Adorjan & R Ricciardelli (eds.). Engaging with ethics in international criminological research. London: Routledge, pp. 13–35

Hammersley, M. (2009). Against the ethicists: On the evils of ethical regulation. International Journal of Social Research Methodology, 12(3), 211–226.

Hammersley, M. (2010), Creeping ethical regulation and the strangling of research. *Sociological Research Online, 15*(4), 16.

Handal, B., Campbell, C., Watson, K., Maher, M., Brewer, K., Irwin, A. M., & Fellman, M. (2021). Human research ethics committees members: Ethical review personal perceptions. Monash Bioethics Review, 39(1), 94–114.

Haney, C., Banks, W. C., & Zimbardo, P. G. (1973). Interpersonal dynamics in a simulated prison. International Journal of Criminology and Penology, 1, 69–97.

Hanson, K., Spyrou, S., Graham, A., Morrow, G., & Taft, J. (2023). Research ethics in childhood research. Childhood, 30(4), 343–359.

Haozous, E. A., Lee, J., & Soto, C. (2021). Urban American Indian and Alaska Native data sovereignty: Ethical issues. American Indian and Alaska Native Mental Health Research, 28(2), 77–97.

Harper, D. (1998). An argument for visual sociology. In J. Prosser (Ed.), Image-based research: A sourcebook for qualitative researchers. London: Routledge Falmer.

Hauser, D., Paolacci, G., & Chandler, J. (2019). Common concerns with MTurk as a participant pool: Evidence and solutions. In Handbook of research methods in consumer psychology (pp. 319–337). London: Routledge.

Healy, J., Hassan, R., & McKenna, R. B. (1985). Aboriginal families. In D. Storer (Ed.), Ethnic family values in Australia. Sydney: Prentice-Hall Australia.

Heath, S., Brooks, R., Cleaver, E., & Ireland, E. (2009). Researching young people's lives. London: Sage.

Held, V. (2006). The ethics of care: Personal, political, global. New York: Oxford University Press.

Herrera, C. D. (1999). Two arguments for "covert methods" in social research. British Journal of Sociology, 5(2), 331–343.

Herschel, R., & Miori, V. M. (2017). Ethics & big data. Technology in Society, 49, 31–36.

Hesse, A., Glenna, L., Hinrichs, C., Chiles, R., & Sachs, C. (2018). Qualitative research ethics in the big data era. American Behavioral Scientist, 63(5), 560–583.

Hintze, M., & El Emam, K. (2018). Comparing the benefits of pseudonymisation and anonymisation under the GDPR. Journal of Data Protection & Privacy, 2(2), 145–158.

HM Government. (2018). Data Protection Act 2018. UK: National Archives. https://www.legislation.gov.uk/ukpga/2018/12/contents

Hochschild, A. (1983). The managed heart: The commercialization of human feeling. Berkeley: University of California Press.

Hokke, S., Hackworth, N. J., Bennetts, S. K., et al. (2019). Ethical considerations in using social media to engage research participants: Perspectives of Australian researchers and ethics committee members. Journal of Empirical Research on Human Research Ethics, 15(1–2), 12–27.

Holliday, R. (2004). Reflecting the self. In C. Knowles & P. Sweetman (Eds.), *Picturing the social landscape: Visual methods and the sociological imagination*. London: Routledge.

Holmes, A. L., Grossi, A. C., Wells, M. L., Chesterman, J. H., & Ibrahim, J. E. (2022). Integrity in guardianship decision making: Applying the will and preferences paradigm. Journal of the American Medical Directors Association, 23(7), 1129–1136.

Homan, R. (1991). *The ethics of social research*. Longman: London.

Homan, R., & Bulmer, M. (1982). On the merits of covert methods: A dialogue. In M. Bulmer (Ed.), Social research ethics. London: Macmillan Press.

Hooley, T., Marriott, J., & Wellens, J. (2012). What is online research: Using the internet for social science research. London: Bloomsbury.

Hope, T. (2004). Medical ethics: A very short introduction. Oxford: Oxford University Press.

Hopman, M. J. (2021). Covert qualitative research as a method to study human rights under authoritarian regimes. Journal of Human Rights Practice, 13(3), 548–564.

Hopman, M. J., Jama, G. A., Zvonareva, Z., Holavins, A., & Anonymous. (2023). Speaking of epistemic injustice: A reply. Journal of Human Rights Practice, 15(2), 374–394.

Hudson, M., Carroll, S. R., Anderson, J., Blackwater, D., Cordova-Marks, F. M., Cummins, J., & Rowe, R. K. (2023). Indigenous peoples' rights in data: A contribution toward indigenous research sovereignty. Frontiers in Research Metrics and Analytics, 8, 1173805.

Hugman, R., Pittaway, E., & Bartolomei, L. (2011). When 'do no harm' is not enough: The ethics of research with refugees and other vulnerable groups. British Journal of Social Work, 41(7), 1271–1287.

Hummel, P., Adam, T., Reis, A., & Littler, K. (2021a). Taking stock of the availability and functions of National Ethics Committees worldwide. BMC Medical Ethics, 22(1), 56.

Hummel, P., Braun, M., Tretter, M., & Dabrock, P. (2021b). Data sovereignty: A review. Big Data & Society, 8(1).

Humphreys, L. (1975), The tea room trade: Impersonal sex in public places. New York: Aldine de Gruyte.

IJsselmuiden, C. B., & Faden, R. R. (1992). Research and informed consent in Africa—another look. New England Journal of Medicine, 326(12), 830–834.

INVOLVE. (2004). Involving the public in NHS, public health and social care research: Briefing notes for researchers. Eastleigh: INVOLVE.

Iphofen, R. (2009). Ethical decision making in social research. Basingstoke: Palgrave Macmillan.

Iphofen, R. (Ed.). (2020). Handbook of research ethics and scientific integrity. Heidelberg: Springer Nature.

Iphofen, R., & Tolich, M. (Eds.). (2018). The SAGE handbook of qualitative research ethics. London: Sage Reference.

Irwin, S. (2013). Qualitative secondary data analysis: Ethics, epistemology and context. Progress in Development Studies, 13(4), 295–306.

Israel, M. (2004). Ethics and the governance of criminological research in Australia. Sydney: New South Wales Bureau of Crime Statistics and Research.

Israel, M., & Hay, I. (2006). Research ethics for social scientists. London: Sage.

Jacobs-Huey, L. (2002). The natives are gazing and talking back: Reviewing the problematic of positionality, voice, and accountability among "Native" anthropologists. American Anthropologist, 104(3), 791–804.

Jankie, D. (2004). "Tell me who you are": Problematizing the construction and positionalities of "insider"/"outsider" of a "Native" ethnographer in a postcolonial context. In K. Mutua & B. B. Swadener (Eds.), Decolonizing research in cross-cultural contexts: Critical personal narratives (pp. 87–105). Albany, NY: State University of New York Press.

Jasanoff, S. (2017). Virtual, visible, and actionable: Data assemblages and the sightlines of justice. Big Data & Society, 4(2).

Johnson, B., & Macleod Clark, J. (2003). Collecting sensitive data: The impact on researchers. Qualitative Health Research, 12(3), 421–434.

Josephides, L., & Grønseth, A. S. (Eds.). (2017). The ethics of knowledge creation: Transactions, relations, and persons (Vol. 31). London: Berghahn Books.

Joynson, C., & Leyser, O. (2015). The culture of scientific research. F1000Research, 4, 66.

Kapā'anaokalāokeola Nākoa Oliveira, K. A. R., & Kahunawaika'ala Wright, A. (Eds.). (2016). Kanaka 'Ōiwi methodologies: Mo'olelo and metaphor. Honolulu: University of Hawai'i Press.

Kara, H. (2018). Chapter 2: Indigenous research and ethics. In Research ethics in the real world. Bristol, UK: Policy Press.

Kara, H., & Pickering, L. (2017). New directions in qualitative research ethics. International Journal of Social Research Methodology, 20(3), 239–241.

Karram Stephenson, G., Jones, G. A., Fick, E., Bégin-Caouette, O., Taiyeb, A., & Metcalfe, A. (2020). What's the protocol? Canadian university research ethics boards and variations in implementing Tri-Council policy. Canadian Journal of Higher Education, 50(1), 68–81.

Kars, M. C., van Thiel, G. J., van der Graaf, R., Moors, M., de Graeff, A., & van Delden, J. J. (2016). A systematic review of reasons for gatekeeping in palliative care research. Palliative Medicine, 30(6), 533–548.

Kau, K., Grama, B., Chaudhuri, N. R., & Recalde-Vela, M. J. (2023). Ethics and epistemic injustice in the global South: A response to Hopman's human rights exceptionalism as justification for covert research. Journal of Human Rights Practice, 15(2), 347–373.

Kay, L. (2019). Guardians of research: Negotiating the strata of gatekeepers in research with vulnerable participants. Practice, 1(1), 37–52.

Kelly, B. D. (2022). Anthropological perspectives on the trajectory from institutionalisation to community care in Irish psychiatry. Irish Journal of Psychological Medicine, 39(2), 121–130.

Kendall, E., Sunderland, N., Barnett, L., Nalder, G., & Matthews, C. (2011). Beyond the rhetoric of participatory research in Indigenous communities: Advances in Australia over the last decade. Qualitative Health Research, 21(12), 1719–1728.

Kennedy, M., Maddox, R., Booth, K., Maidment, S., Chamberlain, C., & Bessarab, D. (2022). Decolonising qualitative research with respectful, reciprocal, and responsible research practice: A narrative review of the application of Yarning method in qualitative Aboriginal and Torres Strait Islander health research. International Journal for Equity in Health, 21, 134

Kent, J., Williamson, E., Goodenough, T., & Ashcroft, R. (2002). Social science gets the ethics treatment: Research governance and ethical review. Sociological Research Online, 7(4). http://socresonline. org.uk /7/4/williamson.html

Kenyon, E., & Hawker, S. (1999). "Once would be enough": Some reflections on the issue of safety for lone researchers. International Journal of Social Research Methodology, 2(4), 313–327.

Khan, S. (2019). The subpoena of ethnographic data. Social Forum, 34, 253–263.

Kidd, I. J., Medina, J., & Pohlhaus, G. (2017). Introduction. In I. J. Kidd, J. Medina, & G. Pohlhaus (Eds.), The Routledge handbook of epistemic injustice (pp. 1–9). New York: Routledge.

Kine, P. (2022, February 16). My journey down the rabbit hole of every journalist's favourite app. Politico. https://www.politico.com/news

/2022/02/16/my-journey-down-the-rabbit-hole-of-every-journalists
-favorite-app-00009216

King, G. (2021). Towards a culture of care for ethical review: Connections
and frictions in institutional and individual practices of social research
ethics. Social & Cultural Geography, 24(1), 104–120.

Kitchener, K., & Kitchener, R. (2009). Social science research ethics:
Historical and philosophical issues. In D. Mertens & P. Ginsberg
(Eds.), *The handbook of social research ethics*. Thousand Oaks, CA:
Sage.

Kleinberg, B., Mozes, M., van der Toolen, Y., & Verschuere, B. (2017).
NETANOS - Named entity-based text anonymization for open science.
Open Science Framework .https://osf.io/preprints/osf/w9nhb

Klykken, F. H. (2022). Implementing continuous consent in qualitative
research. Qualitative Research, 22(5), 795–810.

Kohn, T., & Shore, C. (2017). The ethics of university ethics committees.
In Susan Wright and Cros Shore (Eds). Death of the public university:
Uncertain futures for higher education in the knowledge economy. (pp.
229–249). New York: Berghahn Books.

Kolstoe, S. E., & Carpenter, D. (2023). Head-to-head: Can a one-size-
fits-all research ethics review process work across all disciplines?
University of Portsmouth: Institute of Life Sciences and Healthcare.
https://researchportal.port.ac.uk/en/publications/head-to-head-can-a
-one-size-fits-all-research-ethics-review-proce

Kolstoe, S. E., & Pugh, J. (2023). The trinity of good research:
Distinguishing between research integrity, ethics, and governance.
Accountability in Research, *31*(8), 1222–1241.

Komić, D., Marušić, S. L., & Marušić, A. (2015). Research integrity and
research ethics in professional codes of ethics: Survey of terminology
used by professional organizations across research disciplines. PLoS
ONE, 10(7), e0133662.

Komil-Burley, D. (2021). Conducting research in authoritarian
bureaucracies: Researcher positionality, access, negotiation,
cooperation, trepidation, and avoiding the influence of the
gatekeepers. International Journal of Qualitative Methods, 20,
1609406921996862.

Kovach, M. (2021). Indigenous methodologies: Characteristics,
conversations, and contexts. Toronto: University of Toronto Press.

Kozinets, R. (2010). *Netnography: Doing ethnographic research online.*
London: Sage.

Kozinets, R. V. (2019). *Netnography: The essential geode to qualitative
social media research* (3rd ed.). London: Sage.

Krawczyk, M. M., & Kikalage Dieudonné, J. (2023). To whom does
the knowledge belong? The researcher–researched relationship and
vulnerability in refugee studies. Ethics in Progress, 14(2), 110–129.

Kristiansen, S. (2022). Qualitative online data collection: Towards a framework of ethical decision-making. Qualitative Report, 27(12), 2686–2700.

Kukutai, T., & Taylor, J. (2016). *Indigenous data sovereignty: Toward an agenda*. Canberra: Australian National University Press.

Kuper, H., Hameed, S., Reichenberger, V., Scherer, N., Wilbur, J., Zuurmond, M., Mactaggart, I., Bright, T., & Shakespeare, T. (2021). Participatory research in disability in low- and middle-income countries: What have we learnt and what should we do? Scandinavian Journal of Disability Research, 23(1), 328–337.

Lahman, M. K. E., Thomas, R., & Teman, E. D. (2023). A good name: Pseudonyms in research. Qualitative Inquiry, 29(6), 678–685.

LaMarre, A., & Chamberlain, K. (2022). Innovating qualitative research methods: Proposals and possibilities. Methods in Psychology, 6, 100083.

Landau, R. (2008). Social work research ethics: Dual roles and boundary issues. Families in Society, 89(4), 571–577.

Langston, A., Abbott, L., Lewis, V., & Kellett, M. (2004). Early childhood. In S. Fraser, V. Lewis, S. Ding, M. Kellett, & C. Robinson (Eds.), *Doing research with children and young people*. London: Sage.

Lapadat, J. C. (2017). Ethics in autoethnography and collaborative autoethnography. Qualitative Inquiry, 23(8), 589–603.

Largent, E. A., & Fernandez Lynch, H. Paying research participants: Regulatory uncertainty, conceptual confusion, and a path forward. Yale Journal of Health Policy, Law, and Ethics, 17(1), 61–141.

Larrabee, M. J. (Ed.). (2016). An ethic of care: Feminist and interdisciplinary perspectives. London: Taylor & Francis.

Lassiter, L., Goodall, H., Campbell, E., & Johnson, M. (Eds.). (2004). *The other side of Middletown: Exploring Muncie's African American community*. Walnut Creek: Alta Mira Press.

Latulippe, N., & Klenk, N. (2020). Making room and moving over: Knowledge co-production, Indigenous knowledge sovereignty and the politics of global environmental change decision-making. *Current Opinion in Environmental Sustainability*, 42, 7–14.

Lawton, J. (2001). Gaining and maintaining consent: Ethical concerns raised in a study of dying patients. Qualitative Health Research, 11(5), 693–705.

LeFrançois, B. A., & Voronka, J. (2022). Mad epistemologies and maddening the ethics of knowledge production. In Teresa Macias (Ed.), Unravelling research: The ethics and politics of research in the social sciences (pp. 105–130). Winnipeg: Fernwood Publishing.

Leahy, C. P. (2021). The afterlife of interviews: Explicit ethics and subtle ethics in sensitive or distressing qualitative research. Qualitative Research, 22(5), 777–794.

Lee, R. (1993). Doing research on sensitive topics. London: Sage.

Lee, R. (1995). Dangerous fieldwork. London: Sage.

Lee-Treweek, G., & Linkogle, S. (Eds.). (2000). Danger in the field: Risk and ethics in social research. London: Psychology Press.

Lehner-Mear, R. (2020). Negotiating the ethics of netnography: Developing an ethical approach to an online study of mother perspectives. International Journal of Social Research Methodology, 23(2), 123–137.

Lenton, L. A., Smith, V., Bacon, A. M., May, J., & Charlesford, J. (2021). Ethical considerations for committees, supervisors and student researchers conducting qualitative research with young people in the United Kingdom. Methods in Psychology, 5, 100050.

Lenza, M. (2004). Controversies surrounding Laud Humphreys' Tearoom Trade: An unsettling example of politics and power in methodological critiques. International Journal of Sociology and Social Policy, 24, 20–31.

Leo, R. A. (1995). Trials and tribulations: Courts, ethnography, and the need for an evidentiary privilege for academic researchers. The American Sociologist, 26(1), 113–134.

Livholts, M., & Tamboukou, M. (2015). Discourse and narrative methods: Theoretical departures, analytical strategies and situated writings. London: Sage.

Lomax, H. (2020). Consuming images, ethics, and integrity in visual social research. In R. Iphofen (Ed.), Handbook of research ethics and scientific integrity (pp. 899–915). Cham: Springer.

Loudon, J. B. (1980). Review of Saints, scholars, and schizophrenics: Mental illness in rural Ireland, by N. Scheper-Hughes. Man, 15(2), 404–406.

Lowe, J., & Wimbish-Cirilo, R. (2016). The use of talking circles to describe a Native American transcultural caring immersion experience. Journal of Holistic Nursing, 34, 280–290.

Lowman, J., & Palys, T. (2014). The betrayal of research confidentiality in British sociology. Research Ethics, 10(2), 97–118.

Lupton, D., & Watson, A. A. (2021). Towards more-than-human digital data studies: Developing research-creation methods. Qualitative Research, 21(4), 463–480.

Lynskey, O. (2015). The dual objectives of European data protection regulation. In The foundations of EU data protection law. Oxford: Oxford University Press.

MacDonald, C. (2002). A guide to moral decision making. http://ethicsweb.ca/guide

Macfarlane, B. (2009). (2009). Researching with integrity. New York: Routledge.

Macneil, S. D., & Fernandez, C. V. (2006). Informing research participants of research results: Analysis of Canadian university based research ethics board policies. Journal of Medical Ethics, 32(1), 49–54.

Mapedzahama, V., & Dune, T. (2017). A clash of paradigms? Ethnography and ethics approval. SAGE Open, 7(1):1-8.

Marshall, D. T., & Naff, D. B. (2024). The ethics of using artificial intelligence in qualitative research. *Journal of Empirical Research on Human Research Ethics*, 19(3), 92–102.

Marzano, M. (2021). Covert research ethics. In R. Iphofen & D. O'Mathúna (Eds.), Ethical issues in covert, security and surveillance research (Vol. 8, pp. 41–53). Leeds,UK: Emerald Publishing.

Masson, J. (2004). The legal context. In S. Fraser, V. Lewis, S. Ding, M. Kellett, & C. Robinson (Eds.), *Doing research with children and young people*. London: Sage.

Mathews, B., & Bross, D. (Eds.). (2015). Mandatory reporting laws and the identification of severe child abuse and neglect. Dordrecht: Springer.

Mauthner, M., Birch, M., Jessop, J., & Miller, T. (Eds.) (2002). *Ethics in qualitative research*. London: Sage.

Mauthner, N. S. (2019). Toward a posthumanist ethics of qualitative research in a big data era. American Behavioral Scientist, 63(6), 669–698.

McAreavey, R., & Das, C. (2013). A delicate balancing act: Negotiating with gatekeepers for ethical research when researching minority communities. International Journal of Qualitative Methods, 12(1), 113–131.

McCosker, H., Barnard, A., & Gerber, R. (2001). Undertaking sensitive research: Issues and strategies for meeting the safety needs of all participants. Forum: Qualitative Social Research, 2(1), 22.

McCracken, J. (2020). Ethics as obligation: Reconciling diverging research practices with marginalized communities. International Journal of Qualitative Methods, 19.

McGrath, B. B., & Ka'ili, T. O. (2010). Creating Project Talanoa: A culturally based community health program for U.S. Pacific Islander adolescents. Public Health Nursing, 27, 17–24.

McGuffog, R., Chamberlain, C., Hughes, J., Kong, K., Wenitong, M., Bryant, J., Brown, A., Eades, S. J., Griffiths, K. E., Collis, F., Hobden, B., O'Mara, P., Ridgeway, T., Walter, M., & Kennedy M. (2023). Murru Minya–Informing the development of practical recommendations to support ethical conduct in Aboriginal and Torres Strait Islander health research: A protocol for a national mixed-methods study. BMJ Open, 13(2), e067054.

Menzies, C. R. (2001). Reflections on research with, for, and among Indigenous peoples. Canadian Journal of Native Education, 25(1), 19–36.

Merlan, F. (1997). The mother-in-law taboo: Avoidance and obligation in Aboriginal Australian society. In F. Merlan, J. Morton, & A. Rumsey (Eds.), Scholar and sceptic: Australian Aboriginal studies in honour of L. R. Hiatt (pp. 95–122).Canberra: Aboriginal Studies Press.

Mertens, D., & Ginsberg, P. (Eds.). (2009). The handbook of social research ethics. Thousand Oaks, CA: Sage.

Mero-Jaffe, I. (2011). "Is that what I said?" Interview transcript approval by participants: An aspect of ethics in qualitative research. International Journal of Qualitative Methods, 10(3), 231–247.

Mertens, D. M. (2021). Transformative research methods to increase social impact for vulnerable groups and cultural minorities. International Journal of Qualitative Methods, 20.

Metcalf, J., & Crawford, K. (2016). Where are human subjects in Big Data research? The emerging ethics divide. Big Data & Society, 3(1).

Milgram, S. (1963). Behavioral study of obedience. Journal of Abnormal and Social Psychology, 67(4), 371–378.

Miller, P., Kirkman, G., Timmins, S., Banerjee, R., Panicker, A., Nelson, K., & Ochen, E. (2022). Getting past the gatekeeper: Cultural competence, field access and researching gender-based violence—Evidence from four countries. Power and Education, 14(3), 204–217.

Miller, T., & Bell, L. (2002). Consenting to what?: Issues of access, gatekeeping and "informed consent". In M. Mauthner, M. Birch, J. Jessop, & T. Miller (Eds.), *Ethics in qualitative research*. London: Sage.

Miller, T., Birch, M., Mauthner, M., & Jessop, J. (Eds.). (2012). Ethics in qualitative research (2nd ed.). London: Sage.

Mills, K. A. (2017). What are the threats and potentials of big data for qualitative research? Qualitative Research, 18(6), 591–603.

Mills, K. A. (2019). Big data for qualitative research. London: Taylor & Francis.

Mitchell, W., & Irvine, A. (2008). I'm okay, you're okay?: Reflections on the well-being and ethical requirements of researchers and research participants in conducting qualitative fieldwork interviews. International Journal of Qualitative Methods, 7(4), 31–44.

Mohamad Nasri, N., Nasri, N., & Abd Talib, M. A. (2021). Cross-language qualitative research studies dilemmas: A research review. Qualitative Research Journal, 21(1), 15–28.

Montgomery, J. (2002). Health care law. Oxford: Oxford University Press.

Morey, Y., Bengry-Howell, A., & Griffin, C. (2012). Public profiles, private parties: Digital ethnography, ethics and research in the context of Web 2.0. In S. Heath & C. Walker (Eds.), Innovations in youth research. London: Palgrave Macmillan.

Mozersky, J., Walsh, H., Parsons, M., McIntosh, T., Baldwin, K., & DuBois, J. M. (2020). Are we ready to share qualitative research data? Knowledge and preparedness among qualitative researchers, IRB members, and data repository curators. IASSIST Quarterly, 43(4), 952.

Murphy, E., & Dingwall, M. (2007). Informed consent, anticipatory regulation and ethnographic practice. Social Science & Medicine, 65, 2223–2234.

Murphy, H. B. M. (1979). Saints, scholars and schizophrenics: Madness and badness in western Ireland by Nancy Scheper-Hughes (Book review). Medical Anthropology, 2, 59–93.

National Ethics Advisory Committee – Kāhui Matatika o te Motu. (2021). National Ethical Standards for Health and Disability Research and Quality Improvement. Wellington: Ministry of Health.

National Health & Medical Research Council. (2011). *Research Governance Handbook: Guidance for the national approach to single ethical review*. Canberra: National Health and Medical Research Council.

National Health & Medical Research Council. (2018). *Australian Code for the Responsible Conduct of Research*. Canberra: National Health and Medical Research Council.

National Health & Medical Research Council, Australian Research Council, & Universities Australia. (2019). Payment of participants in research: Information for researchers, HRECs and other ethics review bodies. Canberra: National Health and Medical Research Council.

National Health & Medical Research Council, Australian Research Council, & Universities Australia. (2022). NHMRC open access policy. Canberra: National Health and Medical Research Council.

National Health & Medical Research Council, Australian Research Council, & Universities Australia. (2025). National statement on ethical conduct in human research. Canberra: National Health and Medical Research Council.

Nduna, M., Mayisela, S., Balton, S., Gobodo-Madikizela, P., Kheswa, J. G., Khumalo, I. P., & Tabane, C. (2022). Research site anonymity in context. Journal of Empirical Research on Human Research Ethics, 17(5), 554–564.

Neale, B., & Bishop, L. (2012a). The Timescapes archive: A stakeholder approach to archiving qualitative, longitudinal data. Qualitative Research, 12(1), 53–65.

Neale, B., & Bishop, L. (2012b). *The ethics of archiving and re-using qualitative longitudinal data: A stakeholder approach* (Timescapes Methods Guides Series, Guide No. 18).

Newton, V. L. (2017). "It's good to be able to talk": An exploration of the complexities of participant and researcher relationships when conducting sensitive research. Women's Studies International Forum, 61, 93–99.

Ngozwana, N. (2018). Ethical dilemmas in qualitative research methodology: Researcher's reflections. International Journal of Educational Methodology, 4(1), 19–28.

NHS. (2024). Payments and incentives in research. UK: NHS, Health Research Authority. Retrieved from. https://www.hra.nhs.uk/about-us/committees-and-services/nreap/payments-and-incentives-research/

Nutbrown, C. (2011). Naked by the pool? Blurring the image? Ethical issues in the portrayal of young children in arts-based educational research. Qualitative Inquiry, 17(1), 3–14.

Oakley, A. (1981). Interviewing women: A contradiction in terms. In H. Roberts (Ed.), *Doing feminist research*. Boston: Routledge.

Ober, R. (2017). Kapati Time: Storytelling as a data collection method in Indigenous research. Learning Communities: International Journal of Learning in Social Contexts, 22, 8–17.

Office for Human Research Protections. (2021). International compilation of human research standards. U.S. Department of Health and Human Services. Retrieved from https://www.hhs.gov/ohrp/international/compilation-human-research-standards/index.html

Oliver, P. (2010). *The student's guide to research ethics*. Maidenhead: McGraw-Hill Education.

Olson, R. E. (2021). Emotions in human research ethics guidelines: Beyond risk, harm and pathology. Qualitative Research, 23(3), 526–544.

Orr, E., Durepos, P., Jones, V., & Jack, S. M. (2021). Risk of secondary distress for graduate students conducting qualitative research on sensitive subjects: A scoping review of Canadian dissertations and theses. Global Qualitative Nursing Research, 8, 1–8.

Orton-Johnson, K. (2010). Ethics in online research: Evaluating the ESRC framework for research ethics categorisation of risk. Sociological Research Online, 15(4), 13.

Orzechowski, M., Woniak, K., Timmermann, C., et al. (2021). Normative framework of informed consent in clinical research in Germany, Poland, and Russia. BMC Medical Ethics, 22, 53.

Othman, Z., & Abdul Hamid, F. Z. (2018). Dealing with un(expected) ethical dilemma: Experience from the field. The Qualitative Report, 23(4), 733–741.

Palys, T., & Lowman, J. (2000). Ethical and legal strategies for protecting confidential research information. Canadian Journal of Law and Society, 15(1), 39–80.

Papademas, D., & International Visual Sociology Association. (2009). IVSA code of research ethics and guidelines. Visual Studies, 24(3), 250–257.

Parker, J., Penhale, B., & Stanley, D. (2010). Problem or safeguard? Research ethics review in social care research and the Mental Capacity Act 2005. Social Care and Neurodisability, 1(2), 22–32.

Patterson, M., Jackson, R., & Edwards, N. (2006). Ethics in Aboriginal research: Comments on paradigms, process and two worlds. Canadian Journal of Aboriginal Community-Based HIV/AIDS Research, 1(1), 47–61.

Perlstadt, H. (2024a). Assessing social science research ethics and integrity: Case studies and essays. Cham, Germany: Springer Nature.

Perlstadt, H. (2024b). Tearoom Trade: The ethics of studying social problems. In H. Perlstadt (Ed.), Assessing social science research ethics and integrity: Case studies and essays (pp. 159–181). Cham: Springer International Publishing.

Peterman, A., Devries, K., Guedes, A., Chandan, J. S., Minhas, S., Lim, R. Q. H., ... & Bhatia, A. (2023). Ethical reporting of research on violence against women and children: A review of current practice and recommendations for future guidelines. BMJ Global Health, 8(5), e011882.

Pauwels, L. (2008). Taking and using: Ethical issues of photographs for research purposes. Visual Communication Quarterly, 15, 1–6.

Peer, E., Rothschild, D., Gordon, A., Evernden, Z., & Damer, E. (2022). Data quality of platforms and panels for online behavioral research. *Behav Res Methods*, 54(4), 1643–1662. Erratum in: *Behavioural Research Methods*, 2022 Oct, 54(5), 2618–2620.

Pels, P. (2008). What has anthropology learned from the anthropology of colonialism? Social Anthropology, 16(3), 280–299.

Petrova, M., & Barclay, S. (2019). Research approvals iceberg: How a 'low-key' study in England needed 89 professionals to approve it and how we can do better. BMC Medical Ethics, 20, 7.

Pittaway, E., & Bartolomei, L. (2003). Women at risk: Field research report—Thailand. Sydney: Centre for Refugee Research, University of New South Wales.

Pique, N. (2001). Free and informed consent in research involving Native American communities. American Indian Culture and Research Journal, 25(1), 65–79.

Pink, S. (2003). Interdisciplinary agendas in visual research: Re-situating visual anthropology. Visual Studies, 18(2), 179–192.

Pink, S. (2007). Doing visual ethnography (4th ed.). London: Sage.

Pink, S. (2009). Doing sensory ethnography. United Kingdom: Sage.

Plummer, K (2001). Documents of life 2: An invitation to critical humanism. London: Sage.

Poth, C. N., & Shannon-Baker, P. (2022). State of the methods: Leveraging design possibilities of qualitatively oriented mixed methods research. International Journal of Qualitative Methods, 21, 16094069221115302.

Pratt B., & de Vries J. (2023). Where is knowledge from the global South? An account of epistemic justice for a global bioethics. Journal of Medical Ethics, 49, 325–334.

Prosser, J. (2000). The moral maze of image ethics. In H. Simons & R. Usher (Eds.), Situated ethics in visual research (pp. 116–132). London: Routledge Falmer.

Prosser, J., & Loxley, A. (2008). (2008). Introducing visual methods (NCRM Methodological Review). Retrieved from http://eprints.ncrm .ac.uk/420/

Punch, M. (1986). The politics and ethics of fieldwork. Thousand Oaks, CA: Sage.

Quinn, P. (2021). Research under the GDPR – A level playing field for public and private sector research? Life Sciences, Society and Policy, 17(4).

Quinn, P., & Malgieri, G. (2021). The difficulty of defining sensitive data—The concept of sensitive data in the EU data protection framework. German Law Journal, 22(8), 1583–1612.

Rallis Legal. (2017), *Laws relating to the giving of consent for person with impaired capacity to provide informed consent to participate in research in each Australian State and Territory. Report to the National Health and Medical Research Council.* Australia: Rallis Legal. https:// www.clinicaltrialsandresearch.vic.gov.au/__data/assets/pdf_file/0030 /195537/Laws-relating-to-the-provision-of-consent-for-persons-that-do -not-have-decision-making-capacity-to-participate-in-research.-March -2024.pdf

Raposo, H., Melo, S., & Egreja, C. (2022). Data protection in sociological health research: A critical narrative about the challenges of a new regulatory landscape. Sociological Research Online, 27(4), 1060–1076.

Renold, E., Holland, S., Ross, N., & Hillman, A. (2008). "Becoming participant": Problematizing "informed consent" in participatory research with young people in care. Qualitative Social Work, 7(4), 427–447.

Resseguier, A., & Ufert, F. (2023). AI research ethics is in its infancy: The EU's AI Act can make it a grown-up. Research Ethics, 20(2), 143–155.

Rhoads, R. A. (2020). "Whales Tales" on the run: Anonymizing ethnographic data in an age of openness. Cultural Studies ↔ Critical Methodologies, 20(5), 402–413.

Ribenfors, F., & Blood, L. (2023). To report or not to report: The ethical complexity facing researchers when responding to disclosures of harm or illegal activities during fieldwork with adults with intellectual disabilities. Ethics and Social Welfare, 17(2), 175–190.

Rieger, K. L., Horton, M., Copenace, S., Bennett, M., Buss, M., Chudyk, A. M., Cook, L., Hornan, B., Horrill, T., Linton, J., McPherson, K., Rattray, J. M., Murray, K., Phillips-Beck, W., Sinclair, R., Slavutskiy, O., Stewart, R., & Schultz, A. S. (2023). Elevating the uses of storytelling methods within Indigenous health research: A critical, participatory scoping review. International Journal of Qualitative Methods, 22, 1–15.

Ritchie, J., & Lewis, J. (2003). Qualitative research practice. London: Sage.

Robinson, C. (2020). Ethically important moments as data: Reflections from ethnographic fieldwork in prisons. Research Ethics, 16(1–2), 1–15.

Rodgers, J. (1999). Trying to get it right: Undertaking research involving people with learning difficulties. Disability & Society, 14(4), 421–433.

Romocea, O. (2014). Ethics and emotions: A migrant researcher doing research among Romanian migrants. Sociological Research Online, 19(4), 176–189.

Rose, G. (2007). Visual methodologies: An introduction to the interpretation of visual materials. London: Sage.

Rowlands, J. (2021). Interviewee transcript review as a tool to improve data quality and participant confidence in sensitive research. International Journal of Qualitative Methods, 20, 1–10.

Różyńska J. (2022). The ethical anatomy of payment for research participants. Journal of Empirical Research on Human Research Ethics, 25(3), 449–464.

Rowe, M. (2007). Tripping over molehills: Ethics and the ethnography of police work. International Journal of Social Research Methodology, 10(1), 37–48.

Ruggiano, N., & Perry, T. E. (2019). Conducting secondary analysis of qualitative data: Should we, can we, and how? Qualitative Social Work, 18(1), 81–97.

Saunders, B., Kitzinger, J., & Kitzinger, C.. Anonymising interview data: Challenges and compromise in practice. Qualitative Research, 15(5), 616–632.

Scheibner, J., Lenca, M., Kechagia, S., Troncoso-Pastoriza, R. J., Raisaro, J. L., Hubaux, J. P., Fellay, J., & Vayena, E. (2020). Data protection and ethics requirements for multisite research with health data: A comparative examination of legislative governance frameworks and the role of data protection technologies. Journal of Law and the Biosciences, 7(1), lsaa010.

Schneider, L. T. (2020). Sexual violence during research: How the unpredictability of fieldwork and the right to risk collide with academic bureaucracy and expectations. Critique of Anthropology, 40(2), 173–193.

Scheper-Hughes, N. (2000). Ire in Ireland. Ethnography, 1(1), 117–140.

Scheper-Hughes, N. (2001). Saints, scholars, and schizophrenics: Mental illness in rural Ireland (Updated & expanded ed.). Los Angeles: University of California Press.

Schultze, S., & Mason, R. (2012). Studying cyborgs: Re-examining internet studies as human subjects research. Journal of Information Technology, 27, 301–312.

Schuster, K., & Dunn, S. (Eds.). (2020). Routledge international handbook of research methods in digital humanities (1st ed.). London: Routledge.

Scratton, P. (2004). Speaking truth to power: Experiencing critical research. In M. Smyth & E. Williamson (Eds.), Researchers and their subjects: Ethics, power, knowledge and consent. Bristol: Policy Press.

Sedkaoui, S., & Simian, D. (2020). Developed framework based on cognitive computing to support personal data protection under the GDPR. In D. Simian & L. Stoica (Eds.), Modelling and development of intelligent systems. London: Springer.

Shaw, D., & Satalkar, P. (2018). Researchers' interpretations of research integrity: A qualitative study. Accountability in Research, 25(2), 79–93.

Shepherd, V., Wood, F., Griffith, R., Sheehan, M., & Hood, K. (2019). Research involving adults lacking capacity to consent: A content analysis of participant information sheets for consultees and legal representatives in England and Wales. Trials, 20, 233.

Sherwood, G., & Parsons, S. (2021). Negotiating the practicalities of informed consent in the field with children and young people: Learning from social science researchers. *Research Ethics*, 17(4), 448–463.

Sidaway, M., Collett, C., & Kolstoe, S. E. (2023). Evidence from UK Research Ethics Committee members on what makes a good research ethics review, and what can be improved. PLOS ONE, 18(7), e0288083.

Sieber, J. E. (Ed.). (2012). The ethics of social research: Fieldwork, regulation, and publication. New York: Springer Science & Business Media.

Silverio, S. A., Wilkinson, C., & Wilkinson, S. (2022). Academic ventriloquism: Tensions between inclusion, representation, and anonymity in qualitative research. In Handbook of social inclusion:

Research and practices in health and social sciences (pp. 643–660). Cham: Springer International Publishing.

Singh, G. (2019). The death of Web 2.0: Ethics, connectivity and recognition in the twenty-first century. London: Routledge.

Singh, H. P. (2018). Data protection and privacy legal-policy framework in India: A comparative study vis-à-vis China and Australia. Amity Journal of Computational Sciences, 2(2), 24–29.

Singh, S., & Engel-Hills, P. (2022). Invited peer commentary: Research site anonymity in context. Journal of Empirical Research on Human Research Ethics, 17(5), 565–572.

Singh, S., & Wassenaar, D. R. (2016). Contextualising the role of the gatekeeper in social science research. South African Journal of Bioethics and Law, 9(1), 42–46.

Singi, K., Choudhury, S. G., Kaulgud, V., Bose, R. J. C., Podder, S., & Burden, A. P. (2020, June). Data sovereignty governance framework. In Proceedings of the IEEE/ACM 42nd International Conference on Software Engineering Workshops (pp. 303–306).

Sleeboom-Faulkner, M., & Mcmurray, J. (2018). The impact of the new EU GDPR on ethics governance and social anthropology. Anthropology Today, 34, 22–23.

Smith, L. T. (1999). Decolonizing methodologies: Research and Indigenous peoples. United Kingdom: Bloomsbury Academic.

Smyth, M. (2004). Using participative action research with war-affected populations: Lessons from research in Northern Ireland and South Africa. In M. Smyth & E. Williamson (Eds.), Researchers and their subjects: Ethics, power, knowledge and consent. Bristol: Policy Press.

Smyth, K., Rennie, F., Davies, G., Sillars, M., & Woolvin, A. E. (2016). *Undertaking your research project: Essential guidance for undergraduates and postgraduates*. etips: Research Office Sustainability Studies, UHI Inverness UHI Perth Energy Innovation Team.

Snee, H. (2008). *Web 2.0 as a social science research tool*. http://www. bl .uk/reshelp/bldept/socsci/socint/web2/report.html

Social Research Association. (2001). *A code of practice for the safety of social researcher*. ESRC Government Place Scheme: The British Library https://the-sra.org.uk/SRA/SRA/Resources/Good-Practice.aspx

Social Research Association. (2021). *Research ethics guidelines. Cantebury: Social Research Association*. https://the-sra.org.uk/SRA/ SRA/Ethics/Research-Ethics-Guidance.aspx

Soyini Madison, D. (2005). *Critical ethnography: Method, ethics and performance*. Thousand Oaks, CA: Sage

Spears Johnson, C. R., Kraemer Diaz, A. E., & Arcury, T. A. (2016). Participation levels in 25 community-based participatory research projects. Health Education Research, 31(5), 577–586.

Spencer, G. (2022). *Ethics and integrity in research with children and young people.* Leeds: Emerald Publishing Limited.

Spencer, S. (2010). Visual research methods in the social sciences: Awakening visions (2nd ed.). London: Routledge.

Spicker, P. (2011). Ethical covert research. Sociology, 45(1), 118–133.

Spriggs, M. (2010). Consent in research involving children: The ethical issues. A handbook for human research ethics committees and researchers. Melbourne: Children's Bioethics Centre, The Royal Children's Hospital Melbourne.

Spriggs, M. (2023). Children and bioethics: Clarifying consent and assent in medical and research settings. British Medical Bulletin, 145(1), 110–119.

Stahlke, S. (2018). Expanding on notions of ethical risks to qualitative researchers. International Journal of Qualitative Methods, 17(1).

Steinkamp, N., Gordijn, B., Borovecki, A., Gefenas, E., Glasa, J., Guerrier, M., Meulenbergs, T., Rózyńska, J., & Slowther, A. (2007). Regulation of healthcare ethics committees in Europe. Medicine, Health Care and Philosophy, 10(4), 461–475.

Summers, K. (2013). (Re)Positioning the Indigenous academic researcher: A journey of critical reflexive understanding and storytelling. International Journal of Critical Indigenous Studies, 6(1), 1–13.

Surmiak, A. (2020). Should we maintain or break confidentiality? The choices made by social researchers in the context of law violation and harm. Journal of Academic Ethics, 18, 229–247.

Squire, C. (2008). Approaches to narrative research (Methodological Review Paper 008). Southammpton: NCRM http://eprints.ncrm.ac.uk /418/.

Stanley, L., & Wise, S. (2010). The ESRC's Framework for Research Ethics: Fit for research purpose? Sociological Research Online, 15(4), Article 12.

Strickland, J. C., & Victor, G. A. (2020). Leveraging crowdsourcing methods to collect qualitative data in addiction science: Narratives of non-medical prescription opioid, heroin, and fentanyl use. International Journal of Drug Policy, 75, 102587.

Sweeney, A., Greenwood, K. E., Williams, S., Wykes, T., & Rose, D. S. (2013). Hearing the voices of service user researchers in collaborative qualitative data analysis: The case for multiple coding. Health Expectations, 16(4), e89–e99.

Sweetman, P. (2009). Just anybody? Images, ethics and recognition. In R. Leino (Ed.), Just Anybody (pp. 7–9). Winchester: The Winchester Gallery, Winchester School of Art.

Taquette, S. R., & Borges da Matta Souza, L. M. (2022). Ethical dilemmas in qualitative research: A critical literature review. International Journal of Qualitative Methods, 21.

Tarleton, B., Williams, V., Palmer, N., & Gramlich, S. (2004). An equal relationship?: People with learning difficulties getting involved in research. In M. Smyth & E. Williamson (Eds.), Researchers and their subjects: Ethics, power, knowledge and consent. Bristol: Policy Press.

Tauri, J. M. (2018). Research ethics, informed consent and the disempowerment of First Nation peoples. Research Ethics, 14(3), 1–14.

Thelwall, M. (2022). Introduction to webometrics: Quantitative web research for the social sciences. Cham: Springer Nature.

Thelwall, M., & Sud, P. (2012). Webometric research with the Bing Search API 2.0. Journal of Informetrics, 6(1), 44–52.

Thomson, R., & McGeeney, E. (2018). Protection, participation and ethical labour. In R. Thomson, L. Berriman, & S. Bragg (Authors), Researching everyday childhoods: Time, technology and documentation in a digital age (pp. 39–58). London: Bloomsbury Academic.

Thomson, R., Lacey, A. J., Nasrawy, M., Boddy, J., Morrice, L., & Brannen, J. (2024). *Scoping longitudinal qualitative studies with seldom-heard families* (Report). University of Sussex. Report. https://hdl.handle.net/10779/uos.25574778.v1

Thunberg, S. (2022). Safeguarding personal integrity while collecting sensitive data using narrative interviews – A research note. International Journal of Social Research Methodology, 25(5), 711–715.

Tikly, L., & Bond, T. (2013). Towards a postcolonial research ethics in comparative and international education. Compare: A Journal of Comparative and International Education, 43(4), 422–442.

Tilley, L., & Woodthorpe, K. (2011). Is it the end of anonymity as we know it? A critical examination of the ethical principle of anonymity in the context of 21st Century demands on the qualitative researcher. Qualitative Research, 11(2), 197–212.

Tinker, A., & Coomber, V. (2004). University research ethics committees: Their role, remit and conduct. London: King's College.

Tolich, M. (2004). Internal confidentiality: When confidentiality assurances fail relational informants. Qualitative Sociology, 27, 101–106.

Tolich, M. (2014). What can Milgram and Zimbardo teach ethics committees and qualitative researchers about minimizing harm? Research Ethics, 10(2), 86-96.

Tolich, M., Tumilty, E., Choe, L., Hohmann-Marriott, B., & Fahey, N. (2020). Researcher emotional safety as ethics in practice: Why professional supervision should augment PhD candidates' academic supervision. In R. Iphofen (Ed.), Handbook of research ethics and scientific integrity (pp. 589–602). Cham: Springer.

Toy-Cronin, B. (2018). Ethical issues in insider-outsider research. In R. Iphofen & M. Tolich (Eds.), The SAGE handbook of qualitative research ethics (pp. 455–469). London: Sage.

Traianou, A. (2020). The centrality of ethics in qualitative research practice. In P. Leavy (Ed.), The Oxford handbook of qualitative research (2nd ed., pp. 86–110). Oxford: Oxford University Press.

Traphagan, J. W. (2013). Rethinking autonomy: A critique of principlism in biomedical ethics. New York: State University of New York Press.

Tsai, A. C., Kohrt, B. A., Matthews, L. T., Betancourt, T. S., Lee, J. K., Papachristos, A. V., ... & Dworkin, S. L. (2016). Promises and pitfalls of data sharing in qualitative research. Social Science & Medicine, 169, 191–198.

Tsosie, R. (2020). The legal and policy dimensions of Indigenous data sovereignty (IDS). In M. Walter, T. Kukutai, S. R. Carroll, & D. Rodriguez-Lonebear (Eds.), Indigenous data sovereignty and policy (1st ed., pp. 204–225). London: Taylor & Francis.

United Nations General Assembly. (2007). United Nations Declaration on the Rights of Indigenous Peoples: Resolution / adopted by the General Assembly. New York: United Nations.

United States Indigenous Data Sovereignty Network. (2020), *Principles of Indigenous data governance*. https://nnigovernance.cals.arizona.edu/sites/nnigovernance.arizona.edu/files/resources/US%2520Indigenous%2520Data%2520Sov%2520Principles%2520Working%2520File.pdf

UKRI. (2022). Policy on the governance of good research practice. UK: Department of Science Innovation and Technology. https://www.ukri.org/councils/esrc/guidance-for-applicants/research-ethics-guidance/#skipnav-target

Ulatowski, J., & Walker, W. (2021). Missing in action: Exposing the moral failures of universities that desert researchers facing court-ordered disclosure of confidential information. Educational Philosophy and Theory, 53(5), 536–547.

Ustek-Spilda, F., Powell, A., & Nemorin, S. (2019). Engaging with ethics in Internet of Things: Imaginaries in the social milieu of technology developers. Big Data & Society, 6(2).

Van den Eynden, V., Corti, L., Woolard, M., Bishop, L., & Horton, L. (2009). Managing and sharing data. Essex: UK Data Archive.

Van den Hoonard, W. (Ed.). (2002). Walking the tightrope: Ethical issues for qualitative researchers. Toronto: University of Toronto Press.

van den Hoonaard, W. C. (2020). "Vulnerability" as a concept captive in its own prison. In R. Iphofen (Ed.), *Handbook of research ethics and scientific integrity* (pp. 577–588). Cham: Springer.

Van Teijlingen, E. (2006). Reply to Robert Dingwall's plenary "Confronting the anti-democrats: The unethical nature of ethical regulation in social science." Medical Sociology Online, 1, 59–60.

Venkatesh, S. (2008). Gang leader for a day: A rogue sociologist takes to the streets. London: Penguin Press.

Viney, M. (1980, September 24). Geared for a gale. The Irish Times.

Viney, M. (1983, August 6). The Yank in the corner: Why the ethics of anthropology are a concern for rural Ireland. The Irish Times.

Vlahou, A., Hallinan, D., Apweiler, R., Argiles, A., Beige, J., Benigni, A., et al. (2021). Data sharing under the General Data Protection Regulation: Time to harmonize law and research ethics? Hypertension, 77(4), 1029–1035.

Voloder, L., & Kirpitchenko, L. (2016). *Insider research on migration and mobility: international perspectives on researcher positioning*. London: Routledge.

Waitangi Tribunal. (2011). Ko Aotearoa Tēnei: A report into claims concerning New Zealand law and policy affecting Māori culture and identity (Wai 262). Wellington, New Zealand: Legislation Direct.

Walker, S., & Read, S. (2011). Accessing vulnerable research populations: An experience with gatekeepers of ethical approval. International Journal of Palliative Nursing, 17(1), 14–18.

Waller, L. (2018). Indigenous research methodologies and listening the Dadirri way. In T. Dreher & A. Mondal (Eds.), Ethical responsiveness and the politics of difference. Cham: Palgrave Macmillan.

Walter, M., Kukutai, T., Carroll, S. R., & Rodriguez-Lonebear, D. (Eds.). (2020). Indigenous data sovereignty and policy (1st ed.). London: Routledge.

Ward, R., & Fredericks, B. (2021). Indigenous-led qualitative research. In Yatdjuligin: Aboriginal and Torres Strait Islander Nursing and Midwifery Care (pp. 236–253). Cambridge: Cambridge University Press.

Warwick, D. (1982). Tearoom trade: Means and ends in research. In M. Bulmer (Ed.), Social research ethics. London: Macmillan Press.

Water, T. (2024). Ethical issues in participatory research with children and young people. In I. Coyne & B. Carter (Eds.), Being participatory: Researching with children and young people: Co-constructing knowledge using creative, digital and innovative techniques (pp. 39–64). Cham: Springer International Publishing.

Watts, J. (2008). Emotion, empathy and exit: Reflections on doing ethnographic qualitative research on sensitive topics. Medical Sociology Online, 3(2), 3–14.

West-McGruer, K. (2020). There's "consent" and then there's consent: Mobilising Māori and Indigenous research ethics to problematise the western biomedical model. Journal of Sociology, 56(2), 184–196.

Whitney, C., & Evered, J. A. (2022). The Qualitative Research Distress Protocol: A participant-centered tool for navigating distress during data collection. International Journal of Qualitative Methods, 21.

Whitney, S. M. (2023). From oversight to overkill: Inside the broken system that blocks medical breakthroughs—and how we can fix it. New York: Rivertown Books.

Wiles, R., Charles, V., Crow, G., & Heath, S. (2006). Researching researchers: Lessons for research ethics. Qualitative Research, 6(3), 283–299.

Wiles, R., Clark, A., & Prosser, J. (2011). Visual research ethics at the crossroads. In E. Margolis & L. Pauwels (Eds.), *The SAGE handbook of visual research methods* London: Sage.

Wiles, R., Coffey, A., Robison, J., & Heath, S. (2011). Anonymisation and visual images: Issues of respect, "voice" and protection. *International Journal of Social Research Methodology. 15(1), 41–53.*

Wiles, R., Coffey, A., Robison, J., & Prosser, J. (2012). Ethical regulation and visual methods: Making visual research impossible or developing good practice? Sociological Research Online, 17(1): 3-12.

Wiles, R., Crow, G., Charles, V., & Heath, S. (2007). Informed consent and the research process: Following rules or striking balances? Sociological Research Online, 12(2): 99-110.

Wiles, R., Crow, G., Heath, S., & Charles, V. (2008). The management of confidentiality and anonymity in social research. International Journal of Social Research Methodology, 11(5), 417–428.

Wiles, R., Heath, S., Crow, G., & Charles, V. (2005). *Informed consent in social research: A literature review. Southampton: ESRC National Centre for Research Methods* http://eprints.ncrm.ac.uk/85/

Wiles, R., Prosser, J., Bagnoli, A., Clark, A., Davies, K., Holland, S., & Renold, E. (2008). Visual ethics: Ethical issues in visual research. *Southampton: ESRC National Centre for Research Methods* http://eprints.ncrm.ac.uk/421/

Williams, P. (2020). "It all sounds very interesting, but we're just too busy!": Exploring why 'gatekeepers' decline access to potential research participants with learning disabilities. European Journal of Special Needs Education, 35(1), 1–14.

Williamson, E., Gregory, A., Abrahams, H., et al. (2020). Secondary trauma: Emotional safety in sensitive research. Journal of Academic Ethics, 18, 55–70.

Williamson, I. R., Quincey, K., Lond, B. J., & Papaloukas, P. (2021). Unanticipated voices? Reflections from our ongoing 'adventures' with participant-authored photography, interviewing and interpretative phenomenology. Methods in Psychology, 5, 100062.

Wilson, D., Mikahere-Hall, A., & Sherwood, J. (2022). Using indigenous kaupapa Māori research methodology with constructivist grounded theory: Generating a theoretical explanation of indigenous women's realities. International Journal of Social Research Methodology, 25(3), 375–390.

Woodfield, K. (2017). *The ethics of online research*. Leeds, UK: Emerald Publishing.

Wright, S., Waters, R., Nicholls, V., & Members of the Strategy for Living Project (2004). Ethical considerations in service-user-led research: Strategies for living project. In M. Smyth & E. Williamson (Eds.), Researchers and their subjects: Ethics, power, knowledge and consentBristol: Policy Press.

Wright, A. L., Wahoush, O., Ballantyne, M., Gabel, C., & Jack, S. M. (2016). Qualitative health research involving Indigenous peoples: Culturally appropriate data collection methods. The Qualitative Report, 21(12), 2230–2245.

Wynn, L. L., & Israel, M. (2018). The fetishes of consent: Signatures, paper, and writing in research ethics review. American Anthropologist, 120(4), 795–806.

Xenitidou, M., & Gilbert, N. (2009). (2009). Innovations in social science research methods (NCRM Working Paper). Southampton: NCRM. http://eprints.ncrm.ac.uk/804/a

Yip, C., Han, N. L. Reena, & Leong Sng, B. (2016). Legal and ethical issues in research. Indian Journal of Anaesthesia, 60(9), 684–688.

Yu, B., Liu, Y., Ren, S., Zhou, Z., & Liu, J. (2023). META seen: Analyzing network traffic and privacy policies in Web 3.0 based Metaverse. *Digital Communications and Networks, 11*(1): 13-25.

Yuill, C. (2018). Is anthropology legal?: Anthropology and the EU General Data Protection Regulation. Anthropology in Action, 25(2), 36–41.

Zapata-Barrero, R., & Yalaz, E. (2020). Qualitative migration research ethics: A roadmap for migration scholars. Qualitative Research Journal, 20(3), 269–279.

Zimmer, M. (2010). "But the data is already public": On the ethics of research in Facebook. Ethics and Information Technology, 12(4), 313–325.

Zimmer, M., & Kinder-Kurlanda, K. (2017). *Internet research ethics for the social age: New challenges, cases, and contexts*. New York: Peter Lang Verlag.

INDEX

artificial intelligence (AI)   1, 4,
      122, 137
Alderson, P.   27
anonymity   32, 43, 57, 65–6
   archived research   53
   effect of disclosure of
         identity   38, 59, 72–6,
         112
   identification of research
         participants   8, 58, 66, 74,
         77–80, 135
   online research   57, 59, 130
   pseudonyms   77–8
   research location   75, 78
   visual data   80–2
archived data   53, 115, 131
   consent   114–15
   reputational risk   66–7, 89,
         101
   secondary analysis   131–3
assessing risks to
         participants   84–7
   balancing risks and
         benefits   84
   benefits of research
         participation   59
   costs of research
         participation   89
   emotional well-being   87, 97
   exploitation   90–2
   media reporting   89
   paternalism   85–6
   publication   87

assessing risks to researchers
      84–7
   emotional distress   97–100
   emotional trauma   97
   geographical location   96–7
   reputational risk   100–1
   research in participants'
         homes   97–100
   research topic   101
Atkinson, P.   1, 83, 140

Beauchamp, T.   12, 20
big data   43, 76, 131, 132, 134,
      135, 144
Bloor, M.   93, 94, 96, 97, 99, 100

Chenhall, R. D.   22, 106
Clark, A.   72, 78, 80, 99, 125
common rule   14, 26, 40
competence, *see* capacity
confidentiality   8, 65–77
   accidental disclosure   46–7, 83
   balancing confidentiality and
         data quality   89
   internal confidentiality   73–4
   legal and professional
         responsibilities   28, 67–72
   'off the record' comments   66,
         76–7
   reporting incidents   43–6, 77
   strategies to limit
         confidentiality
         breaches   72–6

consent   37–52, 69, 107–8, 110,
    115–16, 129
  archived data   53
  assuming consent   44–5
  capacity   7, 27–9, 45–6
  children   27–8, 41–2, 45, 50,
    61–2, 93, 127
  collaborative approaches   56
  consent forms   50, 53–5
  covert research   38–9, 48, 96
  gatekeepers   38, 44–5, 141
  Gillick competency   61–2
  online research   55–9
  process consent   42, 47–8
  proxy consent   61–2
  research in public settings   44
  use of material   54, 81
  visual data   29–30
  withdrawing consent   37–8
consequentialist approaches   5,
    19–20, 49
Coomber, R.   14, 54
Corden, A.   78, 79, 100

data governance   118–19
data sharing   44, 82, 121, 122,
    131–4
data sovereignty   136–7, 144
decolonizing methods   122, *see
    also* yarning
digital, e-research and online
    research   16, 43, 122,
    128–31
  geographical boundaries   57
  public and private   129
Dingwall, R.   1, 11, 55
disability   13, 59, 60, 113, 126

Economic and Social Research
    Council (ESRC)   4, 9, 14,
    131
Edwards, R.   109, 114–16
emotional risks   97–8

Epistemic justice   13, 14, 47–9,
    92
ethical decision-making   17–18,
    141
ethical guidelines   7, 17, 23, 130
ethics of care   6, 21–2, 62, 116,
    132
ethnography   56, 105–7

General Data Protection
    Regulation (GDPR)   28–
    32, 77, 134, 136
Gillam, L.   11, 33
Gilligan, C.   21
Global Indigenous Data
    Alliance   136, 137
Grinyer, A.   78, 79, 140
Guillemin, M.   11, 33

Haggerty, K.   14, 15
Hammersley, M.   1, 15, 127
Hanson, K.   141–2
Heath, S.   3, 45, 51, 62
Homan, R.   39
Hooley, T.   55, 56
Hopman, M. T.   47–9
Humphreys, L.   13, 19, 105

imposter participants   55–6
incentives, *see* payment
Indigenous   1, 4, 22, 33, 106,
    119, 126
  data sovereignty   136–7
  informed consent   46–7
  knowledge system   143
insiders   99
Iphofen, R.   15–17, 19, 33, 53,
    65, 71, 78, 88, 95, 97
Israel, M.   12, 15, 16, 18, 20, 24,
    25, 34, 54

Lawton, J.   109–12, 114
Leahy, C. P.   86–7

Lee, R.   71, 74, 75, 83, 87, 89,
     95, 98
legal regulation   25–33
lived experience   41, 105
longitudinal data   41, 49, 114,
     126, 134

Macfarlane, B.   21
Mauthner, M.   15, 132
migrants,   47, 48, 90, 99
Milgram, S.   13, 38, 103–4
moral judgements   4

narrative research   89–92
National Health and Medical
     Research Council
     (NHMRC)   14, 131
Nduna, M.   140
Neale, B.   101, 132–4
new materialist ontologies
     49–50
Ngozwana, N.   106
non-consequentialist approaches,
     see principlist approaches

Olson, R. E.   100

participatory research   126–8
Pauwels, L.   16, 25, 126
payment   52–3, 55, 89
Perlstadt, H.   105, 106
physical risks   95–6
Plummer, K.   90, 91, 141, 142
presentation and interpretation of
     images   39, 80, 88, 125
principlist approaches   5–6, 20–1
professional risks   100–1
Prosser, J.   15, 25, 29, 43, 72, 80,
     81, 125, 126
pseudonymization   77–8
publication of data   81, 87–9
   open access   132
Punch, M.   39

reflexivity   13, 22, 48, 49, 91,
     120, 138
regulation   1, 6–7, 10–11, 16, 18,
     24–5, 40
   history of regulation   14
   GDPR   26–8, 30
   online research   130
Renold, E.   42, 126, 127
research ethics committees   1, 2,
     12–14, 16, 20, 24, 26, 27,
     33, 35, 36, 46, 59, 60, 69,
     85, 139, 140
Rowe, M.   109, 112–14, 132

Scheper-Hughes, Nancy   32,
     116–18
situated ethics   141
Snee, H.   57, 59, 129, 130
Social Research Association   23, 97

Tilley, L.   79, 139
trauma-informed approaches   71,
     91, 99
tri-council policy   14, 26, 33, 46,
     71, 124
Traphagan, J. W.   20, 21, 23
Smith, Linda Tuhawai   122–3

Van den Hoonard, W.   59
visual and creative methods   121,
     124–6
virtue ethics   6, 19, 21–3

yarning   122–3, 136

web 2.0 & 3.0   57–8, 128, 130
Wiles, R.   15, 16, 24, 25, 28, 29,
     37, 43, 51, 69, 70, 72, 74,
     75, 78–80, 82, 85, 88, 89,
     93, 100, 125, 126, 139

Zapata-Barrero, R.   89
Zimbardo, P.   13, 103–5